Discourses on Five Indian Poets in English

Keki N. Daruwalla, Shiv K. Kumar,
Pronab Kumar Majumder, Syed Ameeruddin
and
Aju Mukhopadhyay

Discourses on Five Indian Poets in English

Keki N. Daruwalla, Shiv K. Kumar,
Pronab Kumar Majumder, Syed Ameeruddin
and
Aju Mukhopadhyay

K.V. Dominic

AUTHORSPRESS
Publishers of Scholarly Books

Worldwide Circulation through Authorspress Global Network

First Published 2011
by
Authorspress

Editorial
Q-2A Hauz Khas Enclave,
New Delhi-110 016
e-mail: authorspress@yahoo.com

Marketing
E-35/103, Jawahar Park
Laxmi Nagar, Delhi-110 092
e-mail: authorspress@yahoo.com

Discourses on Five Indian Poets in English: Keki N. Daruwalla, Shiv K. Kumar, Pronab Kumar Majumder, Syed Ameeruddin and Aju Mukhopadhyay

ISBN 978-81-7273-603-3

Printed in India at Tarun Offset, Delhi.

Preface

It is with immense pleasure and satisfaction that I am presenting before you my third book on Indian poets in English. As I have stated earlier through my prefaces, English poetry in general, and Indian poetry in English particularly, have been facing challenges from English fiction. There are a great number of gifted English poets in India who have been constantly ignored by the established publishers, academia as well as readers. The fact that poets are seers and they convey great values and messages through short pieces of writing is deliberately forgotten and never taken into consideration. In this busy, hustling world where people have little time to spare for reading, where visual media enchant the viewers, what suits them most is short pieces like poems and short stories.

The colonial legacy and servitude have not left us even sixty-three years after our independence. The subject experts and curriculum committee of schools and colleges in India prefer Shakespeare, Milton, the Romantics, the Victorians, the Modern and Postmodern British and American poets to Tagore, Aurobindo, Sarojini Naidu, Ezekiel, Kamala Das, and a great number of contemporary English poets in India. If we want our pupils and students to learn about our country—its topography, natural sceneries, ethos, legends, myths, noble traditions and civilisations, urban and rural life, etc.— we ought to teach them poems written by English poets in India. The chief characteristics of our English poetry are that the syntax and vocabulary are familiar to our pupils and students. It is akin to their day-to-day communicative English. So it is the duty of the government to enforce English poems written by English poets in India in schools and colleges substituting British and American poems. The governments and publishers should promote Indian literature in English because only through this medium can India speak to the world; share her ideas, philosophies, traditions, ethos, cultures, emotions, dreams and beauties.

Being an English poet and editor myself, it is my primary duty to promote English poetry in India. I deem it my responsibility to honour my senior poets by exposing the depth, sublimity and beauty of their poetry to the scholars, teachers and such critical readers. My second book of the series was another voluminous one on R.K. Singh, D.C. Chambial and I.K. Sharma—all very reputed, great poets but neglected by the established publishers. The present book consists of critical studies on the poetry of five great contemporary Indian poets in English, namely, Keki N. Daruwalla, Shiv K. Kumar, Pronab Kumar Majumder, Syed Ameeruddin and Aju Mukhopadhyay. The first three hail from North India while the last two belong to South India.

Keki N. Daruwalla (born 1937) is a former IPS Officer who retired as Additional Director in the Research and Analysis Wing (RAW). He was born in Lahore as the son of Prof. N. C. Daruwalla, an eminent professor who taught in Government College Lahore. After the partition his family left Lahore. He obtained his master's degree in English Literature from Government College, Ludhiana, University of Punjab. He joined the Indian Police Service (IPS) in 1958, and eventually becoming a Special Assistant to the Prime Minister on International Affairs. He subsequently was in the Cabinet Secretariat until his retirement. He is also a short story writer and novelist. He has won many literary awards including the Sahitya Akademi Award in 1984 for his poetry collection, *The Keeper of the Dead* and Commonwealth Poetry Prize for Asia in 1987. His poetry books are: *Under Orion*, *Apparition in April*, *Sword & Abyss: A Collection of Short Stories*, *Winter Poems*, *The Keeper of the Dead*, *Crossing of Rivers*, *Landscapes*, *A Summer of Tigers: Poems*, *The Minister for Permanent Unrest*

& Other Stories, Night River: Poems, The Map-maker: Poems, The Scarecrow and the Ghost, A House in Ranikhet, and *Collected Poems (1970-2005)*.

Novelist, short-story writer, poet, playwright, translator and critic, **Prof. Shiv K Kumar** was born in Lahore in 1921. He was educated at Dayanand Anglo-Vedic High School and Forman Christian College, Lahore and Fitzwilliam College, Cambridge. He received his doctorate in English Literature from Cambridge University. He was a Visiting Professor at various British and American universities. In 1978 he was elected a Fellow of the Royal Society of Literature (London). Kumar has published three novels, six collections of poems, a collection of short stories, a play, a translation of Faiz Ahmed Faiz, and several scholarly works. He received the prestigious Sahitya Akademi Award for his collection of poems *Trapfalls in the Sky* in 1987. His poetic anthologies are: *Articulate Silences, Cobwebs in the Sun, Subterfuges, Woodpeckers, Trapfalls in the Sky, Woolgathering*, and *Thus Spake the Buddha.*

Pronab Kumar Majumder was born in 1941. He retired from government service as a Special Secretary to the Government of West Bengal in 2001. He has been editing International Literary Journal *Bridge-In-Making* since 1991. The published titles of Majumder are seven collections of poems in Bengali, his mother tongue, 13 collections of poems in English, six one-act plays in English and a novel in English. Another collection of poems in English is upcoming. He translated about 300 Bengali poems and more than 100 lyric poems of Nobel Laureate Poet Rabindranath Tagore into English and published them in his journal *Bridge-In-Making.* He also edited two *International Anthologies of Poems: 2000 & 2001.* Austrian Literary Circle bestowed upon him, "Degree of Merit" in recognition of his services to literature. "Replica Award" of 2001 was given to him on behalf of *Replica International Literary Journal.* International Poets Academy (Chennai: India) awarded him "Excellence in World Poetry." He also received "Uttarapath" (Sweden) Little Magazine award, 1995. His published titles of English poems in English are:

Dialogue with Time, Replies of Time, Life and Eternity, In the Ruins of Time, Creating Killing Cosmic Time, Where Time is Dead, Time Never Returns to Console, On time UnTime, Sparkles of Time, My India: Through Corridor of Time, Where I is a Noun, Faces of Love, Passage to Peace, Random Poetry, (Upcoming).

Born in 1942 in Andhra Pradesh, India **Prof. Syed Ameeruddin** completed his Masters Degree in English Language and Literature from Aligarh Muslim University in 1966 and joined as Lecturer in English New College, Chennai in 1968 and retired as Head of the Department of English Post-Graduate Research in the year 1995. He is widely published, anthologised, translated and critically acclaimed in India and abroad. He has published six collections of poems: *What the Himalaya Said and Other Poems, The Dreadful Doom to come and Other Poems, A Lover and a Wanderer, Petallic Love Times, Visioned Summits* and *Visions of Deliverance.* He has also published three reputed anthologies on world poetry, namely, *Indian Verse in English, New Voices* and *Voices International.* He visited U.S. twice to attend the World Congress of poets in San Francisco (1981) and in Florida (1985) and was honoured at the Florida Congress as "Laurel Man of Letters." He also visited Bangkok, Thailand, Istanbul, Turkey and Taipei, Republic of China to attend the World Congress of Poets and to chair sessions and read his poems. He also visited several American and UK universities on a lecture-cum-poetry reading tour. He was awarded the Michael Madhusudan Award for literature in 1988. He was awarded the Australia Day Award for literature at Melbourne, for excellence in World Poetry by The Poetry Day Australia International, Australia in the year 1990. He was also awarded with the highest academic honour 'Professor of Distinction' by the Soka University, Tokyo, Japan. He is one of the contributors to the Routledge *Encyclopedia of Commonwealth Literature,* London. He has been elected Honorary Professor of Letters by the Temple of Arts Academy International, New York, USA. He is also the chairman to the Board of Advisors and American Biographical Institute, North Carolina. He is the Founder and President of the world reputed literary organisation, 'International Poets Academy.'

Born in Calcutta (Kolkata) in 1940 and now settled in Pondicherry, **Aju Mukhopadhyay** is a bilingual poet, critic, essayist, biographer, feature and fiction writer. In his professional life he was mainly a banker working as executive of a nationalised bank. He has published 16 books in English 12 in Bangla. He has seven books of poems published in English besides two in Bangla; three books of short stories in Bangla and one in English besides a novel in English. Among his works, essays on Sri Aurobindo and the Mother deserve special mention. He has written their biographies in English and Bangla. Many of his works have been translated in other European and Indian languages and anthologised. Essays and articles on his poetry have been written and published in books. He is an environmentalist and has widely travelled in parts of Europe, USA, Asia and Africa. He is member of large number of literary and environmental organisations. He was awarded Certificate of Competence as a Published Writer by the Writers Bureau, Manchester, UK and awarded Best Poet of the Year-2003 by the Poets International, Bangalore, India. He was awarded the 2007 Editor's Choice Published Poet award by the International Library of Poetry, USA and Excellence in World Poetry Award, 2009 by the International Poets Academy, Chennai. He is a member of the Research Board of Advisors of the American Biographical Institute, who offered him the American Order of Merit. His poetry anthologies are: *The Witness Tree, In Celebration of Nature, The Paper Boat, Insect's Nest and Other Poems, Aju Mukhopadhyay's Poems on Sri Aurobindo and the Mother, Short Verse Vast Universe* and *Short Verse Delight.*

This massive book contains twenty-four articles. The opening article is a curtain raiser to the book, written by P.C.K. Prem, an eminent bilingual poet, short story writer, novelist and critic who has written about two dozen books each in English and Hindi. A recipient of several State and Academy awards and a retired IAS officer, Prem has contributed in this book five more articles on each of the poets. There are five articles on Keki N. Daruwalla, three on Shiv K. Kumar, four on Pronab Kumar Majumder, eight on Syed Ameeruddin and three on Aju Mukhopadhyay.

Before winding up my preface let me express my unfathomable gratitude to the great publisher, Sudarshan Kcherry. He is a unique gem among publishers of the world. To a certain extent, he is another P. Lal, lending his helping hand to emerging and long ignored talented writers, publishing their dreams, not letting money come in the way of promoting talent. Had he not extended his bountiful hand, this book would not have been a reality. Hats off to him and let the Almighty continue to shower upon him strength and benevolence for another five decades ! I wish all readers a real mental feast!

Dr. K.V.Dominic

List of Contributors

P. C. K. Prem, poet, critic, Katoch Cottage (Mian Luder-Mahant House), Chanakyapuri, Palampur-176 061, Kangra, Himachal Pradesh, India.

Prof. Asha Viswas, Critic, B 1, Shivam Complex, Lanka, Varanasi, 221 005, U.P., India.

Jayshree Goswami, Research Scholar, Dept of HSS, Indian School of Mines, Dhanbad, Jharkhand, India.

Dr. Mojibur Rahman, Associate Professor, Dept of HSS, Indian School of Mines, Dhanbad, Jharkhand, India.

Dr. P. V. Jayaraj, Associate Professor of English, Nirmalagiri College, Nirmalagiri PO – 670 701, Kannur Dt., Kerala, India.

Dr. Prasenjit Das, Asst. Prof. in English, Institute of Distance and Open Learning, Gauhati University, Guwahati-14, Assam, India.

Binita Sarma, Counsellor in English, Institute of Distance and Open Learning, Gauhati University, Guwahati-14, Assam, India.

Prof. D. C. Chambial, poet, critic, editor, POETCRIT, Maranda: 176 102, Himachal Pradesh, India.

Dr. Anshu Bhardwaj (Sharma), poetess, short story writer, translator, critic, Professor of English, Arya College of Engineering & Information & Technology, SP-42, RIICO Industrial Area, Delhi Road, Kukas, Jaipur, Rajasthan, India.

Prof. Kurt F. Svatek, Breitenfurter Str, 378/4/40, 1230 Wien/ Vienna, Austria.

Swagata Ray, M. Phil Student, Dept of HSS, Indian School of Mines, Dhanbad, Jharkhand, India.

Prof. R. K. Singh, poet, critic, Dept of HSS, Indian School of Mines, Dhanbad, Jharkhand, India.

Aju Mukhopadhyay, poet, critic, short story writer, 8, Cheir Lodi Street, Pondicherry-605 001, India.

Binayendra Chowdhuri, Poet & Critic, D 57/32-C, Krishna Puri, Sigra, Varanasi-221 010, U.P., India.

Har Prasad Sharma, Poet & Critic, 1012 Janta Flat (Top Floor), Nand Nagri, Delhi 93, India.

Dr. S. Kumaran, Assistant Professor of English, University College of Engineering, Tindivanam, Anna University of Technology Chennai, Melpakkam-604 001, T. N., India.

Dr. Mosam Sinha, poet, critic, Reader & Head, Department of English, CMCA, Teerthanker Mahaveer University, Moradabad (U.P), India.

Rajeev Ranjan, M. Phil Student, Dept of HSS, Indian School of Mines, Dhanbad, Jharkhand, India.

Raj Sree M.S., Research Scholar, Institute of English, Ross Mount, Aramada P.O., Kunnapuzha, Thiruvanathapuram 695 032, Kerala, India.

Contents

Preface v

List of Contributors xi

1. Poetry of Shiv K. Kumar, Keki N. Daruwalla, Syed Ameeruddin, Aju Mukhopadhyay and Pronab Kumar Majumder: Some Reflections 1
—*P.C.K. Prem*

2. *Landscapes*: A Landmark in Keki Daruwalla's Poetry 21
— *Asha Viswas*

3. A Study of Discourse Construction in the Select Poem of Keki N. Daruwalla 39
—*Jayshree Goswami* and *Mojibur Rahman*

4. Policing the Poet: An Ecocritical Study of Daruwala's Nature Poems 48
—*P.V. Jayaraj*

5. Some Reflections on the Poetry of Keki N. Daruwalla 61
—*P.C.K. Prem*

6. Keki N. Daruwalla's Poetry: An Eco-critical Perspective 81
—*Prasenjit Das* and *Binita Sarma*

7. The Sounds of Starved Eros: A Study of Shiv K. Kumar's *Thus Spake the Buddha* 91
—D.C. Chambial

8. Nostalgic Past and Agonised Present in the Poetry of Shiv K. Kumar 99
—P.C.K. Prem

9. The East-West Fusion in Shiv K. Kumar's Poetry 112
—Anshu Bhardwaj

10. Searching Peace and Harmony in an Age of Terror: A Study of Pronab Kumar Majumder's *Passage to Peace* 131
—P.C.K. Prem

11. Time—The Dominant Theme of Pronab Kumar Majumder's Poetry 141
—Kurt F. Svatek

12. Minor Themes Vis-a-vis Time in Pronab Kumar Majumder's Poetry 151
—Swagata Ray, R.K. Singh and *M. Mojibur Rahman*

13. Pronab Kumar Majumder: An Adept in Love Poems 166
—Aju Mukhopadhyay

14. Critical Perspectives on Prof. Syed Ameeruddin's Poetry 181
—Binayendra Chowdhuri

15. Quest for Self: The Poetry of Syed Ameeruddin 195
—D.C. Chambial

16. A Critical Analysis of the Poetry of Prof. Syed Ameeruddln 203
—Har Prasad Sharma

17. Syed Ameeruddin as a Didactic Poet 218
—S. Kumaran

18. Syed Ameeruddin: A Wanderer with a Goal 230
—Mosam Sinha

19. Syed Ameeruddin's Poetry: Visions of a Pilgrimage to the Summits of Deliverance 248
—*O.P. Mathur*

20. An Elevating Spiritual Journey of Grace and Nobility through Syed Ameeruddin's *Visioned Summits* and *Visions of Deliverance* 260
—*P.C.K. Prem*

21. Poetic Style in Syed Ameeruddin's Poetry 274
—*Rajeev Ranjan, R.K. Singh* and *M. Mojibur Rahman*

22. Aju Mukhopadhyay: Voice of the Voiceless 283
—*S. Kumaran*

23. Purifying the Contemporary Inherent Irritants: A Critical Appreciation of Aju Mukhopadhyay's *Poems on Sri Aurobindo and the Mother* and *The Paper Boat* 293
—*P.C.K. Prem*

24. An Ecoaesthetic Rendering of Aju Mukhopadhyay's Poems 303
—*M.S. Raj Sree*

1

Poetry of Shiv K. Kumar, Keki N. Daruwalla, Syed Ameeruddin, Aju Mukhopadhyay and Pronab Kumar Majumder: Some Reflections

—P.C.K. Prem

To critically evaluate the interconnection and lyrical quality with regard to thematic patterns of poetry of these poets together, invites genuine problems. A virtually accurate appreciation is an arduous work if one wants to fully measure the horizons of creativity. To be discreet, appreciation means an affirmative attitude to the creative acumen and sweep of a creator's imagination and intelligence.

Shiv K. Kumar and Keki N. Daruwalla are poets of sophistication and urban background and carry the impact of urban-consciousness with ignorable exceptions. These poets are suavely sensitive and have an enormous strength to use language with ease and effectiveness that even an English author finds it difficult to excel, for, they are clear, direct, and simple but artistically imagistic. They exhibit proclivity for all that is Indian but at the same it is habitually difficult for them to negate the genuine impact of English culture and language and thus they illustrate a few streaks of elitist preference. This unconscious penchant is also their strength. The other three poets, namely, Aju Mukhopadhyay, Syed Ameeruddin and Pronab Kumar Majumder, on the other hand quite comfortably depict awareness of Indian culture and heritage, and use English language as an Indian uses, with all its Indianness which at times does not appeal to the authors earning living by globetrotting, and live neither here nor there notwithstanding claims and counterclaims to the contrary.

The poetry of Aju Mukhopadhyay, Syed Ameeruddin and Pronab Kumar Majumder is relatively incredible for its sense of tranquillity and congenial impact it exercises. Poetic output of these three poets is prolific and it requires tremendous patience to relish the beauty and magnificent reach of their thematic pinnacle. They do not talk in terms of merely rural or urban sensibility but are worried about man's enigmatic life.

A genuine feeling of universality at certain moments appears a little jarring and stridently loud. To follow the pattern of thought in the poetry of these three bards puts a terrific demand on the readers. If Aju is a poet of nature, environment and religious fervour with an extraordinary fascination for Sri Aurobindo, Indian culture and heritage, he is equally worried about the ugly political scenario of India. On the other hand, Majumder is a retired bureaucrat; and has turned a poet-cum-editor. In administrative life, he has witnessed the movement of life in a system. He does not paint a very healthy and encouraging scene. He is fundamentally a poet of themes. His contents of verses are within the reach and intelligence of even a layman. He speaks of time, life, death, anxiety, fear, truth, peace, nature and terrorism. He is individualistic and original.

Syed Ameeruddin is a different poet with an awe-inspiring sense of poetic prowess. He is religious in temperament, secularly undisciplined in poetic methodology, original in poetic throw and many times he takes lyrical liberty in coining words. He is rhythmic in style and favours linguistic autonomy. Each poet, urban in attitude, effectively commands respective poetic territory quite persuasively. These poets lightheartedly provoke and exasperate by desperate obsession with a sage-like demeanour which results in repetition. While Kumar and Daruwalla, living in urban environment, intellectualise life and experiences, Aju, Syed and Majumder deliberate over the mysteries and sufferings of life and try to convey feelings and thoughts in a simple comprehensible language.

Aju and Majumder mostly write short lyrics whereas Syed Ameeruddin is also a master of long verses, and he continues to move quite often from the materialistic to the spiritual and back, and without being burdensome, teaches man the art of living a harmonious life in an age of violence, hatred and treachery. Anxiety about the man's destiny is the hallmark of the poetry of Ameeruddin, Mukhopadhyay and Majumder but they are optimistic and hopeful and touch contemporary issues with sincerity and ingenuity.

❖❖❖❖❖

It is not so in the case of Shiv K. Kumar and Keki N. Daruwalla, stalwarts of Indian English Poetry. In the command over the language, they appear imposing and authoritative without being overwhelming. They impress with the originality of thought-communication which at times does not seem quite fresh but the tonal and sound emphasis makes it natural and quite refreshing. Shiv K Kumar changes a simple situation into an amazing orchestra of images and similes. He hints at an issue, realises sufferings and inner dilemmas of man but without being straight he loves to indulge in articulating feelings and meanings which go well with stylistic convenience. Slow and painstakingly arduous efforts suggest a dithering and lingering approach to life, its mystery and potential solutions. He is obsessed with birth, life, woman and death and these turn him to view life philosophically. Keki N. Daruwalla, a government official, has etched a permanent place in Indian English poetry. He is sharp, direct, cutting, ironical, piercing and contemporary and these characteristics emerge out of an intensity of experience. He knew people intimately while in active service, so one encounters a bureaucratic geniality and a little chill in his poetry. He is bitingly cold and terse, often cynical to an irritating limit, and nurses a foreign attitude at times exhibiting camouflage of emotions and kinship with whatever is Indian. He paints pictures and images in words but at the same time comments on contemporary issues rather scrupulously so that he is not criticised. Basically a policeman, I feel, he is a bit mysterious and opens up rarely while keeping an eye around.

The poets are honest, patriotic and simple without being impudent in poetic art, and if it is otherwise, it is only with slight variations. Kumar and Daruwalla do not create an aura of mystical thoughts and spiritual leanings but apparently they are poets of the world engaged in interpreting destiny of man drawing material out of the earthly existence. Mostly, it is personal experience that generates emotions extending to universality of human experience. It is a journey into the psychological complexities and philosophic deliberations that constitute the rarest of the rare experiential world throbbing vigorously within; and the poets appear to wait for its terrific explosion.

Kumar and Daruwalla have a distinct individual philosophy of life. A sheer touch of powerful imagination gives birth to extraordinary situations out of the commonplace. An insignificant event or incident in life gets a Midas touch and it turns into an experience of a lifetime. Daruwalla and Kumar write poetry with anguished love and passion; and raw cynicism determines their philosophy of life. It is not entirely pessimism. Barrenness and distrust decide man's life according to them with a slight shift in contours of expression. Shiv K. Kumar's "Broken Columns" and Daruwalla's "The Night of the Jackals" are long poems with ordinary incidents but when one reads the poems, it is a breathtaking experience to move with the strong sounds and emphatic punch of the words. One forgets the meaning enshrined temporarily but remembers predominately the engaging sounds of the words.

Shiv K. Kumar not only paints pictures with words but these effectively create sensations of terrific images around. Kumar is a poet of startling images which confuse and baffle a person with rapidity when these concretise feelings or thoughts. Not only is he apt in the depiction of Western sensibility but in an Indian scene also he appears bewitchingly impressive:

> She squats
> on the dust-broomed pavement
> behind a pyramid of mangoes
> washed with her youth's milk

tinctured with the pink rose in her hair.
Through the slits
of her patched blouse
one bare shoulder
two while moons
pull all horses
off the track.

("A Mango Vendor," *Subterfuges* 36)

The poem contains disgusting images of old age and sex-obsessed mentality. The "slits of her patched blouse" and a "pyramid of mangoes" are strong assertion of sexual intentions. An old man may stare but she (the "Mango Vendor") is not attracted. There is double meaning. It is a passionate desire but needs suppression at the non-availability of the right man and there is also a wish to sell mangos. Mango is ripe or...the poet creates a situation and stops. A long poem, "Notes from the Underground" of Keki Daruwalla creates wonderful images of a journey. The images begin with deep ruminations and the consequent haziness is engulfed by frosty relations. The images converge on autumn to arrive at the finale of a not very happy life. The drudgery and unexciting life does not allow a moment's respite. Whatever may be the internal pains and agonies of life, it must end up somewhere in distorted happiness when one confronts 'parched landscapes and rain/parched lips and love.'

An utterly insipid urban life raises questions of identity and destination. It is apparently stimulating but deep down intensely dreary middle or upper middle class mentality that aspires beyond capacity and lands up in total defeat. The poet is remorseful of the despairing life bureaucrats and politicians live, when he observes:

But often the stars
go about their office routine
in the night sky
like glum bureaucrats –
this astral bureaucracy
is even more baffling in its ways
than our central ministries.

("Notes from the Underground," *India International Centre,* Vol. 31, No.4, 2005. 99-100)

It is not that the sophisticated segment of the society is a source of frustration; in another scene the poet paints a terrible picture and thus enhances the distress when he observes:

> Selling kerosene to a crowd
> how aesthetic
> the flame that rides the street.
>
> No end to hoarding
> Breaking open the lockers they find
> A briefcase full of rice.
>
> ("Notes," *Winter Poems* 27)

The poet describes in no uncertain words the man's callousness and brutality in contemporary life. Here selling essential commodities to the poor when the bus halts, is a sign of collective degeneration of society's ethical values. When there is hunger and scarcity then 'the flame that rides the street', and 'hoarding' determine the magnitude and vastness of violence and bloodshed. Perhaps the poet is hinting at years of scarcity when in certain parts of the country there was draught and famine. Those were difficult days for the poor but such occurrences were rare. While the rich fill the lockers and briefcases, the poor grovel and scream in utter misery.

❖❖❖❖❖

Nature gets a different treatment and the poet in Daruwalla quite glumly warns man of the unpredictability and terrible punishment nature hands over to man. Perhaps the poet has in mind, man's indiscriminate and naked destruction he wrecks on nature for personal benefits thereby upsetting the eternal balance:

> Ant suddenly at night
> the north comes to the village
> riding on river-back.
> Twenty minutes of a nightmare spin
> and fear turns phantasmal
> as half a street goes

churning in the river-belly.
If only voices could light lamps!
If only limbs could turn to rafted bamboo!
("The Ghaghra in Spate" *Under Orion* 74-75)

If in the above verse, nature's fury brings havoc, in the lines below it is a playful experience with water. Just observe the lines: 'And miles to the flank, the paddy fields/will hoard their fish/till the mud enters into/a conspiracy with the sun/and strangles them. (Ibid. 76)' Keen observations and conclusions simply amaze. Here the poet's restrained and economical use of words conveys much more than intended. If it is beauty of nature that fascinates the poet, it is also the colossal devastation that shocks him. It is an occasion when there is neither neither celebration nor funeral temper. Keki Daruwalla creates charming images in "Crossing of Rivers" at different points of time and seasons of the year, and then gives startlingly fresh images of a struggle while crossing a river.

And when young blood
Courses along the heart-floor
you take the plunge
and as slivers of glass
explode like flying fish
you close your eyes
clinging to a water skin
or the tail of a bloated buffalo
and lunge and toss long the
rolling spine of the river.
("Crossing of Rivers," *Signatures* 284)

In other words, it is the dilemma of human life that disturbs the poet. Continuity in struggles imparts meaning to life. After braving various obstacles, fighting courageously with many malevolent forces and reaching the destination pushing aside impediments if a man looks back, he is immeasurably thrilled to realise that the beginning is now a past event despite initial hesitation. Thus, for Daruwalla, the river becomes a symbol of perpetual battle, sufferings, alternating experiences of defeat and success; and finally it is the victory that enchants and reinforces belief in life.

Shiv K. Kumar philosophically goes back and measures life of sufferings borne out of guilt and consequent sense of deep remorse. It is a beautiful shift of images. Somewhere guilty deeds chase and in the solitude one begins to comprehend the depths of sufferings. Questions relating to acts of the past and retribution haunt a man when he gravely deliberates over the fall-out of past sins while observing an angry woman in utter desolation; and completely abandoned because of the physical violation. Slowly, a scene opens up and it is revealed that it is somebody else sharing the burden of sins:

He fell for that other woman's
brunette hair, the exuberance
it's that other man now,
dulled by the incessant patter of winter rain,
watching on his window-pane a lustier
drop chase a mere driblet away.

("Karma," *Articulate Silence* 19)

This small verse also contains shades of attempts to touch a religious aspect of life but here the poet desists from making a final judgment. But certainly a few subtle feelings engulf, and ensuing contrition disturbs.

Shiv K. Kumar is at times, confessional and feels strings of guilt catching hold of him quite strongly. But when it is time to emerge out with the truth not substantiated as yet, perhaps ironically he sits back as compunction and repentance overpower:

My clairvoyance prompted me to action.
I bolted, scaled a high rampart to flee
abandoning you to the enemy.
But I loved you most when I forsook you.

merged into yours, ring upon ring.
and I cursed myself for the sacrilege.

("Broken Columns," *Woodpeckers* 16-17)

It is a journey from an innocent childhood to the age of twenty years with all the little trappings of petty sins and great thoughts, of teachings not totally holy; and there somewhere in between live father and mother with satirical remarks, loving gestures, memories and so sceptically 'he camouflages the primal nodes/like a dog covering up his shit.' From here one is startled to find the journey to marriage with all the glitter and flavour but which smell of emotions unholy. Exactly at that hour, suspicions and uncertainties as to the purity and virginity of woman begin pricking; and the terrible thoughts at that moment even challenge his origin and its source. Here the poet curses himself 'for the sacrilege.' In another scenario, he offers a different interpretation to life, if not lived with some amount of purity. Here one gets an inkling of religious hypocrisy. 'I have come to join/the congregation/wash my hands at the same font' are severe indictments of life, the priests live. One is aghast at the thought of a prostitute when pitted against the sanctity assigned to mother and wife. Here the relations look filthy and violated. To a draw parallel appears repulsive. Here one lives between reverence and disgrace when he says:

> On your forspent thighs
> juvenile tourists who had
> only a glimpse of
> the inner shrine
> have left rude etchings
> of name, place and time.
>
> ("To a Prostitute," *Woodpeckers* 32)

This lyric is a trenchant commentary on the steadily degenerating relationship where even family ties are endangered. The sarcasm is much more devastating when the poet observes: 'My wife awaits me round the corner/to reclaim what's left of me (Ibid. 32)'. But then relations in the modern context appear questionable.

At the philosophical and psychological level, Kumar and Daruwalla try to probe life's mysteries in their own way. Daruwalla appears a little obscure and precautious whereas Kumar is ironically melancholic in temperament. If dark thoughts of death continue to haunt Kumar, it is love, loss of love and consequent despair in Daruwalla which raise certain questions about life. Daruwalla's long poem "The Night of the Jackals" has embellishments of sensuousness, love, lust, despair and subsequent loss. At times, a Hamlet-like situation arises while hoping for a union with the woman. It is hard to decide and the wavering attitude lingers, on whether to go or not to go, and hold the woman, as the protagonist visualises a situation where the woman is occupied in miscellaneous chores. At one point, like Shiv K. Kumar, Daruwalla becomes quite obvious when he observes:

> ...with both the kids asleep
> it was eerie, terrifying.
> And if the children had been awake
> she may not thought of me
> for another three months!
> As if in reply
> She presses me harder to herself.
> I enter her
> the way a boat starved of fresh water
> enters a harbour.
>
> ("The Night of the Jackals," *Modern Indian Poetry in English* 28)

The imagery of the last three lines is not only remarkable it is also bewildering with terrific assault of sexuality. As one moves with the long poem, it is evident that the poet is troubled by a feeling of deep loss. This fear of loss is all pervasive when the poet says, 'Have I a touch of the acid-gold?/one month with me, and she is/already talking of dying!' It is death and its thought that constitute a strong imagery in the poetry of Daruwalla.

❖❖❖❖❖

Pronab Kumar Majumder is a prolific poet. He does not boast of a great pattern and rhythm but writes at ease and touches life and its themes in totality. In protracted thought processes and philosophical broodings, Majumder can't escape repetition. He is chastely straight in whatever he says and worldly anxieties keep him impatient. On the theme of love, he writes eloquently in a quatrain without a fixed pattern: 'Love is no

God no deity/She is but caring humanity/In her waking in her sleep/Always her hands does she keep.' ("Stanza 39," *Faces of Love* 10)

Love is a pious and sacred emotion in man's life. Its caring touch makes humanity survive. Love works as a curative agent where tensions disappear: Love is release of emotion/Loves is creation of poetry/Love is release of tension/To get better of energy ("Stanza 124," *Faces of Love* 31). It is like a smoldering ember that refuses to die and love eventually vanquishes enemy whether it lives within or creates troubles outside. If for Majumder, love functions as a great remedial driving force and salvages man from stresses of life and infuses energy, for Aju Mukhopadhyay, it is sparkle divine brightening up the path and only in absolute submission, love is defined without voice or words:

> Love like a flash
> Illumines the life's path
> Blesses with a hush
>
> Love means one
> Love is surrender
> Love is emotion.
>
> ("Zen Poems 4, 6," *Short Verse Vast Universe* 19)

Love is a spring of faith on which peace rests and if man learns the art of love, world peace is certain to make living worth it. In "Haiku 7, 8," *(Short Verse Vast Universe* 3), a similar sentiment excites. Each poet has a different perception about the sensitive feeling of love. For Majumder, love exercises a therapeutic power. All pervasive love leads to world peace that determines theory of love for Mukhopadhyay but for Syed Ameeruddin, love celebrates ethics with an intrinsic divinity. He sings and celebrates the magnificence of love:

> To realise the realms of smithereens realities.
> Every rose that blossoms must fade.
> But before it flickers into nothing
> It must entice and inundate
> Its fragrance to the brimful—
>
> ("Love Song," *Petallic Love Times* 29)

A true realisation of life and ensuing eternal harmony lead men to peace. Love survives in recognising man, humanity, nature, religion, and blessings of life in love—worship; and so man will ultimately discard violence, passions and vanity so reaffirms the poet in "Peace in the Age of Space" *(What the Himalaya Said and Other Poems* 36).

If earnest reconciliatory attitude guides life, there'll be lifelong peace Syed affirms in simple and effective words. Mukhopadhyay imparts fascinating and consoling dimensions to peace. Only a deep and untainted relation with nature gives strength to understanding what true peace is and these sublime thoughts thrill in "Peace Engrave," (The Witness Tree 28). In the 'deeper mysteries' of nature, man can honestly find 'heavenly sight' in 'moonlit peace.' In "Peace," *(Short Verse Vast Universe* 24), the poet dwells upon peace of a different kind. Absence of violence or fear, necessarily do not mean peace but affirmative mindset is supreme in bringing tranquility on earth he observes. On the other hand, Majumder believes in harmonious thoughts of 'togetherness' which can lead man to peace. In "Journey in Togetherness," *(Where Time is Dead* 15) living together is a testimony and assurance of enduring peace. Curiously enough, poet's chief worry is man's peace of mind; and anxiety undoubtedly contributes to fears and terror in man's life. A short verse "Passage to Peace," (*Passage to Peace* 30) conveys a simple philosophy of peace where an injured poet makes a solemn prayer for peace as he harbours a firm belief that one day passage to peace will become a reality. Interestingly, Aju, Majumder and Syed are optimistic about the destiny of mankind and inspire men to live life hopefully.

❖❖❖❖❖

On another level Syed, Majumder and Mukhopadhyay are worried about man's destiny. Many similar thought-currents identify and determine the compass of their poetry. They use words with repeated consistency and try to communicate the surrealistic in life. Mysteries of life disturb and they try to find solutions through highly personalised ideals of life. Questions of life, death and life after death keep disturbing the poets. But one marvelous feature of their poetry is the inveterate faith and confidence in man—a highly encouraging view of life amidst pensively depressing times:

> Life's glory will never stay
> This is not a strange thing I have to say,
> ... ...
> Unaware of everything and anything.
> The claim of knowledge
> In itself is ignorance.
>
> ("Ignorance," *What the Himalaya Said...and Other Poems* 33)

Syed Ameeruddin in the above lines underlines the truth that life at the worldly level is ephemeral and man may brag about intellect but he understands nothing. He lives in ignorance and erroneously claims sovereignty over everything, and that is a huge fallacy. Life is a mysterious 'journey' because man does not know anything and invariably illusion, delusion and speciousness govern man. This thought he elucidates in "Life is a Journey," *(The Dreadful Doom to Come* 36). Life is a never-ending journey and man must go on to find the ultimate reality. The poet's anxieties about the enigma of life and living are quite discernible. He carries forward the strain of thought and emphatically makes out his mission clear. He visits and revisits bizarre and striking areas of serious deliberation and probes into the mysteries of life. Syed is worried about life on earth, perturbed about life after death and then his worries are apparent while making strenuous efforts to understand the predicament of birth and rebirth. On the other side, Majumder majestically talks about life and death and creates an ambience that nothing is to be feared. If man understands these facts and truths of life he can live happily hereafter:

> Life is present everywhere omnipresent
> Death is a pause giving life further voyage
> Death is time-bound life has not time age
> Death is cruel life's love is simply ardent.
>
> ("Life and Death," *Where Time is Dead* 71)

In death man finds life, provided he possesses an intellect to recognise the mystery. Death is just an opening of another life at another moment. Mukhopadhyay defies offensive or negative thoughts, and this psychological attitude speaks eloquently of his love for Nature:

> I will one day leave the earth
> … …
> The enjoyer of the blossoming flowers,
> Silence of the tree,
> Mystery of the whispering wind,
> Under the same canopy?
>
> ("The Witness tree," *The Witness Tree* 41)

He talks of death as a reality and infers it is time to go to another home so that someone else enjoys the music and beauty of nature. Amusingly, the poets do not give an impression of fear and dread on the mystery of death. Again, if one goes into the flow of words below, it is an experience to taste life without bothering the meaning it imparts as one reads "The Existence," *(The Witness Tree* 27). To the poets, nature is also a destructive power. Majumder speaks about the ferocity of nature when it brings annihilation and it is impossible for man to contain nature's fury.

> Sometimes Nature makes an occasion
> To demonstrate how futile it is
> To beef up security measures,
> Earth itself is unpredictable, insecure.
>
> ("Earthquake: Gujarat,"
> *Creating-killing Cosmic Time* 67)

Man not only exploits but contaminates nature; and he knows the truth that he is involved in routine activity. Indirectly, the poets highlight a singular fact that it is man who pollutes and destroys the beauty of nature and this is quite beautifully finds mention in "Beauty: Human: Nature" *(Time Never Returns to Console* 34). The dreadful scenario indirectly tells man of the wrath and panicky fear when nature is angry and causes havoc around. It is almost a visit to hell one experiences.

Mukhopadhyay speaks of a 'civilised man' who disturbs and hurts nature and thus not only dehumanises present but spoils future:

> A civilised man with a nature-lover's zeal
> ... ...
> Moves around in the fringes of the forest.
> Man has axed himself, has gone astray
> Leaving the past through the present to his future way.
> ("About a National Park," *The Witness Tree* 29)

The poets take cognisance of life's relation with nature in entirety and express kinship with rare genuineness. Not for a while poets ignore grace, instinctive Godly feeling and sublimity which an ideal life should have to ensure a harmonious existence. Poetry should ennoble a man with its all-encompassing power of beauty, grace, rhythm, music and faith in life eternal, the poets emphasize. In Aju's words, 'We relish the fun/Before reaching the ocean.' ("Life a river," *In celebration of Nature* 8). Thus the poets are emphatic and confident in the strength of nature as a force which in the ultimate analysis makes life better. Harmony and total forgetfulness in nature, the poets believe help man seek beatitude and eternal bliss.

❖❖❖❖❖

Again, at another level, hostility and conflicts extremely disturb these poets. To establish permanent sovereignty over man and land, a few people work ceaselessly to unsettle humanity and thus perpetuate an atmosphere of anarchy. War-like situations and continuing violence in certain parts of the world are handiwork of selfish people and these sentiments are ably demonstrated in "Skirmishes," (*Creating-killing Cosmic Time* 56). If war-ridden world is destined to live it is man's doing. A politician, a power hungry man, wishes to establish unrestrained domination. Majumder considers democracy, a game of numbers where legitimate expectations of people are crushed. It is an anguished reflection of a sensitive mind on the working of political people. A similar distress is expressed in the "Zen Poems, 8, 9" *(Short Verse Vast Universe* 20) of Aju Mukhopadhyay where the poet reveals a ruthless truth that the politicians usually live in untruth and fabrication and also talks of a virtual disappearance of good persons from the scene.

Socially conscious, Syed Ameeruddin is effusively aware of the cynicism and ambiguity of contemporary world. If politics creates discordant notes in society and brings miseries to the nation, it is also the root cause of sufferings and agonies of man. To be good in this world is treated as a weakness. He rightly points out that 'to be human, is inhuman today, to be inhuman is human today.' A politician is: A maniac/A self-styled and self-lured/Diabolic being…'Despair of our age,' *(The Dreadful Doom to Come* 23). Contemporary man is a fiend—a devil in spirit and temperament—and so he is the reason and cause of miseries and sufferings. In a fanatic attitude, he only hurts and destroys finer instincts in many. The anxiety of the poet Majumder is reflected in the verse "In Wintry Morning" where he says that man's greed for growth and development is polluting a healthy environment which will finally result in total chill in life as he says, We welcome the migratory birds to lesser cold place. But not withering of cold on earthly space. "A Wintry Morning," *(Time Never Returns to Console* 84). Naked commercialisation of natural resources will eventually bring 'cold on earthly space'—a situation where everything will look deserted and inhospitable. Aju Mukhopadhyay raises a strong voice against prevalent inequality. He speaks of a system—probably hints at the country's plight with an oblique reference to world's deplorable living conditions where the rulers have failed to provide a clean government—that does not really work for the downtrodden and this purity of feelings is revealed in "Antithesis". Had this been not the condition, people would have enjoyed life of equality in social and economic life. Thus the poets are worried about the social, economic and political plight of man and question the validity of the system which rules man.

❖❖❖❖❖

Whatever might be the worries of the poets, it is clearly observed that they are patriotic and nationalistic. Without hesitation, the poets glorify India's Vedic culture and heritage. Unmistakably they convey the message that we live if India lives. It is apparent that poets analyse India's pains and trials in historical perspectives. Majumder speaks about the territorial integrity and peculiar identity of the country:

> A nature is respected for the territory it belongs
> Like a bird is recognised by its songs
> Weakness is fragmentation of tradition and culture—
> Respect and honesty key to territorial integrity
> My India stands for cherished identity.
>
> ("Territorial Identity and Integrity," *Through Corridor of Time* 13)

On the other hand, Mukhopadhyay appears to link contemporary issues with nature and environment. He talks of unfortunate disintegrating forces causing threats to the unity of the country. Syed is more enthusiastic in giving vent to feelings and thoughts of patriotism and nationalism by invoking great heroes and areas of teachings in his immortal verse "My India." *(Visioned Summits* 61-62). Syed Ameeruddin is worried about the loss of old splendour, purity, love and virtues of Lord Rama, Krishna and saints of various religions, and thus reaffirms faith in the never dying spirit of love and humanism. These poets consider time as a spiritual force. Aju Mukhopadhyay pays rich tributes to the mystical presence of time. Its sovereignty can't be questioned. If man acts now with a harmonious heart and intellect, he will make life meaningful. Time's movement is eternal and none can stop it if one reads, "With the Time," *(The Paper Boat 4)*. Majumder in an individualistic technique interprets time. Time appears dead when man does not grow and it is then a medium to carry dead bodies to future, he tells. In a philosophic contour, he talks of new areas and meanings of time: 'Life of time is not length of life-time/It is important when life-time is prime/In a stagnant life time is dead /Active life is what time is made.' ("Life of Time," *Where Time is Dead* 10)

Despite impediments, Syed Ameeruddin tries to explain enigmatic life in terms of time. In "Whispers of Beyond" (*Visioned Summits* 71-72) he quaintly attempts to foresee what lies hidden in horizons beyond. One is awakened to a make-believe reality of time. Here time stretches beyond the parameters of past, present and future. One comprehends the mystery but still remains in utter darkness and fumbles for a concrete distinctive image. Remarkable in crafting and coining new words with musical undertones, Syed's indulgence in poetic liberty stirs as imaginative sweep defies restrain.

❖❖❖❖❖

Finally, one finds the poetry of Aju Mukhopadhyay, Pronab Kumar Majumder and Syed Ameeruddin, simple and straight. Aju and Pronab are genuine in conveying contemporary anxieties. Aju is a poet of nature and its beauty and seeks divine solace in nature while making conscious efforts to find solution to teething modern problems. Majumder takes up issues harassing human mind. He deliberates on fear, death, peace, anxiety, love, time, birth, life and life after death, and comes out with multifaceted interpretations and solutions. Ameeruddin is a poet of high sounding words and an astonishing power of echoes words create, continue to reverberate in the ears for a long time. He coins new words lyrically while awe-inspiring images propel readers to another experience. He reflects on the contemporary predicament of human life and in the process moves from the mortal world to the unknown in search of harmony. But these three poets also seem to ignore the complexities of life and the system. They use understandable similes and metaphors and to a large extent they are pedagogic. It is worthwhile to make a mention that poetry of Syed, Aju and Majumder leaves an everlasting imprint of soft sublimity in the hearts and minds like Krishna Srinivas and Raghupathi.

Shiv K. Kumar and Keki N. Daruwalla with urban backgrounds depict contemporary life with all its complexities and predicament where materialism has virtually taken over the man entirely; and the psychological and physical survival is determined by the degree of wealth, ego and self-interest. They are elegant, sensitive and extremely gracious in the use of language, and are also inclined towards the uniqueness of Indian culture and tradition with an elite's exclusiveness. The mystery of birth, life, death, woman and existence disturb and the poets are inexplicably attracted towards the enigma of life. This has shades of despair, frustration and disillusionment in their poetry. They impress with the power of stunning imagery. A journey from the internal to the external world and back constitutes the area of their poetic dimensions, and all experiences struggle to find universality in the essence of personal feelings. Kumar and Daruwalla, in expression of thought and feeling, exhibit sophisticated restraint while depicting realities of life and reveal a dominant virtuosity of great craftsmen, saturated with bona-fide socio-economic and political truth in correct historical and cultural perspective.

As observed elsewhere, to me it appears, many poets of that period particularly of the pre-independence era educated abroad or in English schools—or a product of the metropolitan cities—were inclined towards Western thoughts and habits but in the ultimate analysis when disillusioned they often turned to the origin to locate roots; and that makes a big difference. From this angle the poetry requires understanding and interpretation. If such poets had the impact of T. S. Eliot and others, it is natural if one also analysis the tremendous influence of stunning progress made around in various wings of life. On the other hand, in poetic and intellectual range of these poets, one finds flashes of Ageya, Bharati, Shamsher Bahadur Singh and Narendra Mohan who were giving expressions to contemporary issues man was confronting at that time of history when scientific, industrial and technological growth was making everlasting impact in India.

Works Cited

Ameeruddin. Syed. *The Dreadful Doom to Come*. Madras: Poets Press India, 1974. Print.

_____ *A Lover and A Wanderer*. Madras: Poets Press India, 1980. Print.

_____ *Petallic Love Times*. Madras: Poets Press India, 1988. Print.

_____ *Visioned Summits*. Ed. Krishna Srinivas. Madras: International Poets Academy, 2005. Print

_____ *Visions of Deliverance*. Ed. Krishna Srinivas. Madras: International Poets Academy, 2005. Print.

_____ *What the Himalaya Said...and Other Poems*. Madras: Kalaivendhan Publications, 1972. Print.

Daruwalla, Keki N. *Night River*. Delhi: Rupa Paperback, 2000, Print.

_____ *Under Orion*. Delhi: Rupa Paperback, 2000. Print.

_____ *Winter Poems*. Delhi: Rupa Paperback, 2000, Print.

Kumar, Shiv K. *Articulate Silences*. Kolkota: A Writers Workshop Publications, 1970. Print.

_____ *Subterfuges*. Delhi: Oxford University Press, 1976. Print.

_____ *Woodpeckers*. London: Sidgwick & Jackson 1 Tavistock Chambers, Bloomsbury Way, 1979. Print.

Majumder, Pronab Kumar. *Creating-Killing Cosmic Time*. Kolkata: A Writers Workshop Publication, 2002. Print.

_____ *Faces of Love*. Kolkata: Bridge-in-Making Publication, 2008. Print.

_____ *My India: Through Corridor of Time*. Kolkata: Bridge-in-Making Publication, 2008. Print.

_____ *Passage to Peace*. Kolkata: Bridge-in-Making Publication, 2009. Print.

_____ *Time Never Returns to Console*. Kolkata: A Writers Workshop Publication, 2007. Print.

_____ *Where I is a Noun*. Kolkata: A Writers Workshop Publication, 2008. Print.

_____ *Where Time is Dead*. Kolkata: A Writers Workshop Publication. 2005. Print.

Mukhopadhyay, Aju. In *Celebration of Nature*. Published by Baldev Mirza, 2007. Print.

_____ *The Paper Boat*. Bareilly: Prakash Book Depot, 2007. Print.

_____ *Short Verse Vast Universe*. Pondicherry: Sri Aurobindo's Actions, 2005. Print.

_____ Sri *Aurobindo and The Mother*. Bareilly: Prakash Book Depot, 2007. Print.

_____ *The Witness Tree*. Kolkata: A Writers Workshop Pub, 2000. Print.

Paniker, K. Ayyappa. *Modern Indian Poetry in English*. Delhi: Sahitya Akademi, 1991. Print.

Raghupathi, K. V. *Brave New Wave, 21 Indian English Poets*. Jaipur: Book Enclave, 2009. Print.

Singh, R. A. *Continuity: Five Indian English Poets*. Jaipur: Book Enclave, 200. Print.

2

Landscapes: A Landmark in Keki Daruwalla's Poetry

— Asha Viswas

From 1970 *(Under Orion)* to 1987 *(Landscapes)* Keki Daruwalla has travelled a long distance on his creative journey. The growth of consciousness from the mundane to the vast space of the world of nature, from human subjects and man's creation to objects and God's creation, is a reflection of the poet's maturity of vision. Gone are the mud-scapes of corruption and crime. The hawk that did not let go corruption when it got it between its teeth, now turns its gaze away from the 'descending void' which unfolds 'the rottenness of death unmitigated by maggots' *(Under Orion,* 45), and the 'mass of liquefied flesh seething in fear.' From this 'Inferno' to the 'Purgatorio' of 'fear' and 'angst' of *Winter Poems* to the 'Paradise' of *Landscapes*—this is how one can map the poetic terrain of Daruwalla.

Landscapes is a product of thousands of egoless perceptions, a kind of translation of the visible external world into internal consciousness. It is a poetry where imagination touches the wavelength of the contemplated object. The duality of mind and matter is lost and man and landscape understand each other. About his preoccupation with landscape, the poet says, 'My poems are rooted in landscape which anchors the poem. The landscape is not merely there to set the scene but to lead to an illumination. It should be the eye of the spiral. I try that poetry relates to the landscape, both on the physical, and' on the plane of the spirit'[1]

In another interview he comments: 'I can't help bringing the landscape into my writing whether it is fiction or whether it is poetry—because it is just there. If you have an eye for what is around you, the first thing you will notice is the landscape.'[2]

In his earlier volumes too, Daruwalla's concern for landscape is in evidence. *The Keeper of the Dead* and *Crossing of Rivers* show man and landscape meeting and finding each other. But these landscape poems are the result of intellection which depends on the senses. It is in *Landscapes* that the earlier intellection has given way to emotional response which defeats the senses. The intellect that apprehends also experiences the sensations. At times, the poet rises higher from the sensory confines of sight and sound, time and space.

Interestingly, it is a hawk ready to pounce on its prey that first meets the eye on the cover of this volume. The poet seems to have a great fascination for birds of prey—hawks, eagles and vultures. Occasionally, the reader may find a mallard or a parakeet flying by, but it is the predator birds that outnumber the others. The poet admits that, the depiction of these predator birds is 'deliberate, of course, I mean, the symbolism is very clear: it refers to aggressiveness...'[3] Birds are also regarded as a symbol of the soul. As early as the Rigveda, the sages regarded the human body as a city with eleven gates. 'The immortal soul is the "Hamsa," the swan of heaven who lives in this city as a guest.' One interviewer has traced bird symbolism to Harappan civilisation.[5] But as the bird(s) in the Vedic hymns and in Harappan civilisation or in Mesopotamian myths are not predator birds, it is difficult to accept this symbolism. This recurrence of the predator bird may, perhaps, be attributed to the Parsi psyche. As a sensitive child, teenager or young man, the poet must have seen many of these hawks, vultures and eagles hovering over the 'towers of silence,' where the Parsis leave the dead bodies to be devoured by these birds.[7]

Yet another interpretation could be to regard the predator bird as a symbol of energy. For William Blake lions, tigers, wolves and eagles represented creative, heroic, unrestrained as well as revolutionary and righteously destructive energy. In *The Marriage of Heaven and Hell* Blake wrote: "When thou seest an eagle; thou seest a portion of genius." Daruwalla's predator hawk and eagle too, are symbols of energy at all levels—primal, natural, physical, sexual and creative. They represent the poet's own creative vitality, his poetic genius as well as his angry pounce on corruption. His earlier collection *The Keeper of the Dead* begins with "Hawk" who is 'a rapist in the harem of the sky.' Here, the hawk is opposed to Dove, symbolic of peace. 'Like a black prophecy' the future will be full of hawks who will destroy all those: 'Crying for the right to dream, the right to flesh,/the right to sleep with their own wives.' In the last two lines of the second section of this poem, the poet talks of the slow bringing up of the hawk: '...they feed the hawk by carving the breast/of the quarry bird and gouging out his heart.'

Daruwalla's own comment about these two lines is as follows:

> I would like to say that the fact of the hawk, who is touched by man, the one who is actually trained for falconeering, is absolutely authentic—in the sense that they actually carve out the bird's heart and give it to the hawk; that is how the hawk is brought up slowly." I have read about it. The details are correct; but, of course, I am trying to give them a different dimension.[8]

The last section of the poem is written in the first person. The poet confesses—'The central focus of this particular poem is revealed by the last section of the poem, where I involve myself with the hawk totally.'[9] As a police officer Daruwalla has the first-hand experience of the atrocities committed. Thus he himself wears the predatory mien to victimise the weak.

In "The Fighting Eagles" *(In My Father's House),* the predator birds are compared to soldiers fighting on a hill for a woman or a piece of land—'All their lives they had trained for this. ..turning their screams to the right pitch of hatred.' Yet another collection of poems, *Apparition in April* begins with 'vultures' where 'time is a vulture wing on the glide under a blue sky.' The vultures 'gather like a brewing storm' and the sublimity of the scene has a cathartic effect on baser passions.

In "The People" critics and readers are assigned 'vulture talons.' They swarm 'like a nervous disorder,' can even turn "some pie-dog into Prometheus.' In "Indian Adolescence," 'Vulture urge' has sexual connotations. In *Landscapes*[10] this perspective changes and the predator bird is not only a victim of time that devours all but also a symbol of all consuming time. The seventh poem of this collection "Requiem for a Hawk" presents the predator as a victim.

> ....Now you shift
> from predator-bird to preyed upon fossil
> Witness to a glacier-slow geological drift.

A news item about the discovery of the rock fossil of a hawk triggers off the poet's imagination. Since the fossil was found 'at least a hundred miles away from hawk country,' the poet imagines all the details such as how, while taking 'his rounds' the bird lost its way and came to 'the wrong sky':

> ...the storm came ere he could map
> the country. The perch of air beneath him
> wobbled; the fulcrum snapped.

The fossil of the hawk 'from head to hooked feet' 'entombed in nature's masonry' arouses the poet's sympathy not only for this particular fossilised hawk but for the whole species of birds—victimisers and the victimised, that are ruthlessly killed for the pleasure or palate of the rich. It is this sympathetic tone that pervades this collection of poems. The earlier irony, satire and anger have given place to love that embraces all flora and fauna. The poet, like Coleridge's Ancient Mariner, has attained inner peace and quietitude. It is with this changed softer vision that he perceives each object. There is nothing hard or grating and the poems move in a calmness which is a gift of communion with nature. There is no edge to his voice and the social issues are not incorporated in this collection. The poet comes in the incarnation of a traveller, a spectator and a painter. His seeing and surveying of 'the external object' is closely linked to emotional intensity. He does not present a mere carbon copy with his empirical vision but with his imaginative power he rises much higher. In the very first poem, the poet affirms:

> I have come here not to slake the senses
> but to assuage an old thirst for the sea[10]
> ("Mandwa" 9)

One of the main themes of this collection is the endless, eternal, elusive and haunting change which is an aspect of nature. The essential quality of substance is its spatio-temporal relationship. Everything which is in space has a definite limitation. Similarly, everything endures only during a certain period of time. Poems such as the "Requiem for a Hawk," "The Last Howl," "Wolf," "Migrations" and "The Fall of Mohenjo-Daro" have an explicit reference to matter, which is located in time and space and hence, ceases to be. The past, thus, gets distilled in the present. While the fossilised hawk fell prey to time in the form of storm and tidal waves, the wolf that had, in the past, acquired almost a mythic stature for terrorising children's dreams, is in its turn, terrorised by the gun toting agents of death. The narrator's childhood consciousness was filled with 'half silhouette and half myth' wolf:

> My mother said
> his ears stand up
> at the fall of dew
> he can sense a shadow
> move across a hedge
> on a dark night
> he can sniff out
> your approaching dreams;
> There is nothing
> that won't be lit up
> by the dark torch of his eyes.
> ("Wolf 17)

The brutal killings of the wolves in the present times have destroyed the mythic past. The narrator compares his childhood dreams ('A child's night is a village on the forest edge') to his daughter's dream ('A hedge of smoking gun-barrels rings my daughter's dreams'). The poet laments the senseless killings as well as the deconstruction of a myth. "The Last Howl" is a sequel to 'Wolf and is full of wolf stories heard in childhood. These stories are woven from the black thread of magic and witchcraft:

> As they bayed a moment came
> when sorcerers threw salt in the fire
> and prayed for a spurt in the exorcising flame.
>
> ("The Last Howl")

Here ethnology runs parallel to violence—of man's wilful destruction of fauna. In fact, this chapter of black and white is replaced by a dark crimson stain. Industrialisation, along with its ally urbanisation, is now weaving a different complexion of thought on the loom of time. The last six lines of the poem present the stained web:

> They turned their snorkels to the moon
> and howled for the last time the howl of no hope.
> They sniffed the wind and moved into myth,
> into childhood dreams, allegory, fiction;
> and catching a scent of their own death
> they tracked it to extinction.
>
> ("The Last Howl")

Not only the living creatures, even civilisations fall prey to time, sometimes in the form of foreign invasions. In "Of Mohenjo-Daro at Oxford" and its sequel "The Fall of Mohenjo-Daro," the poet unearths a past. He has a great fascination for the past, for history. He admits:

> I am fascinated with the way people must have lived. I am not really making my poems allegorical for the present. That is facile. It is going back in time and putting your finger on the pulse there.

In "Of Mohenjo-Daro at Oxford," the old archaeologist shares with the poet his reminiscences of unearthing the ruins of a past civilisation. In fact, it is not just one past, but 'nine strata of the city...where pasts had settled over earlier pasts.' Brick by brick that past is reconstructed:

> A Gilgamesh motif on a seal,
> a man fighting two tigers,
> sent me voyaging to Sumer,
> argosies sailing up the Tigris
> laden with Indian cotton;
> a turquoise bead, a lapis Lazuli trinket
> brought caravans from Tabriz and Shiraz,
> the harness-bells jangling, dogs barking
> as the centuries waved to each other,
> on the crossroads.
>
> ("Of Mohenjo-Daro at Oxford")

The eloquent, concrete, visual and auditory images take the reader from place to place and evoke an ambience of colour and sound. But behind this Keatsian sensuousness is the sad reflection that everything, big or small, falls prey to time. The poem ends on a note of haunting sadness:

> I search for memories
> they have swung away like the rooks.
> I dig for words
> and I can't f**
>
> ("Of Mohenjo-Daro at Oxford")

In "The Fall of Mohenjo-Daro", instead of the old archaeologist, the poet uses the dead citizens of the ruined civilisation to narrate the horror of the invasion. Tempted by green pastures, the invaders came, 'hair wind-blown, eyes hard as quartz-flakes.' With their weapons and horses, they laid waste the whole city:

> So now you find us, cozy, calcinated
> in history's forgotten grooves.
> The years will not go round for us
> threshing seasons under the hooves.
>
> ("The Fall of Mohenjo-Daro")

Time encompasses human history. Nature creates and corrodes. Geological catastrophes result in devastation or metamorphoses in the vortex of the material universe. Drought is another catalyst for devastation. In "Migrations" the poet juxtaposes the 'earth cracks seen through blackened stubble' and the starved tribal:

> Tribal—dark and thick-lipped.
> ...ankle, knee and hip-joint
> angling out of his parchment skin.
> He was still and silhouette-black;
> even his eyes didn't move
>
> ("Migrations")

Yet another incarnation of time as the "Mahakala" is in the form of an earthquake. In "Skopje: The Earthquake City," the poet narrates the devastation of Skopje, the present capital of Macedonia, by a massive earthquake in 1963. On his visit to the museum of this Slav city, he finds pieces of the past preserved in the museum—'The coming of Nazis,' the war and the earthquake. 'History is carved,' here 'in disaster eras.' The museum displays a clock too 'that stopped at 0157.' The frozen hands of the clock are an apt metaphor 'for time and the seasons,' that move in a circle. As opposed to this circular movement of time, the linear movement of scientific progress, in the shapes of tunnels and TV towers of the present age, does not augur well for a peaceful future.

In "Suomenlinna," there is no geological catastrophe but the fear of aggression that changes this island across the Baltic sea. Eight thousand soldiers patrol the coast looking out for the 'Russian or Swedish foe.' The imposition of physical force in the form of military occupation of the island and its utter wastefulness irks the poet. Moreover, there is no point in standing on guard duty when no enemy has approached the fortifications for centuries. Tyrannical military power robs its people of peace as the Scandinavian coast has been littered with cannons 'trained against the sea.' Thus a preface for another devastation has been written in the book of history. The poem ends on a sad ironic note:

A beach, people sunning themselves,
children building sand-houses—that's no island.
Battlements on the coast, trained cannon,
a sentry tower, that's an island.
So that nothing can come in
so that nothing can go out.

("Suomenlinna")

"Green Shoots at Volgograd" is another poem that presents a landscape of devastation resulting from aggression:

The mass-grave right there at the memorial
may appear too brutal, but it happened that way.
Those who fought together lie huddled together.

("Green Shoots at Volgograd")

Here, the Nazis are the agents of devastation. The 'unleafing tree' that is planted over the mass grave is an apt symbol for the dea soldiers.

This motif of species and civilisations devoured by time and the thrown like drybones, into the dustbin of history, is repeated again and again. But this does not make Daruwalla 'a poet of hawks, wolve knives and bones' as is suggested by E.V. Ramakrishnan in his review of *Landscapes.* Destruction is only half the picture. The other half is subtly projected by a number of poems that celebrate birth. The creation of new life is presented in all its aspects—the travails of the mother, the infant kicking in the womb, the head coming out, etc. It does not matter whether the birth is that of a human being or of an animal—it is the most mysterious, wondrous sight. It is not only in this collection, but elsewhere too, Daruwalla presents this creative aspect of nature. In the second part of *The Keeper of the Dead,* the poem "To my Daughter Rookzair" presents the labour pains, the infant drawn 'from the weed-bed of the womb.' The poet showers-his blessings on the "supple boned fledgeling". In "For My Daughter, Anaheita" *("Winter Poems")* he repeats the same theme. In the present collection there are three poems about the miraculous event.

In "Gulzaman's Son," the solitary shepherd, ragged about his virility, avoids human company and showers his love and care on his sheep. The moment he reaches the fold, the ewe, writhing in labour pains, 'snuggles up to him and bleats...a thin tremolo of love blanketed by gutturals of pain.' Like an expert midwife, Gulzaman examines her with his heavily greased arms. He knows that 'the lamb is on its way.' An hour later, the lamb is born:

> ...quavery-legged
> and wet and uncertain about
> its rickety, four-pronged hold on the earth
>
> ("Gulzaman's Son)

The birth of a lamb is, in no way, different from the birth of a human infant. In "Lambing" it is the sheep itself that gives an account of the travails in human terms:

> I lie still, knowing pain is next door.
> The lamb is already knocking at the gates,
> kicking away, impatient to shift
> from the pastures of my body
> ....
> I know of failing strength and faltering feet.
> I know I am hungry but I cannot eat,
> for though I am patient
> the lamb within me has turned urgent
> as it twists and strains against my side
> and turns as I rum...
>
> ("Lambing")

The empathy of the lines is more genuine than Coleridge's fraternity with the ass. Daruwalla has drifted far from the 'Scythed fields' of modernism. In "A Pregnancy in the Hills," the expectant mother's belly is described in the register of midwifery:

> Taut as a drumskin
> the belly turns translucent,
> showing its arborescing veins.
> As a trace the capillaries
> the child moves away
> from this bank of your body.
>
> ("A Pregnancy in the Hills")

Lines like these display the poet's excitement and wonder at the prospect of creation. It does not matter whether this creation is in the world of human beings or of fauna. What is important is that the pain and joy of animals are compared to that of human beings. His sympathy for birds and beasts brings him closer to the Romantics.

This circle of creation and destruction shows Daruwalla's philosophic apprehension of the interlocked relation between the two. The event of destruction has a past while creation mirrors within itself a future. These motifs of creation and destruction bring the poet close to Shelley. In his poem "The Cloud" Shelley expressed this unending circle thus—'I change but I cannot die.' Though in this volume Daruwalla does not say this so explicitly, yet the reader may infer it from lines like—'the river flows, ever changing yet changeless' ("Ruminations at Verinag"). In his latest collection of poem *Night River* (2000), the dedication 'For Nainaz and Freyana who came recently into the world and for Khurshid who left,' the poet's acceptance of this circle, of creation and destruction is very clear.

As against this multiverse where everything is tentative, the mysterious presence of nature in solitude, 'Mountains axing down two thousand feet deep' shows that there are objects that have endurance, if not eternity. Poems like "Crossing Chorhoti" and "Ruminations at Verinag" present these enduring objects of nature. Moreover, the landscape, in these poems, encompasses the human and the divine. The trinity of the creator, nature and man is interwoven harmoniously and so is the trinity of the poet's perception, reflection and imagination. In "Crossing Chorhoti," the poet describes the travails of a trek across the Chorhoti pass near the Indo-Tibet border. At 16,000 feet, away from vegetation, the 'night' has 'teeth' and the 'wind' becomes a 'switchblade.' When the tribal compares crossing a pass to bearing a child, the similarity is not that of suffering but of heroism—the heroism of the mother who gives birth as well as that of the one who is born. From a mother's point of view, it is a conscious.heroic deed. It is the giving over of oneself to the life of another that makes it a truly heroic deed. As motherhood involves danger, mountain trekking too involves danger and requires heroism. From the infant's point of view, the transformation from being a water creature living safely in the amniotic fluid into an air-breathing, dependent mammal, will not be easy. If taken consciously, such a journey would be heroic indeed. Traversing the womb wall and mountain trekking need the same heroism:

> We had to reach the pass
> ....We crunched our way across the frosted earth,
> Over the rock-and-bone tundra,
> then up a defile on to a stretch
> of gently rising rock.
> We had transcended even moisture now,
>
> ("Crossing Chorhoti")

At last, the trekking is over and the climbers touch "the top ozone and ether, and a shell burst of light greeted" them, 'fifty Indian peaks erupted.' Here the words, the 'top ozone and ether' and a 'shell burst of light,' have neither the 'inert tone of impersonal phrases' nor 'the incapacity on the poet's part to participate in the scene' as is suggested by E.V. Ramakrishnan in his review of *Landscapes.* These lines are an important evidence of the poet's absorption in scientific accuracy. Daruwalla is a thoughtful, well-read poet with interests that are related to philosophy and arts but at the same time sympathetic with science. Shelley's poems, too, are permeated with such descriptions in which the aesthetics and science merge without any conflict. In fact, the afore-quoted phrases from Daruwalla's poem prove that there is no conflict between reflection and perception. The last four lines of the 10th section of the poem are an apt example of this double vision. The totality of the poet's being is immersed in perceiving the breathtaking beauty of the peaks. At the same time, the hand of the creator is visualised behind this creation of ethereal beauty.

> With snow and the spray-hangover
> of icefalls and the blue of distance,
> as if some god had with a palette-knife
> honed the landscape with ethereal colours.
>
> ("Crossing Chorhoti")

If Kailash remains 'veiled by a cloud layer of white' and Daruwalla cannot penetrate beyond it in order to 'see into the heart of things' (as is commented by E.V. Ramakrishnan in his review) one should know that in the *Upanishads* the Absolute is described as 'neti neti.' There is nothing beyond the veil.

In "Ruminations at Verinag" too, the human and the divine are inseparable. From the skies to the valley, from south to north, the whole landscape wears one colour:

> ....Nothing is bluer, nor ether, nor
> comet-fires
> nor crystal nor sapphire;
> no speculum of a mineral-coloured bird
> is so intense. This blue dot is the word
> in its womb chamber...
> Even the air above it becomes a blue vibration.
>
> ("Ruminations at Verinag")

The place is said to be visited by the blue-necked Shiva and his consort Parvati, 'Perhaps with chilblained toes they came in the summer-thirst of their passions.' Parvati is the Godly ideal of the chaste wife. Shiva and Parvati (Shakti), the cosmic male and female represent conjugal love. Shiva also stands for primal energy—the blue flame.

From this mythico-divine love, there is a shift to human love. One finds a male ambience in Daruwalla's earlier works. One may find references to 'razor-shaved legs,' 'Her torso...double fried eggs,' or a 'Vanilla-pudding face' *(Apparition in April).* In *Landscape,* for the first time, the poet celebrates conjugal love in all its tenderness and beauty. Far from being a purely physical, earthly passion that bums, this love is calm and brings peace:

> ...your hair trailed over my face and pieced
> together the bruised bits of my being...
> The light from your eyes
> Phased the darkness out.

This love has the peace of the five elements—the earth element arises out of touch, from 'the waters of...body' the water element, air from love's ccstasy, fire from 'the light from...eyes,' space corresponds to 'the sky above...your hair trailed over my face.' Thus the five elements and are five senses, the human, the divine all merge in a humanised love which is never a transgression. The serenity of the landscape also adds to the calm and peace attained by the lover.

The sequence of six poems "The Round of the Seasons" (In the footsteps of Abhinanda and Yogeshwara) imitates Sanskrit love poetry. These poems do not have the ironic edge which one finds in Nissim Ezekiel's love poems which are also written in imitation of the Sanskrit love poets. In Daruwalla, each season is a metaphor for a mental or physical state.[11] In "Vasanta" (Spring):

> A bird alights on the leafing lotus bed
> thinking it is an island.
> Bathing on the ghats,
> shawled in mist, she finds
> bees moving towards her breast-tips.

The image is as soft as a whiff of gentle breeze in the Indian spring season. The words have a touch of a painter and the expression is a picture filled with the season and its warmth.

In "Grishma" (Summer), the forest fires match the fire of passion. Like an antelope trapped in forest fire, the lover loses his way 'in the forest of your limbs, under the black rain of your hair.' 'Varsha' (the rains) is associated with nocturnal trysts. Daruwalla follows the Sanskrit poetry convention of the woman going to meet her lover on a rainy night which enhances the erotic mood. However, the poem is less concerned with the meeting of the lovers, it pays more attention to the loneliness and sadness of the lover separated from his beloved. In "Sharad" (Autumn), the season makes no change to the feelings of love: 'Is lightning necessary for those smitten by lover's lightning?' In "Hemant" (Early winter) tpo, 'it is a season for arrivals' of lovers. In "Sisira" (Late winter), the pen picture of the woman, leaving her lover in the early hours of the morning, is painted with aesthetic strokes:

The one that had slipped from his string bed
Light as a dawn breeze,
the colours of the east
streaking across her love-bitten face.

("Sisira")

Daruwalla's forte is imagery and the lines present a collage of shape and form through colours and nuances. There is perfect harmony between impression and expression.

In the anonymity and impersonality of the women of these six poems, Daruwalla follows the Sanskrit love poets. These poems can be compared with Nissim Ezekiel's poems written in imitation of the predecessors, the Sanskrit love poets. While in Ezekiel there is an obsession with female protuberances, in Daruwalla it is totally absent. In Ezekiel, the descriptions of female^ anatomy are graphic and uninhibited. In Daruwalla they are suggestivk and wrapped in decency. While Ezekiel's women are urban, in Daruwalla all love-making takes place in a pastoral background as is indicated by the very title of the sequence "The Round of the Seasons" ("In the footsteps of Abhinanda and Yogeswara"). Ezekiel describes various types of women classified on the basis of their love-making. There are the bashful coquettes, the initiatoress, the wanton, the harlot, the formidable, etc. These emotionless women in Ezekiel have no warmth and they are associated with urban defilement and debasement. Daruwalla consciously makes a departure from this particular characteristic of modernism which makes everything devoid of meaning. When one loses faith in everything, even love is reduced to mere friction of skins. Daruwalla's love poems retain the romance. His women are not the by-product of the indifferent, callous, rotten city. Though the women in these six poems are not presented as chaste wives because the emotion of love manifests itself in extra-marital relationship as is the convention in Sanskrit love poetry, yet even this love retains the tenderness and beauty of human passions.

Part two of the collection is entitled *Oxford and After*. Daruwalla has been called "The Poet of North India."[12] He confesses:

> I used to shun non-Indian subjects because I did not feel I could write about them.... My earlier ambitions... were conditioned by my small town mentality.[13]

In this collection, the poet writes about his visits to England, Eastern Europe and Scandinavia. "Coming into Heathrow" describes the initial 'euphoria' and subsequent disenchantment with 'nylon furs and electric fires.' In 'Christmas Eve Walk,' the poet feels like 'one lone expatriate flake of snow.' Memories from India crowd in to make him nostalgic for his own country:

> I think of Indian evenings,
> shrill with cricket and bull-frog-burp,
> the banyan tree whose arbours fill with rooks...
>
> ("Christmas Eve Walk")

The last four poems of this collection present another sequence. These poems describe different phases in the life of the American poet Ted Roethke. The first poem of this sequence is about Otto Roethke, the father of the poet who cared more for the plants in his greenhouses than for his son. The sensitive son could not forget the slights he suffered:

> He's old enough to feel the hurt
> Crawling on fours, tugging in dark
> on bristly stem with bruised hands
> ...while orchid, rose and carnation
> are tended by the father, who
> does not know he has lost a son.
>
> ("The Father Florist")

Otto Roethke's death had a traumatic effect on the son. This is the theme of the second poem "Grass and Wind." His loneliness and loss of faith in God made him seek refuge in alcoholic drinks. The poet's attacks of hyperactivity and disorganised behaviour are the subject of the third poem—"Breakdown." "The Season of Light" presents the peace and happiness that Roethke eventually found after his marriage to Beatrice O'Connell in 1953. The last two lines of this poem:

> Later in day Light came and knocked:
> Eternity was manifest.

are an apt conclusion not only for this poem but for the *Landscapes.* None can remain an atheist in landscapes like these.

Like Vikram Seth's *Golden Gate* (1986), Daruwalla's *Landscapes* too, makes a complete departure from modernism. In its love for nature, love for the past, love for mythic lore, emotional intensity, lack of irony and satire, the collection shows the poet moving away from the sand-dunes of modernism towards greener pastures.

Notes and References

1. Ramakrishnan, E.V. "Poetry of Knives and Bones": A Review of K.N. Daruwalla's *Landscapes.*
2. Personal interview with Geeti Sen, in *India International Centre,* Quarterly, 1984, 234-35.
3. *India International Centre,* 230.
4. *Hymns of the Rigveda,* Tr. Ralph T.H. Griffith, 1971, Varanasi, Chowkhamba Sanskrit Series, IV, XL, 5.
5. In her interview with Daruwalla, Geeti Sen comments: I am reminded of the beautifully painted jars of the late Harappan civilisation, from cemetery H, where they have birds and peacocks painted around the rim of the large jars. These were placed in cemeteries so the birds were a symbol of the after-life.... These particular jars are given as evidence of the belief that people believed in the soul, as visualised in the form of the bird. *India International Centre,* 230.
6. Daruwalla in an interview comments: I think, according to some Mesopotamian myths also, the soul is the bird itself; and the soul flying away is like a bird flying away. *India International Centre.*
7. Piloo Nanavutty, in her book *The Parsis* explains the meaning of "Towers of silence" in the following words: The English phrase, "Towers of silence," for the original Dakhma or Dokhma was coined by Robert Xavier Murphy...in the late 19th century. As the Achaemenians held sacred the three elements of earth, fire and water, the corpse could neither be buried, burnt or immersed. Dead bodies were, therefore, exposed on mountain tops, or placed in towards specially built for this purpose...the tower is a massive structure of solid stone—divided into three rows of shallow, open receptacles. The first row is for the males, the second for females and the third for children. There are holes in the inner side of the

well through which rain-water is carried into four underground drains at the base of the tower...connected with four underground wells-pieces of charcoal and sandstone are placed at the end of each drain.... Thus, the rain-water passing over the bones is purified before entering the soil, in keeping with the ancient command that the earth shall not be polluted.

(The Delhi Parsee Anjuman, 1992, Appendix B).

8. *India International Centre,* 229.
9. *India International Centre,* 229.
10. Daruwalla, K.N. *Landscapes* (1987; Delhi: OUP), 9. All subsequent quotations from *Landscapes* are taken from this edition only.
11. de Souza, Eunice. *Talking Poems: Conversations with Poets,* 1999. New Delhi: OUP, 49.
12. de Souza, 50.
13. de Souza, 50.

3

A Study of Discourse Construction in the Select Poem of Keki N. Daruwalla

—Jayshree Goswami and Mojibur Rahman

The present paper intends to study the discourse construction of "Caries." This poem by Daruwalla has been interpreted on the discourse model provided by Halliday.

According to Halliday and many other functional linguists, anthropologists, sociologists as well as philosophers of language, language study cannot be successfully fulfilled without considering the situation of context, for it is constrained and influenced by the situation of context. These practitioners stress that the study of words, utterance even whole chunks of discourse, cannot be appreciated without the convention of contexts among them. Context can well be understood from Norman Fairclough's interpretation of discourse, "the ways of representing aspects of the world—the processes, relations and structures of the material world, the 'mental world' of thoughts, feelings, beliefs and so forth, and the social world."[1] In addition, Halliday claims that the context of situation is obtained through a systematic relationship between the social environments on the one hand, and the functional organisation of language, on the other, which can be best understood in terms of 'registers'. Register, a semantic concept, is very important because it is seen as the linguistic consequence of interacting aspects of contexts, which halliday calls 'field, tenor and mode.' These three contextual features help in constructing an idea about the texts' purposes and reasons, as well as its structure, and the adequate use of language in the text. Field refers to the topics and actions which language is used to express; tenor indicates the language users, their purposes, and their relationship to each other. Mode stands for the channel through which communication is carried out.

Caries

1) First when the teeth got caries
2) They stuffed them with silver.
3) The relief! Earlier even politicians
4) as they talked to him
5) took their hankeys to the nose!
6) Now he didn't have to chew
7) cloves or cumin seed
8) or perfumed areca nut.
9) He didn't have to daub his clothes
10) with pungent perfumes of *kewra* or rose.
11) For the manholes in his mouth were plugged.
12) His own kisses were welcome now;
13) the girls wanted more!
14) Beyond the friction and the skin of sex
15) he probed for feeling. It dawned on him
16) that in the absence of stink, ideals
17) are almost within reach. Fleeting aberration.
18) Ideals always were at hand he discovered;
19) you only had to reach for your pocket book!
20) His half-truths had an edge over his rival's now.
21) His clichés were backed by better amplifiers.
22) His smile was more toothsome.
23) The people he bombarded with his grapeshot lies
24) were more vulnerable.
25) The election was already in his pocket!

26) Then it stank again.
27) Shards of mutton and decaying leaf
28) sawed away at the cutlery of the mouth
29) and caries came gunning
30) through the portholes of the gums.
31) This time, they said, we must
32) stuff the mouth with gold;
33) over the chasm we must build a bridge,
34) cap the front teeth with a gold crown
35) and wrap an enamel-skin around them
36) so that they look natural.
37) In the city his house remained as it was,
38) cows and goats tethered in front,
39) open drains flowing all around,
40) clogged with offal and spinach-leaf.
41) People must still think that he was
42) simple, one of them.
43) only in the bedroom air-conditioners hummed
44) and thick rugs covered it wall to wall.
45) And he started asking friends
46) What are those swiss banks?
47) How the hell do they operate?
48) He has enough now, but whenever the mouth is empty
49) the teeth go clack, clack, clack.
50) They are an appetite which has calcified
51) along the jawline.
52) Now it is not the mouth which stinks;
53) only hi swords,
54) like maggots from the body
55) Of overripe fruit.[2]

Poem as Discourse

Field, Tenor, and Mode of the Poem

In the poem 'Caries,' the field of the poem is expressed as verbal art. It represents the Indian socio-political scenario, which is unscrupulous and reprobate. The background and the predominant image, the speaker's mood, the relationship between the narrator and the protagonist form the sub-field.

The tenor is expressed through the relationship of the narrator with the character. In the poem, the relationship is expressed through the pronouns 'they' and 'he'. It indicates that the narrator does not share an intimate relationship, but as appears from his tone is cynical of the protagonist's acts. The purpose of the narrator is to unveil the true nature of the character. The poem exhibits the play between the appearance and the reality, and the narrator attempts to demonstrate this play being played by the Indian politicians.

The mode is expressed through the textual function. The poem is a satirical poem which has a predominant image of caries. Moreover, the form adopted for communication is free verse.

Analysis of the Poem

In the first stanza, the persona elicits an issue of caries. This noun apart from upholding a denotative meaning also functions at the connotative level. The noun exhibits an affiliation of the Indian political leader with the decayed human anatomy of teeth. The entire decayed mouth shares an implied relation with the Indian political system.

The discourse is in a narrative mode with instances of dialogue. The speaker or the third person narrator is an Indian citizen, who is aware of the contemporary Indian political scene. The discourse begins with a description of a past decayed, diseased state of teeth as denoted through the words "first when", and "earlier". Both these words have the feature {+ past} and at the same time it hints at an influential change later on. Further, the context or the situational background of the discourse is explicitly denoted through the noun "politician" (line3), and 'The election was already in his pocket!' (line25). This is also because the expressions "Earlier even politicians" (line 3), 'as they talked to him' (line 4), and 'took their hankeys to the nose!' (line 5) denote the affinity of the character with the politicians. It is found that the discourse mentions an abnormal condition of teeth, as it is afflicted with caries. Nevertheless, what is worth examining is the remedy adopted to confront this diseased state. The character prefers stuffing the teeth with silver {+ornamentation, +deception} which results in 'the relief!' The exclamatory expression hints at the success, and the immediate pleasure out of the deceptive act. Further, we notice that the household remedies like chewing of 'cloves or cumin seed/or perfumed areca nut.' daubing clothes 'with pungent perfumes of kewra or rose.' hints at the Indian setting. So the politician belongs to India.There are certain lexical items in the firth stanza which relates to the ideational meaning of caries. They are 'manholes' (line 11), 'stink' (line 16), and 'Fleeting aberration' (line 17). Similarly, there are also a set of lexical cohesive item that relates to the superficiality. They are 'silver' (line 2), 'perfumed areca nut.' (line 8), 'pungent perfumes' (line 10), 'absence of stink' (line 16), and 'Ideals always were at hand' (line 18). The gap between deception and reality, and the predominance of deceit over verity also hints at the gullibility and imbecility of the citizens as they fail to apprehend the real motive of the politician. The discourse intimates a shift of noun, from the noun caries to the noun manholes; from a small decay to a sewer. The shift signifies the intensity of corruption, degeneration, and contamination inherent in the character, as well as the system that advocates it. Thus, the character realises:

> that in the absence of stink, ideals
> are almost within reach. Fleeting aberration.
> Ideals always were at hand he discovered;
> you only had to reach for your pocket book!

The entire discourse is an ironic realisation of ideals by the character. Two expressions are contrasted here, they ere 'stink' and 'ideals'. This is something ironic as the narrator intends to present a view that is not acceptable in the normal code of conduct. What is unacceptable is the equation of 'absence of stink' with the realisation of ideals. The narrator seems to be cynical of the character's attitude in 'Ideals always were at hand he discovered;/you only had to reach for your pocket book!' Associating ideals {+grand} with pocket book {-grand} conveys the lowliness and commercialisation of these ideals.

In the next stanza, the narrator depicts the activities of the character after he has acquired sham to hide his genuine nature. The outcomes of his trickery are:

> His half-truths had an edge over his rival's now.
> His clichés were backed by better amplifiers.
> His smile was more toothsome.
> The people he bombarded with his grapeshot lies
> were more vulnerable.
> The election was already in his pocket!

The force and urgency in the tone suggests the urgency and intensity of the actions.

The words like 'rivals', 'amplifiers', 'bombarded', 'grapeshot', and 'vulnerable' relates to the ideational meaning of 'violence' therefore, suggestive of the violence adopted for winning the election. Apart from violence he also takes recourse to half-truths like smile and lies {+false} that resulted in apparent accomplishment of his goal—'the election was already in his pocket!'

To begin the third stanza it is commendable referring to a comment of the narrator in the first stanza, which is 'Fleeting aberration'. Therefore, the third stanza bespeaks of the failure. It is because the true self 'came gunning'. Like in the first stanza, in the third stanza too, there are many lexical cohesive items related to caries. These are 'shards of mutton and decaying leaves' as well as 'carries came gunning'. This time silver was not adequate, so a change is required, a change that was suggested in the first stanza.

> This time, they said, we must
> Stuff the mouth with gold;

There is a shift in the time sequence, from the past description of the actions the focus shifts to the present, along with an emphasis on the modal verb 'must'. The use of this modal indicates that stuffing teeth with gold is a necessity. Gold {+ ornamentation} is a cohesive item that shares affinity with silver (1st stanza), though gold is esteemed for a higher value than silver. Nevertheless, the meaning of gold deviates from the usual code, and attains a specific meaning in the context. In this stanza gold signifies that the character should put up a mask of honesty, honour, and dependability, so that he can appeal to the masses.

> over the chasm we must build a bridge,
> cap the front teeth with a gold crown
> and wrap an enamel-skin around them
> so that they look natural

The entire discourse intimates dissimulation. In order to hide his pernicious and fallacious deeds the leader cloaks his acts with gold or falsehood. Building a bridge over the chasm suggests that the differences between the leader and the populace should be resolved. Furthermore, in order to make his guile look natural he must wrap an enamel skin {+ natural} for restoring the natural colour of teeth, or the cordial relationship. What is significant is the pronoun 'we', as it indicates the involvement of not one leader, but of many.

Lexical items in a discourse as a chain can link paragraphs or stanzas closely and tightly. The lexical items really as a chain play a key role in connecting the first stanza with the second, third, and the fourth stanza of this poem together in a cohesive order with logical ideational meaning. It also connects the fifth stanza skilfully. In the fifth stanza, the narrator describes further falsehood. The dichotomy between truth and falsehood generates irony in the stanza and the duality in public and private life denotes the hypocrisy of the character. The character maintains a projected self:

> In the city his house remained as it was,
> cows and goats tethered in front,

> open drains flowing all around,
> clogged with offal and spinach-leaf.
> People must still think that he was
> simple, one of them

The character adopts the dingy and decayed lifestyle to make his self look more natural. Once again, there is a switch in the tense from present to the past. This is to evince the present change and contrast. The dull scenes {+ decay} like 'open drains flowing all around', 'clogged with offal', and 'spinach-leaf' shares cohesive affinity with the carries. The belief people must still think 'he was/simple, one of them' is a sarcastic comment on the gullibility of the citizens, who fail to distinguish between right and wrong, appearance and reality, and good and bad. The word 'still' further enhances the sarcasm and at the same time denotes that they have been deceived in the past, is still being deceived, and will further be deceived in the future. Next, the ironical character sketch is made subtle by contrasting the earlier deplorable images with the modern comforts. Thereafter, reconstructing the thematic play between reality and illusion:

> only in the bedroom air-conditioners hummed
> and thick rugs covered it wall to wall.
> And he started asking friends
> "What are those swiss banks?
> How the hell do they operate?"

The first two lines share the semantic parallelism with the play between gold/silver and the carries. The concealing of the air conditioners {+luxury} with the thick rags {+poverty} re—exemplifies the deception. The dialogue 'what are those Swiss banks?/how the hell do they operate?' relate to the contemporary socio-political situation of India where the dishonest industrialists, scandalous politicians, and corrupt IAS, IRS, IPS officers have deposited in foreign banks in their illegal personal accounts a sum of about $ 1,500 billion, which have been misappropriated by them. This amount is about 13 times larger than the country's foreign debt. The reality is the Indian economy has been stripped of its wealth.

The speaker's last comment on the character is worth examining. The comment brings out the true picture, the attitude, and the perception of the leader

> He has enough now, but whenever the mouth is empty
> the teeth go clack, clack, clack.

The words 'enough' and 'now' relate to the success achieved by the leaders. The need for money and luxuries is exhibited in the statement 'whenever the mouth is empty/the teeth go clack, clack, clack.'

The reference to the teeth 'as an appetite which has calcified' denotes the unaccounted money and the associated greed of the leaders. The persona ends his final comment with a dilapidated image.

> Now it is not the mouth which stinks
> only his words,
> like maggots from the body
> Of overripe fruit.

Conclusion

The poem illustrates the prevailing corruption and the loopholes in the political system that on one hand facilitates the prosperity of the leaders and the deplorability of the nation on the other. There is no direct reference to any one political leader but an implied reference to all the criminals, dishonest, and debased men who use guile to win the faith of the citizens. The duplicity and guile, which resonates in all the stanzas, are referred through the cohesive items along with the images associated with the noun 'caries'. They anticipate and exhibit the decay and debris. The mode of discourse helps in demonstrating the satire as well.

References

1. Norman Fairclough, *Analyzing Discourse—Textual Analysis for Social Research.* (Oxon: Routledge, 2003) 124.
2. Keki N. Daruwalla, *Winter Poems* (Bombay: Allied Publishers Private Limited, 1980) 53-54.

4

Policing the Poet: An Ecocritical Study of Daruwala's Nature Poems

—P.V. Jayaraj

Nissim Ezekiel's reference to Keiki N Daruwala's poetry as one containing 'the energy of the lion' befits the latter's engagement in naturalism. A significant number of Daruwala's poems contest the role and status of man in relation to the varied aspects of nature. The poems manifest the world of realism with which he tries to identify himself. Therein lies the relevance of an ecocritical approach to the selected poems of Daruwala spanning a later phase of five years, i.e. between the years 2000 and 2005.

It won't be out of place to note that the poems discussed below were all composed after Daruwala's retirement from the Indian Police Service, in the rank of a Secretary to the Government of India. In his early years he had donned the uniform in the state of Orissa, to which cadre he belonged. Later he went on deputation to the central government where he remained till superannuation.

If the early poems of Daruwala evince the spirit of controlled aggression, the latter verses present the reader with a much mellowed temperament, highly sedate and reflective. But in both phases of his career as versifier, we find Daruwala's undying love for the ecosystem whereby he is prompted to consider his culture as its manifestation or sometimes to use it as a metaphor for culture.

It would be rather oversimplistic to define ecocriticism as merely the study of the relationship between literature and the physical environment. However, it is comparatively a new theory that originated in the west and one that still continues to be treated as an emergent movement. Its most remarkable feature is its rejection of the notion, unlike the other commonly known theories, that everything is socially or linguistically constructed. Therefore, nature really exists as an entity which affects man according to his acts and intentions. As issues directly relevant to green studies, one can say that nature, culture and the states in between are all real. Theorizing the outdoor environment as a series of adjoining and overlapping areas, it moves gradually from nature to culture in the following way:

The first area comprises 'the wilderness' where we have deserts, oceans, and uninhabited continents. The second one is 'the scenic sublime', consisting of forests, lakes, mountains, waterfalls, etc. The third is 'the countryside' filled with hills, fields and woods. And lastly, the fourth area is 'the domestic picturesque' presenting parks, gardens and lanes. A mental progress through these environmental areas take us from 'pure nature' in the first to a condition of 'culture' in the fourth. The nature poems of Daruwala do not exclude any one of these four areas in their attempts to create a cosmic order, readying to sacrifice the anthropocentric world for the sake of an ecocentric one.

The vulnerability of the narrator pitted against the all-pervasive nature is well illustrated in many of Daruwala's verses. A short poem like *I Walk the Sands, No Sirens Sing*, exposes the hapless condition of man as a victim caught among the natural forces that refuse to deliver what he craves for. He is in league with the dusk as well as the sea (with whom he identifies himself at differing points of time) in his struggles to fix his destiny. The world of nature is a great leveler in that the elements fuse with the mythical characters like Osiris and Isis to consider man as only one of the many benefactors in a universal order. The human witness realises that though it is his "destiny—to merely sizzle, fret and fail" (Daruwala 10), such a bearing of failure is celebratory in tone and mood.

A similar stance finds expression in another short poem enlightened *Goddess I Am Lonely Now*. The narrator pines for the company of the planetary constellations like the Pleiades, Orion and a natural satellite, the moon, who are instrumental in providing him with the sustenance of love in the material world. But the failure to strike a unifying chord with nature is suggested in the last stanza: 'Love's desertions, they are swift,/ as star clusters incline and shift,/My lovers like Orion drift./I drift alone (10).

The poet's attempts to connect the past with the present are very often exemplified using nature as an anchor. In *Notes from the Underground*, the degree of soreness of the physical separation from a life partner is scaled down considerably when nature gives him hope through 'that thin smoke of mist/over the iron-grey waters of dawn,/icy waters of cold dawns' (19). There is the juxtaposition of the human life within and the elements without. The celebrations within the bar—comprising smoking, womanising and drinking—cannot be sustained in the face of the cold wind burning like acid outside. Partying perfunctorily, the narrator fails to gain any kind of enjoyment as he is seated 'between betweens,/to the left of voices/to the right of memory' (16). As his thoughts float into the slow silence of air currents, time hangs heavily about him and he detaches himself from the human world of merrymaking with an 'autumn-leaf detachment' (16).

Sooner than later, he realises the futility of trying to pour out his feelings to the typewriter or the computer, where the storage in its chip-memory could be embarrassing. The limitations of the man-made machines are brought out by pitting them against the potential of the sea which preserves and nurtures a wealth of marine life.

The narrator pities the fact that his beloved missed out on their regular trek up the mountain which used to give them a kind of proximity to the stars in the sky. Sometimes the heavenly bodies behave like glum, unsympathetic bureaucrats in government ministries in claiming the lives of unsuspecting humans. The flowering of the trees and the return of the grass on the mountain slopes rest on the generosity of the rains, capable of creating a paradigm of parched lips and love.

But the ultimate peace of understanding is reached when the narrator's dreams, like the awareness of absences and the power to know the good from the bad, move like the thinnest veil of mist over water. His spiritual union with his spouse is akin to the 'murmur of a spring of underground water' (19).

Underwater Notes, written after revisiting a dream, lends the reader further insight into the binary opposites of temporal desolation versus spiritual companionship. The poet begins with his cold loneliness in a warm house where the materialist setting is dull and uninspiring like the frost smudging the windows. Life is compared to a voyage in the hull of a tossing boat drifting towards an unspecified horizon. Existence is a gloomy forest full of darkening leaves underneath a darkening sky. The only way in which the poet can alleviate his desolation is by partitioning his time in different slots of nature's caves. 'The sea is the present/The forest is the future./Speech is present tense/Echo is the future' (21). The poet stresses the point that the current acts of man find their repercussions in the days to come. He has reposed more faith in a natural life when he admits that 'Unsure on land/you take to the sea' (21). Besides voyaging, he also opts for his 'flirtations with altitudes'(21) and hence goes up the Karakoram ranges at Siachen to turn one with the elements.

The history of the homeless Palestinians who loved and lived upon the bare desert sands is summarised in a tribute entitled *To a Palestinian Poet.* Empathising and sympathising with a poet robbed of his vineyard by ideologically opposed forces, he is reminded that history joined hands with nature to further it. It is no use railing childishly against one's destiny, 'against the pitiless heavens' (22). The desert sands are a great leveler as both the warring communities have suffered a state of exile for hundreds of years. But the excesses of this fellow poet, which includes 'measuring the sky with chains' (23), is condoned as he is a mere child of nature.

Fish symbolises the helpless victims caught in the play of natural forces. Despite its amazing size and strength, this marine creature is killed and carried to the shore by the great sea herself. The poet acknowledges the remarkable personality of the dead fish by graphically describing its distinct traits: 'her tin coloured barnacles/and long threaded rose moles/patterned on her body' (27). The translucent eyes of the fish suggest that it is only half aware of the state of its body. The tide repeatedly lashes its fury against the carcass of the fish for a lòng period of time, but to no avail. Thus the fish turns out to be a representation of corporal beings, who undauntedly carry on their lives though they are oblivious of the uncertainties of their present or future.

Poem for a Granddaughter is a tender advice to all of humanity to learn to love nature and her manifestations. The poet creates a near perfect pastoral ambience for his granddaughter to sleep and wake up to. The darkness of the night is quieter than the day as even the chittering cricket has left for peaceful 'sleep,/Wrapped in leaf and dream and bark./ The night was made for slumber deep' (29).

The child is urged to dream in her sleep, as it is lighter than an insect's wing to cover up her eyes. It is quiet as silence, yet it sings of hope, friends, play and fun and thus excites the brevity of the innocent child's past. The poet has introduced the phenomenon of dream as a perfect device for wish fulfilment. According to the poet, 'If you lived near the sea/You would have dreamt of sail and mast./If in the hills, you would have dreamt/Of shepherd, flock and valleys green,/Of rivers clean as burnished glass,/And watched the salmon go upstream'(29).

The poet tries to correct the notion that the night holds several terrors. A unique kind of stillness, a dog's lone bark or the cry of an owl shouldn't worry us to believe in ghosts or ghouls. The pantheistic world view of the poet is evident here as he exhorts us to enjoy the starry, black night instead of yielding to superstitions. Remember that 'A thousand worlds are looking down/On our small world which is so small/So small and round,/It could fit into one glove/these vast worlds that fill the sky' (29). A sense of gratitude to the dark night for having made possible the observation of, say, the shooting meteors, is symptomatic of the scientific temper that grows concomitant to the enjoyment of nature.

A dexterous mixing of the elements is achieved in the short poem, "Sky, River". The poet considers options other than a dream or meditation in order to gain something more than mere answers that the two are capable of giving in their individual competence. 'Looking into the still river/which is not still' (339), the poet finds 'the sky translated there' (339). A viewer feels that along with the unmoving river (which is not actually at rest) the sky gives the impression of progress. But it proves to be false as the sky remains where it was in the blue river bed. This is different from what we have in a mirror or a mere pool of water. Yet, the poet fails to know the exact reason for the sky to throb in the current under the stillness of the river. We have here an earnest disciple of nature looking puzzled at its mysteries. The advocacy of a biocentric view is evident here, as the poet recognises the non-human world as having value independently of its usefulness to human beings.

The disciple makes a "Century-end Prayer" to the Lord to maintain the biodiversity of the universe and help all species to lead a secure and peaceful life, in tune with the moves of nature. A prayer to God is meant to save the birds and animals from the machinations of man, who is notorious for upsetting the ecosystem of the earth.

The poet hopes that the arctic birds, living in liaison with the friendly polar winds, would survive at least for the next hundred years. At the same time, the poet expresses his ignorance about 'bird-life near the Poles/as birds are about good and evil' (341). He wishes his ignorance could also be equated with such innocence.

But the poet's prayers are not exclusively directed—with the help of the Pole Star—towards the life in the distant lands and oceans. He returns to the warm rain country to make a similar prayer for the rhinoceros trundling through the mire for millenniums. 'May the beaver and the porcupine /burrow their way/to their underground haven./And may the elephant shed his tusks/so that we don't shed his blood' (341).

Before ending his prayer, the poet makes one small appeal on behalf of the tiny but significant sparrow. The birds that live in close communion with humans have very often lost their natural habitat on account of the sophistication of the latter. Hence in a 'skylight prayer, Lord:/May the sparrow know glass/ from the crisp air outside' (341).

The poet attempts to unify religiosity with romance in the poem "Going Down the Night River". A Parsi, who toils in the heart of the city throughout the hot day, returns in the evening to the meager consolations presented in the form of a Zoroastrian prayer in the fire temple. He realises that, to gain a substantial peace, he has to get hold of oars and row down a river in a boat. But it is next to impossible for a city dweller trapped in a flat, high up on a building. He can only embark on his solitude and take recourse to the envisaging of scenes from nature as a poor substitute for the lived experience. He craves for the tempting hills, the rice terraces and the blue river against the brown stone bed, 'singing a different note/each time it swarms over a stone' (290). There is an intertwining of religious passion and sexual love under the auspices of nature when the Zoroastrian harps on the ardour of love rushing on and on like the river that he can never enjoy in his urban existence. He is convinced that love has to coil around something, like a vine around the almond tree, to make it flower. In the absence of choices, he pitifully takes comfort in the thought that 'a dream is as good a raft as any/to take you down the night river' (290).

"The Room" is another dream sequence in a similar mode where the follower of Zarathushtra employs his religious rites to know the soul of nature. The dreamer goes up a hill to reach a large room with only three walls. The architect wanted it that way in order to make the missing wall open up to a vista overlooking a river. On reaching the river, the narrator finds hundreds of strangers squatting in line for a meal on plantain leaves and leaf-cups. While retracing his steps, he observes a shepherd girl without her flock, and an old man with a monk's head reminding him of some of his ancestors. When the shepherd girl shouts, two hunting dogs rise and snap to herd the flock of sheep. That call which was 'older than the Dead Sea scrolls,/older than Zarathushtra (292), lighted up the river's flanks and caused an almond tree to flower with love as well as the sheep bells to move towards the dreamer through the open gateway. The poet suggests that it was the observance of the religious rituals closely identified with the festivities of nature that presented him with the fruition of hopes and wishes even in a dream.

The dominance of the spirit over the mind is exemplified by the verse "Dream Log". Despite a tense search in the black—mirror-river, the poet fails to trace his face. The angst is heightened by the thoughts over the likelihood of the search going waste with nothing to find. Initially, the poet feels that the loss of his face could be explained with the help of the all-pervasive mist. But then he realises that the mist is associated with the spirit that hangs like a drape over the whole valley and which 'defines the core of whiteness' (291). Hence the poet makes a general appeal to the spirit of the mist/river/mountain to find his face for him. The poem acknowledges the power of nature/spirit to define the true face/character /identity of man.

The search for the long lost face continues in "Melons". The poet attempts to quench his thirst for melons from a merchant stationed at a river bank that gets steeper enough to darken the waters. The depiction of the melon seller as one sent by a Djinn flown in from Samarkand concretises the significance of nature as the only substantial relief for the despondent man. The poet's chat with the melon seller enlightens him about the presence of abandoned river beds, who look like parents from whom their daughters have separated after marriage. Pondering over the state of those brackish puddles, the poet leans over one of them, 'only to find, reflected,/in a shallow scoop of water,/(his) long-lost face/on a bed of moss' (294). Nature has taught him, through its antiquated veneer, how to know himself from his past.

The unending search for the substantial self fostered by nature continues in "Contradictory You". The poet is convinced that it rests in all the varied manifestations of nature. It remains in the waters which the rains caused to collect; in the ferns that fan out; in the vegetable dyes where colours are a dialect and the darkness is a language. It is found in the night 'grained with the milky way/and granuled with stars' (301) or in the flicker and the spray of lights and waterfalls. The narrator considers it to be the wharf where his ship is berthed. Possibly, it could also be the rock where his ship gets wrecked. The poet ends his tribute with a reference to the 'blue trance of the mountain and the fever of the valley' (302) as well as the rain-rinsed morning as the possible sites for his metaphysical search. The poet seems to suggest the monistic faith in which the world and its creatures are seen as one substance or one organic body.

The poet has composed a set of verses entitled *Island Poems* that reveal his deep-set devotion to one of the most abiding manifestations of nature, namely, the sea. He begins the first one, "Prologue", with the assertion that such a poem is an island in itself as heartburn and frost burn—the afflictions of the mind and the body—lie outside the paper on which it is composed. 'The outer sense field lacks all relevance—/the dying planet's pyrotechnic rage;/the basti's fingers round the forest's throat—/leave these dialectics to another age' (311). The time taken to shape a poem is as slow as the gradual thickening of a coral in the thickets. Time is reduced to the basics like sundown or star-set. The versifier tells us that the painfully slow composition of a poem is similar to an island creating its own 'prosody' while the sea ebbs and surges alongside the rush of the winds. The blood-beat of the poet has to slow down in tandem with the rhythms of the tide.

He assures us that all island poems are more or less identical with regard to their timbre, temper and pace. 'offloaded here in time, and outside time,/as we know it, the islands fell in place;/hump flowering with forest, beach seething in sand' (312). If the poem is not true to the spirit of the sea, it will suffer salt burn and sunburn; and sooner than later it will get separated from the moment and the place that gave it birth.

"Coral Poem" takes us to a wilderness of leaf and prop root, of loam and fallen tree. They refer to islands dreaming and 'waking to beaches/of white encircling sand' (312). They are encircled by calcified shrub and striated, cellular coral as bulbous as the brain. The coral on that island is depicted as 'million-fingered, million-nailed,/million-jointed' (312). The exercise of picking up such shards of shattered reef is analogous to the mode in which an etymologist lifts Sanskrit words from the debris of island languages. The attempts to decipher the subtle integrants of the corals testify the poet's faith in the didacticism of nature.

"Ross Island brings" out the historicity of the landscape under purview. The mode in which the ruins of the ancient buildings on the island have been conquered by the wild growth of nature is indicative of the dynamics of coextension: 'Intricate as snake bone/fierce as tentacles/the ficus roots drape themselves/over crumbling parapet and wall' (313). It is an island on which the stillness of the past cohabits with the kinetics of the present. The spotted deer nibbling at groundnut in the dragonfly infested morning with the wind roosting in the palms is juxtaposed against the inoperative bakery, Jap bunkers of the World War era, dilapidated houses of officials, and derelict desalination and ice mineral plants in addition to a cemetery with a roofless chapel.

"The Night Ferry" offers the reader with a scintillating pictorial description of a romantic island nurtured by the gifts of the breezy sea, which is 'blue mirroring blue' (314). Its beach, designed like its girdle, is a corselet of white sand indented by an 'unflanked, unwalled cave of solitudes' (314) that has nothing to reveal except the fact that the absence of alligators makes it safe for visitors. The blossoming mangroves have started flowering yellow and mauve in order to drape the white beach. The island drips with shadows as the old fleshy trunks get wreathed by shadows. The innocuous vivacity in the play of sun lights is brought out in the refraction of the broken prose of the verse:

> Where the skyline burns
> The spyglass
> Frays into opacity.
> Then scraps
> Of lilac clouds
> adrift
> at dusk
> Trailing

Tendrils of light
the night ferry
green-lit on starboard
its phosphorescence
letting its green hair down,
chugs
into the Phoenix Bay (314).

Vignettes look like a sub-section of the *Island Poems* in that they continue to glorify and deify nature through the graphic delineation of islands enjoying the siege of the seas. The first poem in the series is given an incomplete title—"*A Dream Is* Also" –to suggest the poet's unrequited love for nature. The dream is also an island as it is surrounded by the swirling waters of myths that are ingrained in human memories. The dream can also be likened to an allegory, though the poet distrusts the hierarchy of veils and masks that one has to pass through during the makeover from one form to another. He rues the fact that by the time one has decoded the allegory, the dream and the memory of it 'have both swept past/like a fish-shoal wrapped/in a darkening current' (315).

The *déjà vu* that entails the repetition of identical experiences from nature in dreams is explained in "Of Fullness". Initially, the nights might look full due to the dreams that steam through them. On the other hand, the days are full 'because of new skylines, new shoals, new tides' (315). Sooner than later, the nights turn empty as the sea—nature—satiates your sensibilities to such an extent as to make your dreams look unsolicited.

The domineering influence of nature is emphasized in the terse lines in "What the Sibyl Said". Man might feel rather enigmatic when the sibyl—the unnamed inner voice—warns him about the transience of islands, whose self-absorption teaches him that it is the same as solitude.

"Island Notes", the last and the longest in the collection, teaches us the virtues of naturalism as practised on an isolated island, free from the pitfalls of anthropocentric interests. The poet is convinced that laughter was invented on the islands and shipped to the mainland where man must have distorted it to suit his dissimulations and hypocrisies. The sea embracing the island must have rolled around sunlight and laughter, though the same cannot be said about the dark rainy nights that make the poet homesick. Just as the sea is quick with ferries, the night is quick with dreams. The poet creates a synesthetic effect as he describes the wind skimming the sea tide to turn it blue enough to paint a thousand worlds for the gull to fly through them. The poet states the key design that keeps the universe together: 'Distance is the warp, blue the weft' (317).

It is not merely for the sake of glad animal pleasures that one spends his days and nights on an island. It can also be a solemn period of introspection. The island teaches him the way to avoid considering all aspects of life in terms of symbols, since 'symbols become dead words and slow down a language' (317). He probes the relationship between the island—nature—and human aspirations when he describes how the lifting of the island's anchor is concomitant to the lifting of the anchor of our dreams to make it disappear.

The island, which personifies longing, haunts the poet with memories and daydreams after his return to the mainland. It is a scheme of 'the ego's nimbus blotting out the sky' (317). Since his experiences on the island are a kind of reality that is too subtle for verification, the poet cautions us not to judge everything with an ideal certainty of understanding.

The observation of Jonathan Bate in relation to Wordsworth's *The Excursion* can be applied to Daruwala's nature poems as well: 'everything is linked to everything else, and, most importantly, the human mind must be linked to the natural environment' (Kerridge 536). Daruwala's poetry doesn't attempt to escape permanently from the anthropocentric viewpoint to migrate to another ecocentric world. But he is aware of the existence of other viewpoints as well.

Daruwala doesn't believe that the landscape depicted in his poetry should function merely as locale, milieu or representation. He is convinced that the non-human setting is present not merely as a composing device but as a presence that begins to suggest that human history is drawn in natural history. The human interest is not understood to be the only rightful interest. Human accountability to the environment is part of the moral course of Daruwala's nature poems. Some sense of the environment as a course of action rather than as an invariable or a specified set is inherent in the texts composed by him.

The imaginings of the poet to renounce modernity for a more natural, simple and innate way of life helps him to augment his level of self-awareness and teleology (the sense of life as movement between an origin and a goal). But evidently a rural retreat offers the protagonist only a temporary sanctuary. A flight from urban peril is followed by a consoling bucolic break, which heals the narrator and prepares him for a return to his original habitat. Therefore, we find Daruwala's sensibilities being constantly policed by the immanence and transcendence of nature, to which he owes a great deal in the growth of his mind as a poet.

Works Cited

Barry, Peter, *Beginning Theory*, Manchester: n.pub., 2002.

Daruwala, Keiki N. *Collected Poems 1970-2005,* London: Penguin, 2006.

Kerridge, Richard, "Environmentalism and Ecocriticism" *Literary Theory and Criticism*. Ed. Patricia Waugh. Oxford: n.pub., 2006.

5

Some Reflections on the Poetry of Keki N. Daruwalla

—P.C.K. Prem

I

Keki N. Daruwalla is a Parsi with nine collections of poems. Knowledge of Parsi's history and legends influence Daruwalla's poetry and one also finds fragments of myths of Hindus, Christians and Muslims. He is a vastly read man. One finds folklores, tales and myths of Africa at times, which are conveniently observed in the thought currents, and this helps interpreting contemporary life. His poems contain charms of philosophic outpouring and each collection is a genuine mirror of contemporary life. The frequent use of words like dark, light, night, water, river, bird and vulture are symbolic and can be interpreted differently. If some words tell man of light, generosity, good mind, righteousness in life, piety, well being, immortality, etc. a few words depict evil spirit also. If these are qualities of a Hindu mind, the said virtues are also very close to Zoroastrians. Like Lord Rama, Ahura Mazda (the Lord of Light) also symbolises these eternal values and if human beings obey the holy commandments, there can be no vice or sin in the life of man. These thoughts continue to determine the mind of the poet. Here, he is not different from other poets but it is the treatment that speaks of his unique poetic strength.

Daruwalla is modern and there are glimpses where he finds consolation in ancient myths. The contemporary age of uncertainty and ethical degeneration with profusion of violence and corruption disturbs him. Daruwalla is worried about contemporary life of man. His anxieties of modern life are reflected in almost all his collections.

So far, he has authored more than 12 books, mostly collections of poems and a couple of fictional works. His significant books are: *Under Orion* (1971) *Winter Poems* (1980) *Night River, The Keeper of the Dead* (1982) *Landscapes, A Summer of Tigers* (1996), and *The Minister for Permanent Unrest & Other Stories.*

One of the most influential voices in Indian English Poetry, Daruwalla is worried about life, its dilemmas and contemporary location of man. In the delineation of landscapes, he is quite at ease and there appear plenty of rural touches. Here, an attempt to critically examine *Under Orion, Winter Poems* and *Night River* has been made. The poetry shows as mentioned elsewhere pessimism born out of sufferings, hatred, violence and corruption and these currents create a sort of misery and anguish in poetry. He looks at life in totality and there he tries to arrive at a philosophy of life.

Daruwalla is a poet of sophistication with wide-ranging experiences and has the influence of urban-consciousness with ignorable exceptions. He is insightful and uses language with suave effectiveness. He is clear, direct and imagistic. At times, his lyrics are abstract. He is inclined to Indian culture and heritage but interest in English culture and language remains intact and he turns elitist which might appear snobbish. His unconscious penchant for English style and attitude does not irritate but adds colour to poetry. The poet graciously moves from one thought to another and in the process history and myths intermingle. He is striking and authoritative without being overwhelming. He impresses with the originality of thought-communication which at times does not seem quite fresh but the tonal and sound emphasis makes it natural and quite refreshing. When he takes up nature as a subject, depiction of landscape, water, rivers, hills and valleys is superb.

Daruwalla understands the tonal and sound value of words while graphic capturing of scenic details, remind one of Tennyson. On the other hand, intellectual and philosophic areas of Daruwalla are quite vast. There is nothing romantic about the poems. Melancholy, anxiety, hopelessness, defeat, death and sex with host of modern ailments chase him. His thoughts and ideas with doubts about the destiny of man despite impact of various religions and myths, do speak of an age not very happy and optimistic. He, like many urban poets, takes us back to poets like Eliot, Pound, Auden and a few others who did not believe in romanticism or intense religious sentiments but exhibited vigorous intellectual prowess with flashes of metaphysical wanderings. Intellectual poetry is usually linked with cynicism and sarcasm and that could be termed as a great drawback. In that case, noble exploration of virtues and apparent love for qualities of life seem suspect and needs to be avoided if it is so. Extreme intellectualisation leads to evaluative conclusions but it also speaks of ego and arrogance. There is a thin line of demarcation between his thoughts and feelings. However, efforts have been made to look at Daruwalla from different angles as to how he looks at life. Scathing irony, sufferings and death are the prominent features of his verses. There are invisible and sneering efforts not only to irritate finer sensibilities but the lyrics also frustrate man's attempts to keep hopes alive.

II

One observes intensity of irony with depth of melancholy and sufferings are quite evident. His sarcastic looking at things shocks. It also provokes him to think deeply about life and existence and the principles which often govern an ordinary life. Keki N. Daruwalla is aware of the burning issues a common man faces in life. In "Notes" he paints a dismal picture of hunger, thirst, scarcity and greed. It simply depresses. The poet appears sharp and disillusioned when he observes utter dissoluteness in the conduct of men. "Notes" in *Night River* is a disappointing and reproachful picture where hopes, struggles, failures and birth get mixed up and confusion prevails as nothing is clear. It is story of deceit in all walks of life: "The ultimate aspiration:/an exact forgery/of the ideal" shows life is empty, corrupt and without meaning. Living appears phony that adopts a hypocritical approach. Here conspiracies determine life where love is an arrangement, and life is just a movement of dreary hopes to death. It is waiting for the ultimate end of depressing life and wishes but that too is not exactly death:

> The bird of life and bird of death,
> must, among other things, fight.
> … …
> I want the two birds
> always fighting
> or always making love,
> or half the time fighting
> and half the time making love.
> ("Notes," *Night River* 47-48)

An agonising life lives in love, violence, failure and futility. In different words, the painful current continues to flow in this poetry. In fact, pessimism and futility worry poets of urban areas most of the time. Life for a common man is dreadful. The images depress when in an area of scarcity, a bus arrives with the essential commodities. It sells necessities of life. One gets everything in a queue. One is pained to see when the poet observes:

> No end to hoarding
> Breaking open the lockers they find
> A briefcase full of rice.
> ("Notes," *Winter Poems* 27)

It is an irony that in an age of plenty people are still not getting enough. It is greed and corruption in a welfare state, he hints at. The miseries are indescribable. This thought returns to the poet after sometime. The viruses of greed, covetousness, loot and corruption are evident in "Graft" in more telling words:

> The pity is even the decent are corrupt
> those who walk hospitals with a silent tread
> who leave the car to stop urchins fighting
> a doctor who has brought you back from the dead.
> … …
> And hand don't flame when they accept the bribe.
> Palm-lines are impervious to change.
> ("Graft," *Under Orion* 81-82)

Here irony is intensely painful. When Daruwalla wrote this poem greed, corruption and such vices were prevalent but were not evident. At that time, bribery and hunger for money and fall in ethical values had begun to show signs with the slow disappearance of the first generation of great leaders who struggled hard so that we may live in a free country and who had in mind 'service to the people and nation' as the motto. At that time also some honest people must be feeling a terrible corrosion of ethics. Public life in the sixties had begun to degenerate is quite evident here. Now after many years, if one looks back and forth, the emerging trauma shakes righteous and honest people to the marrow. The contemporary society thus, despite glittering growth and progress has only eaten up the vitals of Indian ethical value-system. This sickening thought possibly defies all remedial measures.

It is pertinent to say that when urban poetry began to take roots, India was already a free country and was forging ahead brushing aside all obstacles whether social or economic or religious. Leaders had a clear cut vision. Soon systematic planning started. People experienced hardships, anguish of relations lost in some regions and issues of emotional adjustments. But they were not disillusioned for, they knew that hard work was a key to success. If those initial struggles and sufferings of a nascent nation are interpreted as causes of pessimism, futility, loneliness and vacuity then it is difficult to believe. For, in India at that crucial time, life moved on to the destination with hopes.

In such conditions, the poet is anxious about the life of women. On the life of a woman in Indian society, the impact is more severe and committing suicide is the only recourse left to her. In rural areas, pet animals strengthen economy but in famine, farmers are forced to sell even 'First utensils, then silver anklets, lastly cattle,/A pregnant cow/was sold for seven millet cakes.' Again a terrible picture emerges when the poet enhances the anguish when he says:

> There is no red-light area in the town
> where starving daughters can be sold.

The river bank comes to the rescue,
its sand soft as volcanic ash.
("Notes," *Winter Poems* 27)

Not only man's heartlessness and cruelty are underlined but it is collective degeneration of society's morality which appears disgusting. Perhaps the poet is hinting at years of scarcity when in certain parts of the country there existed draught and famine. Those were difficult days for the poor but such occurrences were rare. In "Chopper Poems" the poet again speaks of hopes, disillusionment and empty assurances as people suffer during drought. It is an awful picture of scarcity. People scramble for little things. A scene outside is of total barrenness, pale figures and blank eyes. Everything is reduced to figures and numbers. There is hunger and thirst. The face of earth is terribly scorched. Human bodies in rags look burnt up and black. Those air surveys by the authorities appear not only encouraging but they fill people with disgust, for, promises and meager help do not provide relief. As the chopper flies over, the fields look 'marooned patches of bristle/holding their root-hugging soil'. The miseries are intensified each moment. But irony gives intense pain. Amidst words and deeds of benevolence there is failure, defeat and sadness.

People in a state of pessimism and hopes bleak, continue to live and imagine that prayers might relieve much of the sufferings.

A man kneels beside his bullock,
his knee sinking into the ploughed earth,
his hands dark with prayer.
A lucky grove
around a horse shoe pond;
a hummingbird
that trembles like a cello.
("Chopper Poems," *Night River* 56)

Poetry of Daruwalla is rich in thoughts and it disturbs feelings and re-energises dormant philosophic tensions. He never allows man to live in peace but guides him to find true meaning of life, anarchic conditions, corrupt times and violent temperament.

III

Winter is symbolic of chill, long da rk nights, shivering of passions and tearing of cozy nights in icy bed when love is cold, lethargic and indifferent. It is more a question of attitude. Man's internal world is totally shattered and is overshadowed by dark forces of melancholy. This is the result of outer sufferings in life. Here drought, corruption and death enslave and wound man.

In an entirely different scenario, the poet talks of nauseating opulence and insensitive attitude of the wealthy people. In a five-star living, it is a fashion to talk of scotch and cocktails, automobiles and air-planes, for they are possibly unaware of the lives of commoners or may be they do not look at kindly on their pitiable conditions. It is a disgusting human behaviour but it is quite normal. The poet observes:

> He talks of chicken so tender, it needs
> a pediatrician; suggests succulent meats
> spiced and gold-grilled over live charcoal:
> lamb chops, ox tongue, a rhino's teat.
>
> ("Paradise," *Winter Poems* 31)

The poet is aware of the tragic end of life of activity and seeming meaningfulness. Living in shadows of hopes and dreams amounts to incessant sufferings in life. Deep longings pester and still life aspires for eternity. Again a blind drive to abysmal depths of the unknown stalks a man with the ideas of devils and killers where history is merely a farce, and thus life appears not only mocking and incongruous but miserable.

> There are blood poems that take you to the knife,
> and death poems that give you
> a vulture's eye-view of what the vulture sees;
> and poems that mark themselves out
> for a particular locale:
> grey wall behind you and guns in front.
>
> ("The Poem," *Night River* 83)

Life of sordid physical pleasures, carousing, sex and sensual experiences just sum up the life of affluent people, the poet says. If he exhibits disgust, there are also moments when poets experience some flashes of happiness. "Living on Hyphens" is an attempt to reach those areas of joy and delight when he says that a man ought to adjust 'Between dream and landscape/and between dream and the dark blood.' Will power and patience are required so that man is in a position to analyse different attitudes of life tossing between hopes and failures where there is enough anarchy, violence and dichotomy in the system. One must know his place or else he will encounter difficulties. The world exists with a set hierarchical order and here 'a man must arrive/at some sort of understanding' for this will lead him to some kind of happiness. The poet does hint at happiness but it is in ironical fragments. Not total, not in little pieces and yet there is some derisive current in making it complete. One lives in bafflement when life is calculated and manipulated while examining the limits of 'a sky of feeling/... and a different sky of history/over each separate past.' Daruwalla's poetic sweep does not stick to one thought or feeling. It subtly wanders from on point to another. What a paradoxical shift but it does fascinate:

> Between the face and the mask
> that looks better than the face;
> between love for the land
> and hatred for the times
> between the smog one lives in
> and the hope one lives on;
> a man, a woman
> must come to an understanding.
>
> ("Living on Hyphens," Night River 7-8)

A painful hiatus stays on as man tries to fill the gap between desires and achievements. While worried of happiness in life, he finds dreariness always accompanying and then he thinks of nation and land.

IV

Reading Daruwalla's poetry is an enriching experience where one encounters realities of life with harsh, immensely hurting and unrelieved agonies. He deliberates on the sufferings of life and thinks over corruption, violence, hatred, conceit and pusillanimity. If he creates impressions of melancholy, he indirectly tells man to stand up against odds and fight out. The real world exists within and it must be protected, he appears to emphasize. He is thoughtful and at times looks visionary as earthly realities interact. He arduously tries to understand life but correct interpretation eludes. Violence and hatred in "Rumination" make him pensive and serious. Evils of life continue to haunt and this is probably the cause of death idea, at times not intense and depressing. A little morbidity appears repulsive as sick sentiments intervene.

> I can smell violence in the air
> Like the lash of coming rain—
> Mass hatreds drifting grey across the moon.
>
> and again he avers:
>
> Death I am looking
> for that bald bone-head of yours
>
> ("Rumination," *Under Orion* 85)

Again the poet is just a normal human being with natural weaknesses and failings when he calls 'But it's in flesh and flesh-tissue/that my destiny lies/and slowly corruption takes hold.' Flesh and soul do appear to determine destiny of man. It is flesh that breeds corruption but to get away from the lure of fleshly pleasures is impossible for a man. It leads to an end, foul smelling and disgusting. Its disgusting smells can not be eliminated as death is a certainty.

> The drift as it comes to us now
> Is aroma stench nausea
> jostling each other
> In the morgue-verandah another queues up
> her nose sliced off, her long punctured
> (It is a three-word story
> Infidelity, irate husband.
>
> ("Rumination," *Under Orion* 85)

An utter failure of man to value relations is quite visible. It is tribal instinct of violence that treats woman as a low human being. Man's hatred, violence and deception are quite evident. Violence can disfigure human body and emotions. The corpse of a woman lying on the verandah of the morgue—a victim of her husband's jealousy, presents a grisly look with her nose sliced off. Man is yielding to the ultimate fate. Man's inhuman treatment undoubtedly is quite apparent but it also reveals man's hidden brutal instincts.

> Man is so pliant, adaptable. Bury him
> and he is steadfast as the earth.
> Burn him and he will ride the flames.
> Throw him to the birds and he will
> Surrender flesh like an ascetic.
>
> ("Rumination," *Under Orion* 85)

The poet thinks for a long time and observes an obvious impact of rain on each object of nature. It has a cleansing influence. Dirt and dust disappears and vision is so transparent and clear. It seems the poet tries to offer a vision of the unknown. The feelings of violence are just relegated to the background offering some relief.

> I look around for a cleansed feeling
> the kind you experience
> walking in a temple
> after a river bath.
> I cannot find it.
> I have misplaced it somewhere
> in the caverns of my past.
>
> ("Rumination," *Under Orion* 85-86)

Time and again, the poet is anguished at the ruthless behavior of man. He may be living a life of pleasure and awesome richness but unfortunately he treats man not on equal terms. If affluent life is equipped with power which is quite usual in contemporary life, then the poor has no hope or brightness in life. He can only live in miseries as money with power turns cruel, brute and inhuman. As no love or compassion is left, people are treated with utmost scorn and abhorrence. Curfew is an instrument the state uses in times of disturbance to silence people who are least involved in anti-social activities.

Vandalism of a few wicked and shrewd people results in disrupting normal life. It is power of the minority that cripples life and emotions of the majority.

> Plug all the cracks.
> Fear, love and hate must crumple where they are.
> Nerves exposed upon the tarmac must be backed.
> ... ...
> The stress in on silence. A man may die
> but the body shouldn't thud. From the broken skylight,
> light spills on the road like a patch of blood.
>
> ("Curfew 2," *Winter Poems* 41)

Man behaves with grace and decency outwardly as is the habit of hypocrites for, there might be atrocious violations of human rights in sickening orgies but there is no scope for debate. Eventually, feelings just lie low and dead because in silence, hope of life seems possible. Daruwalla is a master of creating terrific images with raw and murderous humour. To the poet the state power appears a symbol of terror, cruelty and apathy.

A similar thought occurs with ferocity and ugliness where words, voices and smiles are forbidden when the state exerts pressure and power. It is a scenario of darkness and death that shadows the activities of men. In "Variations" irony and raw humour stalks. A dry, disdainful and skeptical death haunts peace loving people and:

> The place is agog with eyes—
> holes drilled in the darkness
> and stuffed with malevolent jelly.
> ... ...
> They shake their heads and say
> 'we want evidence'
> How can I explain
> that there can not be any evidence.
> For when the state rapes
> The streets are empty.
>
> ("Variations," *Winter Poems* 45)

Threatening and malicious designs of the state are revealed. If abominable and heinous crimes are committed, the state needs evidence or else if thc state perpetrates a terror-regime, the evidence is nowhere. The horror is intensified when the poet vividly but painfully recaptures mechanical operations of how law is made and approved as he observes again in "Variations" that 'This is order/the corpse and the coffin-maker/ at their places.' It is a perennial chase by pains and miseries which make man's life painful. To what extent the state power can go and create terror in the minds of the people, is a horrid and bone-chilling experience. Particularly, when a policeman describes such events and experiences of the exercise of state power with callousness, these assume outrageous proportions.

V

At heart Daruwalla is a sensitive poet but outwardly he keeps a strong posture which collapses the moment he talks of violence, terror, state power and hardnosed men in society bereft of finer sensibilities. He feels perhaps that many sufferings, pains and predicament of man are creations of intellectuals. The thought of curfew appears for the first time in "Under Orion." Curfew reminds of death, destruction, fear and violence. It is the iron law that brings peace and here the poet is ironical while in the mind he has a peaceful democratic set up which is often promised to the people.

> Trailing the siren comes the iron law;
> you clamp the curfew on the outskirts now,
> on the outer fringe,
> the outward striate of this whorl of madness.
> What the hell is it, you wonder;
> Curfew or contagion?
>
> ("Curfew in a Riot-torn City," *Under Orion* 15)

It is the cruelest face of state power to subjugate people for the wrong doings of a few iniquitously bad people. Only the innocent people suffer but state is least worried.

Poet is conscious of what happens around and paints a true picture without attachment. It is easily made out that the poet is pointed, cutting, ironical, piercing. He is ruthless when talks about contemporary life. If he is dreary and insensitive with an ironic touch, one can safely conclude that such characteristics emerge out of an intensity of experience. He knew people intimately while in active service so one encounters a bureaucratic geniality and a little chill in his poetry. This is quite apparent in poems. He is bitingly cold and terse, often cynic to an irritating limit and also nurses a foreign attitude exhibiting camouflage of emotions and kinship with whatever is Indian.

Daruwalla paints pictures and images in words but at the same time comments on contemporary issues rather scrupulously so that he is not misunderstood. He is cautious in lyrics as the images open up new meanings and while he keeps an eye around. When he talks of life, death, sex, hunger, thirst and poverty, he is mostly ironical. Not only he takes pity on the life of poor but also denigrates the rich people with power who often accelerate the pace of self-aggrandizement and greed with little scruples. These burning thoughts disturb the poet and around these issues, a philosophy of apathy, hatred, violence, futility, death and waste is born.

Certain important burning issues do not escape the eager eyes of the poet. It was during early days after forty-seven that many reforms were initiated so that socialistic pattern of society is fortified. Emphasis was obvious on the poor and the landless. Poet's patriotic feelings are expressed in poems like "Collage I" where he talks of great events and men like Ravi Shankar and Tagore and at the same time he does not forget to mention Mahesh and the Beatles. The Beatles's craze was quite noisily clear in late sixties. Ironically the poet speaks of imitations. He looks at things rather sarcastically when a foreigner talks of Indian culture and philosophy when he quotes the *Bhagavad Gita* and Krishna. Perhaps he has in mind that people here do not much follow the immortal teachings of Lord Krishna. Even social reforms that are undertaken are described with some derision and ridicule.

> Who say we have done nothing?
> We have abolished zamindari
> and liquor and English
> and driven out the whores from the G. B. Road.

... ...
We have inaugurated crematoriums
with an unclaimed corpse.
("Collage I," *Under Orion* 53)

One discerns painful stroke of irony and hypocrisy which determines mind-set of many when he says: 'Some day, here/ the sun will refuse/to light the path for lepers. (Ibid. 54)' In the name of development, numerous sham practices come into existence without bothering about the morality. Irony and utter contempt for life are visible in this lyric. In "Collage II" the poet talks of meaninglessness, death, sex, corruption and futility:

Mother, you are floating foetus
on a larval bed
around which we thrash abut
'black colonies of summer fish.'
Corruption is the chemistry of flesh
No wonder the senses suppurate, passions putrefy.
("Collage II," *Under Orion* 56)

In one of his finest verses "Bombay Prayers" Daruwalla talks of life in urban areas in its totality. Indirectly, here he is philosophic. A constant feeling of anguish is experienced while one reads the poem. In a surprisingly interesting but sardonic play of words, he paints multidimensional pictures where man is dissected, hated and glorified which at the end, leaves everyone disillusioned. Here a master craftsman is at work. The protagonist is an egoist and can not bear with those who are lowly and poor, dull and stupid, sick and ugly when he says: 'The road, I feel/should be stratified so that/I rub shoulders only with my kind.' One is aghast to realise the intensity of hatred for the sick and handicapped.

The very next lines exhibit disgusting feeling of sex and lust. That is life, he means to suggest. The poet is conscious of the indifference and coldness of people who are engaged in certain noble professions when he observes:

I am the doctor who bangs his doors shut
on a queue of waiting patients.

Urban life, at heart, is not humane and kind but here cunningness, chicanery and deceit are evident. Not only meanness is nakedly clear in words 'I dial their dreams late at night' but one is curt and devilish. This world is harsh and here only promises which will never be realised are handed over. In a setting of high sophistication, instead of simple water, bottle is assured. The irony remains alive whether it is liquor or mineral water for, a wealthy man can not think of life in simple images.

> Yet I tell the blind of the light to come
> and hold out for the thirsty
> the promise of the bottle.
> Lord, slowly, inexorably,
> I am adopting your vices.
>
> ("Bombay Prayers," *Winter Poems* 67)

Hypocrisy and distrust stay on in life with masks of truth and sincerity for personal consumption. The poet's visions are gory, lusty and dangerous. Violence is surfaced for it is difficult to 'stand up/to your heavy weight-will.' If the poet speaks of the 'dunghill of fulfillment' and creation of species 'in your image', it is absolute selfishness and greed with a thought of sex and violence. Thoughts of spreading benumbing insipidness is the doctrine of this life so it is better to:

> Put dead fungus in their brains.
> so that their heads don't rattle,
> so they can't hear the stone in your words,
> nor see it forming in you eye
> a monster-cataract moving across the eye of the world.
>
> ("Bombay Prayers," *Winter Poems* 67)

The world to poet appears inhabited by corrupt people and there is no choice left. Here the movement of the people is monstrous and poisonous and bodies emit foul smell. There are prayers for a sterile generation. To contain population explosion, the remedy lies in clearing the uterus for years. It is an obvious reference to many half-hearted attempts made to contain population explosion because politics of votes hampered efforts of well-meaning persons. The poet hints at the malicious and evil thoughts that continue to hover over in the world. As if this is not sufficient, it is an utter act of treachery that measures relations. In a dreadful scenario of barrenness, sterile generation, corrupt souls and bodies with dumb and fungus-grown heads and unfulfilled ambitions, the poet observes:

> I shall still hope for favours.
> A year of toil,
> … …
> But once a year during harvest time
> let me walk home
> with a few stalks of light.
>
> ("Bombay Prayers," *Winter Poems* 67)

A thought of utter futility shocks. One is simply baffled by the amount of distorted hopes and dreams, images of recurring assurances ultimately proving false, indulgent passions for worldly pleasures in a mechanical life where love is just a rancid feeling. Then images of lust and sex invade 'within caressing distance/so that we can indulge our strength/in resisting temptation/and our weakness in surrendering to it' do not paint an encouraging picture as:

> Each man thinks he is an
> oasis of disenchantment
> in a world of illusion.
> Our illusions are precious.
>
> ("Bombay Prayers," *Winter Poems* 70)

Out of absolute disgust, disillusionment and failure, sterility of hopes and frailties of love, there is still a ray of hope left and the prayers to the Lord become more forceful. In utter desperation, meaning of life is hazy as much desired change also eludes. So life is a huge tragedy for the poet in the present context.

VI

What one gets in little fragments is a truncated philosophy of life where sex, death, questions of birth and death, futility, distrust and treachery assail living. Total ego and self-interest determines man's existence. It is life of politics in values and it is politics of corruption and lethargy in ethics with naked apathy towards system and its apparatus. That way it is dismal picture of contemporary life. This sad note is the strength of many poems of Daruwalla and a bewildering concrescence of various thoughts and ailments continues to permeate many verses. This distressing thought again appears in "Of Sages". The poet's description of sages is superb. Apt words give sounds which amplify meanings. This short lyric is about holy men engaged in the service of the king so that the empire remains intact. The holy men not only train *vish kanyas* –the poisonous damsels—but ensure that the king is not harmed. These deadly girls, in the past were meant for the enemy for they knew he would die the moment he cohabited with *vish kanyas*. Now these conspiracies have assumed different shapes in the contemporary scenario. The politics of using women for political and personal purposes still pollutes ethical lives, if any, of men-who-matter in modern life. The poet observes:

> And they went forth with their gourds
> called kamandalus, and their fire-tongs,
> looking amongst caves
> for the echoes of some lethal chant
> or some demon lost in penance,
> seeking immortality
> or worse, eternal virility.
>
> ("Of Sages," *Night River* 5)

Many images confound the readers. A simple sage becomes intense and fierce when he trains poison wombs for the enemy while keeping postures of a holy man. Then, begins a search for some immortal seed so that it grants virility to man. A subtle hint to an epic is apparent which ultimately resulted in total annihilation of a family. Or is it a hint to men who only require women, sex, power and money in life. Here we also find how modern rulers try to finds ways and means to perpetuate rule by adopting disastrous methods of dirty politics. Finally, it is sex and lust proving fatal when he observes:

> And the first that the poor fellow
> busy with his vish kanyas,
> would know of all this
> was when his navel or his loin cloth
> would of a sudden, start smoking.
>
> ("Of Sages," *Night River* 6)

The poet is not as simple as he appears, in poetic art and if it is otherwise, it is only with slight variations, as abstraction and obscurity puzzle. Daruwalla hardly ever baffles with mystical thoughts and spiritual leanings but is often engaged in interpreting destiny of man in a complex contemporary situation. He meticulously draws material out of everyday life; and man's mind and deeds act as the sources. Personal experiences generate emotions extending to experiments on life and its origin where dreariness and crudities stare man. It is more a journey into the psychological complexities and philosophic deliberations that constitute rarest of the rare experiential world throbbing vigorously within; and the poet appears to wait for its terrific explosion.

Daruwalla cherishes a distinct philosophy of life and this is perceptible in his poetry. A touch of imagination gives birth to extraordinary situations out of the ordinary. An insignificant event or an incident in life gets a magic treatment and it turns into an experience of a life time. One is reminded of Shiv K. Kumar another doyen of urban poetry. Daruwalla and Kumar write poetry with anguished love and passion; and raw cynicism determines their philosophy of life. It is not entirely pessimism but it is barrenness and distrust which decide man's life for that reason with a slight shift in contours of expression, the poets believe. Shiv K. Kumar's "Broken Columns" and Daruwalla's "The Night of the Jackals" are long poems with very ordinary incidents but when one reads the poems, it is an incredible experience to move with the strong sounds and emphatic punch of words. One forgets the meaning enshrined temporarily but remembers predominately the engaging sounds of the words. Daruwalla's contemporary themes relate to man and society. Mostly ironic in tone and tenor, he finds awful inconsistencies in Indian living style. This naturally leads us to detect contradictions in words, deeds and philosophy of life but the evolution of thought fascinates. He deals life at many levels with a huge arsenal of images and thus keeps the narratives engaging.

To me it appears, most of the poets of that period with urban background were inclined towards Western thoughts and habits but to find roots they often turned to the origin. It happens that creative artists return to roots quite often. It is also an experience to absorb influences of various cultures. These poets had been influenced by T.S. Eliot and others as observed elsewhere. While talking of Daruwalla's poetry, one easily recalls poetic sensibility and intellectual scope and strength of Ageya, Bharati, Shamsher Bahadur Singh and Narendra Mohan (all forceful voices in Hindi poetry) who were also deeply worried about the fate of man in the contemporary life when astounding progress was visible everywhere. Here I believe that the poets may use any language but surprisingly the depth and scope of feelings and thoughts at the experiential level almost remains unaffected. Deeply rooted in Indian culture and ethos, poets like Rizvi, Chambial (with a number of rural images), R.K. Singh and Manas Bakshi are poets of urban sensibilities and undoubtedly their poetry is in the tradition of Shiv K. Kumar. To a great degree Prem like Chambial and others, is not an exception.

Daruwalla excites, instills satisfying and provoking dreariness; and a sense of miseries which cause a few disturbing ripples within. By hurting feelings and thoughts, he stirs inner tranquillity and harmonious feelings. He talks of contemporary fall in qualities of life and ethical vacuum without intentions to educate and leaves one to understand the hidden import. The poet had varied experiences of life while in government service and knows many weaknesses and pitfalls of the system and this encourages him to reflect on life cautiously. He is astutely aware of the injustice, corruption and immorality in life and tries to give an authentic intellectual explanation which shall always remain his strength.

Works Cited

Daruwalla, Keki N. *Night River*. Delhi: Rupa Paperback, Reprint. 2000. Print.

___ *Under Orion*. Delhi: Rupa Paperback, Reprint. 2000. Print.

___ *Winter Poems*. Delhi: Rupa Paperback, Reprint. 2000. Print.

6

Keki N. Daruwalla's Poetry: An Ecocritical Perspective

—**Prasenjit Das** and **Binita Sarma**

As one of the radical voices in post-independence Indian English Poetry, Keki Nasserwanji Daruwalla, popularly known as Daruwalla, needs no introduction. In the introduction to 1980 anthology of poetry entitled *Winter Poems* he wrote: "What Indian poetry needed was... a modern sensibility in confronting the confusion, bewilderment and disillusion of the times" (Mehrotra 160). As many critics would have liked to argue, his experiences in professional life provide his readers with a feel for the turbulence and confusion of the modern life in India of the metropolis, the provinces and the hinterland. This paper is a deliberation on the experience of reading some of the major poems of Daruwalla. However, most of the poems we have chosen for analysis are taken from his collection *Landscape*, although references will be made to his other significant poems that serve the purpose. We also intend to explore the ways in which his poetry seems to have moved towards an 'ecocritical' concern in recent years. For analysing this, we have extensively borrowed from the ideas of Lawrence Buell who is often considered a pioneer in American 'ecocriticism.' His books *The Environmental Imagination* (1995) and *The Future of Environmental Criticism: Environmental Crisis and Literary Imagination* (2005) have made 'ecocriticism' an explicit method of analysis.

The most notable aspect of Keki N. Daruwalla as an Indian English poet is that he is not following the conventional mode of using English as a medium to explore his 'Indian' sensibility. His poetry addresses the world and its various affairs with its sights and sounds, tastes and cultures expressing the unity in diversity. The poetic self in most of his poems is continuously in conflict with his conscience for which a vein of irony often runs through his poems and yet they exhibit the hue of Indian culture. Especially, his poetry in *Landscape* (1987) makes an effort to parallelly represent the contemporary and the global. His 'landscapes' extend from the small town of Banaras to the modern metropolis of Bombay, but finally, his poetry transcends the geographical limitations and mirrors the world of kingdoms and rivers. It is like a man telling his gory tales to his fellow men. The famous Indian poet-critic Nissim Ezekiel praised his work as an 'impressive evidence not only of mature poetic talent but of literary stamina, intellectual strength and social awareness'.

In his "Decolonised Muse," Daruwalla also reflects on the nature of his poetry like this: 'Looking back I find that the compulsion to mark out an identity for myself must have been very strong. Since one was writing in English, it should be all the more evident that it was an Indian writing. Just bringing an Indian sensibility... is not enough. The poem had to be securely fastened to an Indian setting [...].' Such an opinion based on a strong sense of Indian locations can also be put forward as the mark of his Indianness. Along with this, the conglomeration of the local and the global is also another striking example of his engagement with world affairs.

Daruwalla's is a myth of culture and his approach is characteristically anthropocentric. This 'Map Maker' of Indian poetry touches upon the contemporary issues such as poverty, traditionalism and spiritualism without any trace of sentimentality. His strong imagism and flexible narrative drive further strengthen his anti-traditional approach. Subsequently, there is a growing sense of nostalgia for wilderness and the primitive. Equally noteworthy is Daruwalla's indebtedness to Hindu and Muslim traditions, which can be traced in a long poem like "Crossing of Rivers" in his collection of poetry by the same name. Now it is pertinent to mention here that in

Daruwalla we can never have the regionalism apparent in the writings of Raja Rao. Resorting to the native spirit, Daruwalla throws his critical spectrum over the world of events. In *The Map-maker: Poems* (2002) for example, he experiments with monologues and narrative verses where there is a sense of adventure in the themes exploring the transition in time and space. He even takes an ironic stand to the multi-layered conflicting realities of lives in India. However, it is his 'landscape poems' which most powerfully exemplify his preoccupation with diverse cultural, historic and mythic landscapes of India. But, his fascination with the inner worlds and his philosophical speculations over time and space also help in locating the meditative structure of his poems. While his *Winter Poems* (1980) addresses the contemporary issues of national and international disasters, representing India of the terrible drought, starvation and food riot, the *Landscape* (1987) critically observes the cultural changes that took place as a result of various socio-economic, cultural as well as political upheavals in India. Through his telescopic vision, Daruwalla tries to locate the socio-historical and cultural factors that become the causes of changes in civilisations.

One cannot deny the fact that Daruwalla's vision of the future is essentially pessimistic. His poetry announces the inevitability and advent of the approaching doom. The senselessness of the time and guilty conscience can be exemplified through the following examples from the poem "Breakdown": 'All pasts are full of losses,/so was his. He recalled father's face/through glass-window coffin./Hare-guilts, shames,/ moles scurried as he moved in.' Again, the growing sense of loss, anxiety and hunger find its expression in the following lines of "Lambing": 'the lamb within me has turned urgent/as it twists and strains against my side/and turns as I turn against the straw rick.' And, things are all rotten as the poet expresses in "Mandawa": 'In the meadows of love/crowbar and crucifix,/ the beat of death/in the flowering heart of life.' Such radicalism of Daruwalla is best expressed through the narrative energy which is used to portray post-Independence India as 'a landscape of meaninglessness'. Consequently, he asks in the poem "Collage II": 'Then why should I tread the Kafka beat/or the Waste Land,/when Mother, you are near at hand/one vast, sprawling defeat?'

So, it is obvious through the examples cited above that Daruwalla strikes a creative tension between the image and the statement, and makes a scrutiny of the contemporary time and civilisation. One can clearly trace the vision of rottenness of post-Independence India mainly in the 'landscape poems' with all its fragmentariness, meaninglessness and disillusionment. Because, he offers a concrete picture of the fragmented world where things are falling apart, where 'no one remembers seeing a myth die'. At times, it appears to be a mystery for him as there is hardly any scope to make an escape. His "Mandwa" is an excellent example of this characteristic conflict where the death of the baby-whale signifies the death of innocence and purity. His Bombay is a 'black yeast', with a wall of 'rotten muscle'. The sky, the land and even the wind is turning hostile and wild. The wind 'wheezes in through shuttered slats as if a lung of the night were pierced by a glass sliver'. In "Striving's End", the poet finally acknowledges that 'God, death and love all are striving's end'. Similarly, his poems like "The Earthquake City" and "The Fall of Mohenjo Daro" trace the death of civilisation, and delineate a sense of horror and impending disaster.

So far, we have seen how Daruwalla has made himself a sentinel of the decaying world. Seen from the point of view of nature, many of his poems are Wordsworthian so far as the philosophical portrayal of nature is concerned. Yet his legacy of poetry is not confined to the genre of Romanticism. Unlike most of the Indian writers, his decolonising myth of nature is a deliberate attempt to address the conscience of the people through language and imagery. The pantheistic significance can be traced but in the poems' mystery prevails, and this debunks the conventional myth of Romanticism. His 'landscapes' carry the message of death and decay. Still, his anti-colonial approach is essentially a reaction to green Romanticism of Wordsworth which should not necessarily mean—fancy or romance. As G. Huggan says, Romanticism may not be synonymous with romance. It is exactly at this moment that we intend to argue that Daruwalla's sense of Romanticism is more eco-critical and eco-Marxist in approach. It is an exploration of the anti-colonial dimension of Romanticism which is very often associated with desire, and this serves the sentiment of the exploited and the disempowered. A Marxist reading of Daruwalla's poetry, on the other hand, will certainly exemplify its anti-colonial and post-colonial stand. Then, it will not be an exaggeration if we call his romanticism an eco-socialist vision of the landscape.

Now let us consider Daruwalla's poems in the context of the recent environmental turn in literary and cultural studies, which has emerged as a self-conscious academic movement in the recent decades. In his preface to the book *The Future of Environmental Criticism*, the noted eco-critic Lawrence Buell argues that 'ecocriticism' studies the endangered state and uncertain fate of life on earth and its implications in literary and cultural studies. Although we tend to assume that the literary-environmental study is actually based on the notions of eco-criticism, the movement's increasingly heterogeneous nature, especially its increasing engagements with metropolitan or 'toxified' landscapes, challenges its early preoccupations with literatures of nature and preservationist environmentalism. So, it is almost mandatory that while discussing the so-called environmental turn in literary and cultural studies, we feel the need to clarify points, liked how and why something called eco-criticism emerged, what its distinctive concerns are, how it is invested for environmental imaging and representations and how the construction of 'nature' is frequently used as part of art as well as of lived experience. Implicit also in such enquiries is the question of the usefulness of the ways in which this contemporary movement called 'ecocriticism' or 'environmental criticism' established itself differently from its previous counterparts. For example, we can take a close look at William Wordsworth by exploring the various ways we find him referring again and again to nature. But, a contemporary reader, informed of the latest developments in contemporary 'ecocriticism', may also tend to read that Wordsworth's was not just a love for nature but a 'proto-ecological knowledge and environmentalist commitment' (Buell 12). Moreover, the recent developments in literary theory will help us re-consider the work of art as a 'text' demanding an objective treatment from its readers. Consequently, the assumptions of environmental criticism too can be best explained by addressing how the readers examine a text as a part of the 'natural system' of which they themselves are a part. In this context, let us once again quickly refer to Lawrence Buell who has argued that any text, to be environmentally oriented, must be dealing with a few important points like:

a) the non-human environment is present not merely as a framing device but as a presence that begins to suggest that human history is implicated in natural history.
b) the human interest cannot be understood as the only legitimate interest.
c) human accountability to the environment is part of the text's ethical orientation.

Pointing out to what Buell has said, we would like to argue that all such ideas seem to have played important roles in the writings of Daruwalla. Going a step further we can even join hands with Anis Bawarshi who has, in his *The Ecology of Genre*, argued that genres and texts are themselves arguably 'ecosystems,' not in the narrow sense of the text as a discursive 'environment,' but in the broader sense that texts 'help reproduce socio-historical environments' in stylised form. Indeed, an individual text must be thought of as environmentally embedded at every stage from its germination to its reception (Buell 55). However, such a statement of the text looks very radical and ambitious if we try to apply it in our analysis of the poetic 'texts' of Daruwalla and seek to explain that his texts sought to project certain 'eco-systems'.

Drawing from this theory, it is now possible to argue that the trends in environmental criticism have greatly influenced contemporary world-literature, both explicitly and implicitly, and the writers are now more self-consciously engaged with an ecological concern. Our claim is that this is no different with Daruwalla. It is interesting to note that his *Landscape* extends from the ancient kingdom of Kalinga during the reign of great

Indian emperor Ashoka to the overwhelming contradictions of the modern metropolitan cities like Mumbai as well as the small-towns of India like Benaras. But, it will be too simplistic and reductionist if we say that Daruwalla's is just another form of environmentalism. Subsequently, it can never be an exaggerated claim that he conforms to an Indian form of 'ecocriticism'. His poetry makes us feel 'ecocritically' about nature and they urge us to preserve nature which is overtly dehumanised. This is an apt claim because we the contemporary human beings are actually facing ecological problems in today's society. Naturally, his 'baby-whale' reminds us of Coleridge's 'albatross' which had to face the atrocities of men and finally caused the dilemma of 'life in death' in the mind of the Ancient Mariner—another early example of the Romantic concern for ecological imbalance. There is a strong reality behind Daruwalla's conforming to writing comparatively long poetry as he seeks to narrate local history which is lost due to environmental as well as other reasons. He is not merely against killing but is vehemently against the destruction of the natural habitats following human motive of exploration. Although the symbolic meaning of the 'wolf' is the poet himself, there is also an implication for the preservation of external nature. As the poet writes: 'The wolves have been slaughtered now./A hedge of smoking gun-barrels/rings my daughter's dreams.'

So, Daruwalla has debunked the myth of nature and examined the man-nature relationship from an 'ecocritical' perspective. In contrast to Wordsworthian 'landscapes' Daruwalla's is not a fertile one but a dead vegetation with all its rottenness. He is pessimistic in that he offers a parallel treatment suggesting that the decay of nature will finally result in the death of human civilisation. Thus, the ethical orientation of Daruwalla is highlighted. His poems delineate the inhuman activities of men and its adverse effect on natural resources for the sake of profit. Almost each word image of his poems conveys the same message of the dying generation. Hence, the purpose of our discussing his poetry from an 'ecocritical' perspective. While considering his poems, two distinct trajectories in his 'ecocritical' perspective can be identified: one being his satirically potent voice against modern technological developments which have polluted the entire human environment and habitat, the other being the loss of the natural habitats for all natural objects which has caused tremendous ecological imbalance in the human environment. Unlike D.H. Lawrence and Ted Hughes whose significant animal poems are invested towards the portrayal of the 'natural' world of birds and beasts, Daruwalla's animal poems are to be seen as more powerful for its hidden and symbolic meaning. The beginning of the poem "Requiem For a Hawk" aptly begins with such a hidden meaning: 'According to a report, the discovery of a rock-fossil of a hawk has/considerably intrigued both geologists and ornithologists. A well-known/bird-watcher disclosed that the sea coast where the fossil was found was at least a hundred miles away from "hawk country" (News item)". Human civilisation began with the men-nature relationship. Gradually human beings learnt how to exploit the natural resources for all-round development of mankind. But, mankind today in the name of making profit and progress, has dehumanised nature inviting critical responses from concerned activists as well as writers. This is quite obvious in the poetry of Daruwalla, who like a social activist, relates the violence in nature with the violence in human life.

Taking up the first trajectory, we see that since time immemorial, human beings are causing all sorts of atrocities on nature and with the advent of technology this has become even worse. Daruwalla leaves no scope to criticise this mentality as available in one of his historically-oriented poem "The Fall of Mohenjo Daro." This poem prophecises the death of a civilisation which has contemporary relevance and which is made explicit in the lines: 'There was no escape, the high treble/of their neighing paralysed us;/their wheels marked furrows/over our squirming backs.' The same sense is further extended in the other poem "The Earthquake City" where he discusses the menacing impact of technology and the imminent loss of a promising future: 'Having carved history into disaster eras/the museum saw to it that the present spoke/through tunnels and TV towers. Meet the future/gentlemen; plate-glass and factory smoke.' But the most vehement 'ecocritical' attack on the present technologically advanced civilisation is available through his presentation of Bombay as 'toxified' and as 'black yeast'. The living conditions have not at all changed. If on one side, Bombay is exemplified as 'the lepers, the acid-scarred, the amputees' from which the narrator turns his face, on the other side, Benaras is unforgettably evoked as the place 'where corpse-fires and cooking-fires/burn side by side', even while the sacred river Ganga flows on ("Boat-ride along the Ganga").

While discussing the other trajectory, where he is seen preoccupied with preserving the natural habitats for the animals, we can argue that the tranquillity of Mandawa beach is seen interrupted by the death of a baby-whale which was finally thrown back into the sea: 'The night passes in baby-whale talk,/a baby-whale which came in/with the foam and outstank the city,/till the fire-brigade cut it up/and threw it back into the ocean./When you come to the sea/your nightmares have to adjust.' A similar attempt has been made in the poem "Fish are Speared by Night" in which the 'Flashlights stab the sea' and 'the fish is skewered and forced down the spear-head, still threshing the sand.' Subsequently, in "Requiem For a Hawk" and "Wolf" we find that the killing of natural instincts can even serve as the potential for worse violence. The hawk is sought to be tamed and trained by men but the attempt to tame nature is totally nullified by the futility of taming the wild. Once again, this idea has been expressed in the poem "The Last Howl" like the following: 'All the hungers of the world were caged in their bellies/and hungers for the wild./After the last rabbit had bounced out of his hutch and the porcupine had shed his quills.'

Daruwalla's non-human world is not only symbolic but the reality that serves the setting for his thoughts. In him the poetic text itself transforms into an ecosystem and his ethical structure surrounds his sense of strong environmentalism contributing to the development of contemporary 'ecocriticism'. He should be credited with intertextually combining realism with 'ecocriticism' as he has proved that human history is always implicated in natural history. One of the most dominant characteristics of Indian poetry of 1970s and 1980s, is the change in focus. To expose the actual Indian experience, the poets have used techniques and expressions reflecting not the perceptions of the poet on himself/herself, but the actual hazards of the community life. Consequently, their poetry reveals more of the environment, of other lives, of the problem of daily living. Daruwalla has gained tremendous significance exactly for these issues and his sense of location and range of subject matter reveals an extraordinary reading experience. Poems like "Nights of the jackals", "Hawk" and others in "Crossing of Rivers" and "Keeper of the Dead" show a sharp awareness of the variety of Indian life and a skeptical view of North-Indian societal reality. As Bruce King has observed, the concern with exactness, social activism, perception of environment, forthrightness and the evaluative compassion of poets will be characteristic of many writers and critics who have been associated with Ezekiel and Daruwalla's sensibility is actually aware of and committed to the present-day socio-political and cultural reality. If poetry must show an awareness of the physical and human landscape then Daruwalla's 'eco-poems' can be cited as the fitting examples of Indian Poetry in English in the last three decades.

Works Cited

Buell, Lawrence. *The Future of Environmental Criticism: Environmental Crisis and Literary Imagination.* USA: Blackwell Publishing, 2005. Print.

Mehrotra, A. K., ed. Twelve Modern Indian Poets. New Delhi: OUP, 2004. Print.

7

The Sounds of Starved Eros: A Study of Shiv K. Kumar's *Thus Spake the Buddha*

—D.C. Chambial

Shiv K. Kumar is a major poet writing today, and the corpus of his poetry has indubiously made him the leading poet of the contemporary age. He started writing late in his career of a successful teacher of English literature. Having taught literature in Britain and the USA, his career reached its apogee as a Vice-Chancellor, Osmania University, Hyderabad, the highest rung of life in the academic world. He has more than eight volumes of poems. The present study is restricted to his seventh volume, *Thus Spake the Buddha,* with scant references to his other volumes, to study his quest for love (Eros) in its various connotations, primarily of sexual overtones.

The word "Eros" comes from the Greek mythology. Eros is the god of love. Hesiod proclaimed him as one of the primeval gods born of chaos. Later he was said to be the son of Aphrodite. Eros is depicted as a beautiful winged youth carrying a bow and a quiver of arrows like Kama (his arrows have flowers), the Hindu god of love. Though the word pertains to pure platonic love, but in its various connotations, it also suggests mild carnality or sexual love—a love for the flesh. In its psychological connotations it is the life instinct, based on the libido, sublimated impulses, and self-preservation; hence, also sexual love or desire.

As a 'late bloomer' in poetic world, he was, as the circumstances reveal, driven to poetry to seek sublimation of his emotion of love after he was deserted by his wife in 1966.

Then, he was in the prime of his life, realising and relishing the heights of achievements one after the other on the ladder of professional success. This was the time when he needed emotional satiety at home, but there came a sudden stroke of fate in the form of the divorce of his wife. He felt completely shattered and turned to poetry for emotional outlet. Under this impact of cerebral strain, his poetry has invariably shown, in the words of Bijoy Kumar Das, 'a luxuriant growth and sustained development' (17). Eroticism is not a derogatory term, but an essential primordial instinct with all living things. Therefore, its mention in literature is as integral to literature as to life. Literary works are not only the figments of one's fancy, but also 'open up to the reader hidden vistas in man's life' (Mordell 1). Here the word 'man' suggests the writer.

What we come across, here, in the book under study, began with his first anthology of poems: *Articulate Silences* (1970) wherein his predilection for this kind of imagery and theme can be seen in his lines and phrases such as 'nipples smeared with gold dust-powder' and 'weaving endless cycles of/desire and Pain' (20), and 'The other hunger forages/for silken thighs' (21). There is no end to such emotional vent for Eros. All other anthologies of his poems are replete with such imagery and references. Such mentions do not, in any way debase his poetry, but raise it to higher altitudes of poetic perfection. Now let us turn to the study of *Thus Spake the Buddha.*

The first poem, entitled "A Gorilla at the Zoo," in, speaks about the eternal sin of tasting of the forbidden fruit (sex) in these words:

> Not that he'd ever sinned—
> nor have ever done it behind bolted
> door, in shame and secrecy'
> Then why are his eyes half-shut
> lost in thought
>]over his disinheritance? (2)

In this poem the persona refers to the great Fall of Man and his disinheritance from Paradise, the theme of Milton's epic *Paradise Lost* and applies it to the Gorilla that he sees at a zoo. Adam did not commit this sin in any modern room by bolting the doors lest the people notice his shame; the reference to "behind bolted/door" very explicitly states that it pertains to the persona, who tries 'questioning every premise' (1) of his own life through Gorilla. As these lines tell that this Gorilla has not committed any such act of which he should be ashamed, yet he is lost in some thought: 'his eyes half-shut.' Perhaps, he is contemplating about his 'disinheritance,' not the aftermath of his own disobedience but of some one else. The poet begins by negating the commission of the act which ultimately led to Adam's Fall and human misery and death in this world of human inheritance. However, the very mention of the act/sin 'behind bolted/doors' debunks obsession with unsatiated Eros.

He himself admits in "Thus Spake the Buddha" that 'The way to satiate a yearning/is to sublimate it' (3). Psychology teaches one to seek sublimation of one's inhibitions/obsessions to free oneself from them. Once an individual is emancipated from these, he comes to his normal life that he was leading in an abnormal way. Desire, on the other hand is like 'an unbridled stallion'—here the simile of horse suggests sexual virility and again directs the boat of critical study towards the same goal post: unsatiated eros. In the second stanza of this poem, he talks about 'Body's appetite' which again pertains to sexual hunger and the persona's carnal starvation. When one is sexually starved one feels highly agitated and is prepared to challenge even the strongest of the strongest as these lines evince: 'Body's hunger, like a crocodile's belly,/can hold rock, metal/and a virgin's thigh' (5).

The same atmosphere continues in "I was Old Before My Birth." Here the persona, even while in womb could see his father's changing moods from morn to night: his angry mood in the morning, his drinking at nightfall, 'and at night, he summoned all the angels/to witness his ecstasy/as mother cooed under him, in bed' (6) is obvious manifestation of sex act suggested by the word 'ecstasy'. The persona continues: 'I could also count upto seven—the entire gamut of his sins' (6). The range of father's sexual virility is very lucidly displayed.

The premise of Eros is explicit in 'Listening to Beethovan's Sixth Symphony.' The influx of a lover is proclaimed by a bird: 'a woodpecker starts knocking/at Juliet's window/to announce her Love's arrival' (8). And, in her moony moments, she takes long to open her door to welcome him: 'A long pause, as if she needs an aeon/to dress herself for the rendezvous,/a constellation in her hair,/a sunflower's smile on her lips' (8). Her movement in the room towards the door is described: 'she glides across the marble floor,/trailed by her satin gown/drunk on ambrosia' is suffice enough to betray her romantic ecstasy.

In "Voices at Night," the persona talks about 'a tiger's mate' and 'frogs' mating calls' (16). He uses the word 'mate,' first as a noun and secondly as an adjective. At both the places, it connotes a sexual companion/partner. In the first image, the poet writes:

> A cat's monosyllabic mewing
> as it recalls how, in one of its nine
> previous lives, it was a tiger's mate.

And, in the second '... the frog's mating calls/after a brief down pour,' the urge becomes powerful as in the case of frogs in rainy season. The apex of yearning is reached in the last stanza of the poem when the persona muses:

> The rose bush's tapping
> against my rear window, relays whisperings
> from a woman who once ambushed
> me with her red throat.

The desire for a woman, which developed through references to cat and frogs, ultimately ends in alluding to the woman who had seduced him with her powerful passion. The phrase, 'red throat,' hints at the passionate self of the woman at that particular moment. The word 'ambush,' points to the wild chase like the heroine of Shaw's *Man and Superman*: she wanted him and when he appeared she didn't want to lose the opportunity at hand.

In 'Which of My Selves do You wish to speak to?' the same character retires into a reverie:

> ... the moon's shadow lingers
> on my window pane, stirring memories
> of a face from my childhood,
> it's time for an intimate dialogue, (17)

The last line, quoted above, very unequivocally betrays his itch. The atmosphere is romantic. It drives him to past memories of his childhood love which is followed by the longing for 'intimate dialogue.' In "Stress," another poem, he hears father's mumbling in dream, instructing the son to read the *Gita* and welcome a 'call-girl' in philosophical equipoise. No difference between a call-girl and any other lass of her age. The question is only the sublimation of the urge that haunts his mind. These philosophical advices are 'Easier said than done.' He seeks diversion from this moralising discourse of *Gita*.

Sexual undertones are also manifest in the poem, "Honeymooners' Lane, Kodaikanal." With the fall of the day the lovers/honeymooners come out to this lane at Kodaikanal. In the growing darkness, they look like shadows:

> As it's time for the sun
> to retreat behind the veil,
> shadows appear down a lane
> that curves like a scimitar, flanked
> by wild flowers. Each shadow saunters,
> arm in arm with another,
> emancipated from time and space. (29)

The persona describes this carefree movement of the lovers lost in their own world as cupids and psyches in the veil of darkness and inebriated by the aroma ensuing from "wild flowers." The slow, 'arm in arm' movement of the lover's calls for comparison with cupid and psyche in Keats's "Ode to Psyche":

> They lay calm-breathing on the bedded grass;
> Their arms embraced, and their pinions too;
> Their lips touch'd not, but had not bade adieu,
>
> (Garrod 211)

But, as the lover, here, lets his hand slink down the 'nape of a neck,' his this movement is lovingly restricted, because

> ..., there'd be time
> to consummate the ritual later,
> in deluxe room at the Hill view
> that has witnessed scenes
> from Konark and Khajuraho. (29)

The poem is rich in its imagery of love. The persona, as an omniscient, watches all this to derive pleasure for his lovelorn and sex-starved psyche from this spectacle 'in deluxe room at Hill View' hotel that has love-making 'scenes' aplenty 'from Konark and Khajuraho.'

The sex-starvation sits heavy on the persona's consciousness when, in "Stopping under the Traffic Lights," he hears

> ... a voice in the air:
> it's not the red alert against the phantoms
> of guilt, nor the green signal that tempts one
> towards a mirage ...(30)

Whatever, he sees/encounters reminds him of the temptation in Heaven and the commission of sin: desire/temptation and caution move side by side. Even the consummation of 'the ritual later' is no more than 'a mirage' in this world of *Maya*.

The element of beauty is sure to shake even the seat of saints. The persona, in "Watching the Rain from my Balcony," while watching the rains wants to know that was if the rain drops were tears:

> ... is it some saint in tears
> who fell fro a woman with the eyes
> of a gazelle. Twenty years of meditation
> squandered away. (32)

Beauty is sure to shake not only the thrones of kings, but also the seats of saints. The saint, in the poem, squanders away his twenty-year long *tapasya* (meditation) 'for a woman with the eyes/of a gazelle.' She appears more powerful in her temptation for him than all the meditation he has been practising for the sake of seeking *moksha* from this birth-death-birth cycle and mystic unity with the Divine one.

Bearded goat has always been associated with masculine virility. This imagery is used for exhibiting the dormant desire in "Anxiety." The persona fears sexual assault on his daughter and feels concerned:

> That goat-bearded young man
> with a scorpion tattooed on his chest—
> how can I salvage my daughter
> from his dark shadow? (33)

To increase the acerbity of the fear, the persona sees 'scorpion tattooed on his chest.' Scorpion is a very poisonous insect. The 'goat-bearded young man' appears to him dangerous for his daughter and thinks about the way of protecting her from him: 'How can I salvage my daughter/from his dark shadow?' Even his shadow seems dark/ominous. He feels much concerned with the safety of his daughter. There is a change in Kumar's thinking with advanced age; he, now, does no more think of 'curves like scimitar,' and moving "arm in arm" or any gazelle eyed beauty in company but feels concerned about the ladies belonging to him.

"The Sea from the Cottage on the Beach" has Eros expressed in the imagery derived from the sea and sea animals:

> .... A pair of young seals,
> just initiated into love, glower at these
> intruders, then retreat into the depths
> for cover. But as darkness cleans up
> the beach, they are back to caress
> each other's flanks, smooth as
> the crest of a chrysanthemum. (36)

Now, the persona looks from a cottage at the beach, wherein he is sojourning, to the amorous caresses of the animals in the sea to get some sublimation of his similar sentiments. Love-making is a private affair. None would tolerate any intrusion in it. So, this 'pair of young seals,/just initiated into love,' glare at the persons who come to the beach for picnic and perturb them in their love-making. They, feeling disturbed, go back to the deeps of the sea, but the fall of night, when these people leave the beach desolate, the young seals return to caress each other in perfect solitude till their commotion of love.

Thus, the corpus of this article amply evinces that the protagonist is haunted by Eros. For its fulfilment, he seeks its sublimation in such images as are related with such biotic acts. This comes home to the readers of Kumar when they come to know that his wife divorced him in 1966 and he faced a traumatic situation, when he was 45 years of age (b. 1921). We also realise the purpose of his turning to poetry and the domination of erotic images as 'an expression of the innate feelings of his protagonist' (92) what Prabhat K. Singh, a scholar of his poetry, rightly contends.

Works Cited

Das, Bijoy Kumar. *Shiv K. Kumar as a Post-colonial Poet*. New Delhi: Atlantic, 2001. Print.

Britannica Ready Reference Encyclopedia. Vol. 3. New Delhi: Encyclopedia Britannica (India) Pvt. Ltd. & Impulse Marketing, 2005. Print. Text selected from *Britannica Concise Encyclopedia* by the editors of the Encyclopaedia Britannica, Inc. Special Edition for South Asia.

Garrod, H. W., ed. *Keats: Poetical Works*. London: OUP, 1973. Print. Rpt. of *Oxford Standard Authors* series. 1956.

Kumar, Shiv K. *Articulate Silences*. Calcutta: Writer's Workshop, 1970. Print.

___ *Thus Spake the Buddha*. New Delhi: UBS Publishers' Distributors Pvt. Ltd., 2002. Print.

Mordell, Albert. *The Erotic Motive in Literature*. New York: Collier Book, 1962. Print.

Singh, Prabhat K. "The Poetry of Shiv K. Kumar." *A Passage to Shiv K. Kumar: From Agony to Ecstasy*. New Delhi: Sarup & Sons, 2001. Print.

8

Nostalgic Past and Agonised Present in the Poetry of Shiv K. Kumar

—P.C.K. Prem

If one goes into the background of earlier Indian English poetry, it becomes fairly clear that the earlier poets had to struggle hard in order to make a dent in the Indian psyche particularly the elites of an age, where it was not trouble-free to go against the current of existing thought; and the thoughts and ideology which exercised a certain charisma in the minds and intellects. Shiv K. Kumar is among the tall poets of that era, who always struggled hard between two mindsets and tried to establish a definite reconciliatory posture where it was an endeavour not to hurt Indian sensibility and cultural moorings. Mostly based in urban areas, many poets of this age did try to highlight Indian problems arising out of the foreign governance. Obviously one finds restraint, discipline and cautious depiction of sentiments and social issues troubling people. Shiv K. Kumar is not an exception. He is a prolific writer and has given wonderful poems, novels and short stories to the literary world. Truly, he is one of the finest and brilliant Indian English author.

Shiv K. Kumar is a poet of terrific images and at times one is dumbfounded at the rapid sequence of release of varied images. A reader has to work hard to reach the intellectual, imaginative and imagist's acumen of the poet. Dr Atma Ram observes: 'The poem emerges naturally from a nebulous conglomeration of images. It is always a floating image that gets frozen in his mind—so his poems tend to think in terms of images and symbols. For him, each poem chooses its own diction. According to him, the East-West confrontation is the most distinctive feature of modern Indian-English Poetry. In this respect, this branch of literature transcends national ramifications' (60).

When Dr Atma Ram says that it "transcends national ramification" he probably means that it is not only a genuine Indian English Poetry but goes beyond the country now without colonial hangover. I.H. Rizvi and N.F. Rizvi briefly observe, 'Kumar is an original poet, though he has been influenced by some poets like T.S. Eliot. The range of his themes is very wide and his treatment of subjects is original.' (*Origin, Development and History of Indian English* Poetry 70). As one goes into the depths of Kumar's poetry one learns that he is chiefly worried about life and so preoccupation with the concept of life and death continues to haunt. It is also a painful journey with overbearing thoughts of 'woman' and 'suicide' for the poet, and he observes sufferings around and makes efforts to emerge out victorious but is partially triumphant; and then he turns to religion and spiritualism without becoming vocal or enthusiastic.

On the one hand, the poet appears morose, thoughtful and lonely as ideas of life, death and sufferings invade sensitivity, on the other hand when he thinks of women it makes him quite sensuous, soft and eloquent. To escape from the unsympathetic realities of life he finds consolation in abstract ideas. It is in total abstraction that one has to find the gist of poet's thoughts and his anxiety for man's sufferings. Kumar is occupied with the thoughts of death, women and at times worldly sufferings and suicide; and alternately he moves from the outer world to the inner world of man. In other words, the poet many a time goes back to past and recalls poignantly each moment and then lives in the present and finds solace in sufferings, primarily internal. It is the inner battlefield where he fights out for viable existence. On the themes, the poet handles, I.H. Rizvi and N.F. Rizvi say, 'Love, sex and marriage cover a considerable portion of Kumar's poetry. To him love and sex are one, and in this respect he seems to have been influenced by D. H. Lawrence's theory of love as enjoyment of sex. He believes in the fulfillment of sexual urge.' (ibid. 70)

He knows that a man is involved in the awful monotony of life without ever knowing that it will lead him nowhere. Life's sufferings and pains will force him to seek deliverance from the agonies. When the poet talks of 'The easiest path to renunciation/is to paralyse memory's cell,' it is:

> To accost the past suddenly
> down a blind alley
> with memory's lancet eyes
> but no defensive weapons,
> is to be trapped into rapid provocation
> to recount all one's losses and gains,
> making renunciation
> a mere chimera.
>
> ("Renunciation," *Articulate Silences* 18)

Man's life moves between past and present with sufferings and little joys pursuing unremittingly, and man is invariably engaged in building up a possible defense but still gets pushed into the persistent arithmetic of life while calculating gains and losses. The sufferings do disturb man while he wishes to run away from the 'torrid zones of turbulence.' Elsewhere, when he talks of 'weaving endless cycles of/desire and pain, satiety and ennui/his beatific smile surpassing all understanding' (Buddha at a Night Club, *Articulate Silences* 20) he hints at an unexciting life where nothing tempting is left and so life has to be lived perhaps with a doze of pleasure. If the poet philosophically talks about life, sufferings and imminent death, it can also be construed his attempt to escape from the callous realities of life. But then philosophers are seldom happy and this is exactly the message, Kumar wants to give. He is pessimistic and yet wishes to continue the fight through disseminated sensibility and audacious courage of the inner man. This attitude suddenly catapults him to thoughts of death as a means of liberation from the miseries of life:

> For thirteen days, say the Hindus, the departed
> soul hovers round its earthly habitat, and
> so for thirteen days, I have communed with the
> spirit—whenever a door handle rattle, a
> nipping wind howls, the dog whines or the
> blue-bells clang, I feel her presence within me.
> Immanence is an attribute of God.
>
> ("An Encounter with Death," *Articulate Silences* 34)

The poet in many poems talks of death and tries to find its meaning and scope. He knows it is a continuous search for meaning. D.C. Chambial makes pertinent observations when he says that the poet '...wishes to know more about life and death before dying. It may take the whole span of life to learn about it. Now he is ready to welcome death before dying. He reconciles himself with death as the natural end of somatological existence. For him this fear becomes therapeutic and evaporates as death turns into a welcome friend.' *(Indian English Poetry and Fiction 149)* One wonders if the poet draws out sadistic pleasure out of such raucous expressions about life, death and the chasing pains. One finds powerful sounds of words before confronting the real message. Interestingly the last lines—'I feel...of God'—speak of a perennial truth though an agnostic intellect may refuse to accept. A similar strain continues in "Siesta," in a more cogent, clear and graphic beauty:

> Halfway through my life
> I feel the burden of pain, unbearable,
> Even my tears cannot mitigate.
> ... ...
> It is napping—so am I.
> All doors of perception sealed.
> Mid May drizzle and the wind whistling.
>
> ("Siesta," *Losing My Way* 20)

Here lucidity and perceptible simplicity are wonderful even though nothing is said to create intensity that tortures but still the realistic picture captures the authentic spirit of bliss in amnesia. But poet's encouraging attitude is quite evident when he wants to find a few moments of joys by evading burden of life in nature's gifts. A distinctive beauty pervades "Lightning," p.48. Here, the poet attracts with the thought and beauty of words. In another short lyric, the poet talks about the contemporary selfishness ruling the minds of people in a highly confessional style:

> I see another face on the opposite side,
> wan with the same dread. Maybe
> I should let him make the first move.
> Always easier for me to wait
> for someone else to lead the way.
>
> ("Crossing the Street," *Losing My Way* 51)

One finds unique coherence in the four entirely different images that the poet creates, leading directly to the contemporary ruling temper of naked egoism among people of all hues.

Poverty, exploitation and hunger disturb him as he describes the miserable living conditions of people working day and night for the rich in "Rickshaw–Wallah." Disgusting luxuries and opulence at a few places also unsettle the sensitive mind of the poet. He understands the sufferings of the hardworking people but hates bragging like a leader who talks of socialism but refuses to adhere to its tenets. The words obesity, tattered, mother-hen and chicks are superbly used to convey a thought with perfect adroitness:

> he computes the patches
> on the street's tattered shirt.
> Beyond the municipal precincts
> in a slummed roost
> the mother-hen is gagging
> her chicks' full-throated cries
> for a few grains of rice,
> their last supper.
>
> ("Rickshaw-Wallah," *Subterfuges* 46)

To understand poet's modern-day perception is an experience. Intense urban feelings and sophisticated living, restrain the poet to say certain painful realities of life in direct language. He paints a scene and in remarkable use of metaphors and images reflects on the prevailing rut in the society. The modern administration of justice is time-consuming, agonising and redundant for it is ultimately the poor man who suffers:

> Born out of the moon's eye—
> tender, omniscient, lithe-limbed—
> justice was ambushed mid-air,
> pulled down to these chambers
> then nourished on casuistry and deferment.
> Now she speaks a dialect nobody can understand.
> ... ...
> On the rickety wooden benches,
> the waiting pilgrims have left
> their bones for their progeny to collect.
> ... ...
> It's the long wait that kills
> the lover, the cancer-patient
> and the petitioner.
>
> ("The Hazari Courts, Delhi," *Trapfalls in the Sky* 23)

In a democratic socialistic country justice should be the basis of a clean life but it does not happen. The poet is trenchant, unequivocally true and pained as the people suffer and wait for justice for years, nay from generations to generations and the lethargic courts stand still. If the poet hints at the 'Kaurava-Pandava land wrangle' it speaks of a modern dilemma. When the poet says in the same verse that '...I already see your son, and his/and his—all queued up/brandishing the same petition/ for a speedy redress,' it is a sadly irremediable disease that plagues the Indian society and body-politic.

He is aware of the maddening life styles and crazy urban expansion in concrete structures causing despair and disillusionment. It is a search for an escape route for a better pasture to live life peacefully which is now a near impossibility, the poet appears to tell:

> Darkness drips from the decapitated lamp-posts—
> the squall lashes
> at the naked glasspanes.
> Sitting in the porch
> I wonder if this city

too is doomed.
In mid-spring
birds lie still
under the memories of a winter
that had raised too many questions.

("Alternatives," *Cobwebs in the Sun* 31)

Another critical mental disease relates to utter individualistic propensity to live life and here disconcerting situations arise which threaten the very foundations of a sound system in personal relationships. Questions of identity disturb. At times one feels existence being reduced to a mere 'wall poster' or a 'call girl'. The first image is terrifically lazed around in sensuousness:

Between one bed and another
the call-girl smoothes out
the dabbled folds
of her self
to let the sun charge it again
with the will to be.
But night coins in too soon
to claim its tithe.

("Identity," *Cobwebs in the Sun* 38)

It is shocking to notice that life becomes so despicable, preposterous and comical when even images humiliate existence but then the poet in Shiv K. Kumar is master of such word-paintings while poet's eyes epitomise life in wider perspectives.

Kumar is ruthless in describing a life of futility where identity even if luxurious, appears lustily dirty as in "Identity" but surprisingly while he speaks of people on the pavement in Bombay, he is equally heartless and candid in depicting a scene that puts a question mark on the civilised world while telling sardonically of the 'fallen angels':

Lying cheek by jowl ...
they look like corpses waiting to be dumped
into a mass grave.
... ...

> Day is for sweating—
> For shoe-shining, foraging for crumbs from dust-bins,
> For pan-handling, or wiping the windscreens of cars
> As the traffic freezes at the red signal.
> ("Pavement-sleepers of Bombay," *Woolgathering* 22)

Life of the poor in different images is vividly created when he describes their shocking living conditions of punishing nights and toiling days which in fact sum up the meaning of life for these dwellers but still an unspoken quietness makes them happy. Amusingly, rich people do not live in peace but in vacuity, the poet appears to say and the woman in "Mercedes" exemplifies it. The poet appears to show sympathy to pavement-sleepers when he says: 'that while an empty belly's prayer/is echoed by the stars, the priest's vespers/never rise beyond the cathedral's dome/because these sleepers are only fallen angels…' The utter emptiness is quite evident when the poet tells that the prayers do not go beyond dome. It also underlines the hypocrisy and falsehood in the life of urbanites.

If in "Broken Columns" the poet appears confessional, in "O Delhi!" he is reminded of the old beauty and warmth of the city even if it was not so comfortable itself when it felt mutely pangs of partition times and here too his tone of confessional attitude is quite visible. The poet seems to recall that he had entered Delhi years back like an exile and 'It was a frigid morning, the sun bundled up/in a grey shawl of mist, the breeze probing/the bones marrow…' but Delhi opened its warm gates despite the chill outside to 'welcome indoors a fugitive from another land./I savoured your hospitality.' Here, the poet is hinting at the horrifying experiences of partition days during which people suffered physically, spiritually and economically in cold-blooded uprooting from original land. At that time the city was 'like the contours of a virgin's torso—taut and scented…I was like another Adam inheriting/a new Garden' after 'Riding the crest of amnesia.'

Kumar is graphic and ingenuous in social and historical perspective. It appears he underwent horrific mental and physical agonies during those excruciating days. Next moment, he is disappointed at the decline of a beautiful place as people began to play with it in a haphazard manner. Now to him it is a city of 'sagging udders' and 'plastic dentures' and it is loosing its old glory and sinking slowly to the 'earth's epicenter.' The poet quite rightly or perhaps out of habit, is not straightforward but reveals truth of history in innocuous hints. He talks of communal discords, of bigotry, of discrimination, of pollution, of cow-politics, of various cunning devices to linger on with life, of rituals of big men visiting Ghats and pleasure resorts, of justice while dumping the victims (one thinks of "The Hazari Courts, Delhi," *Trapfalls in the Sky*) and of so many diseases originating out of contamination. It is an intellectual bewailing but gives shocking moments. Here, making a departure from expression of hopeful despair, the poet stunningly appears a little optimistic:

> I prophesy that you too will fall
> like Nineveh and Babylon
> and so new Indraprashtha will rise
> from your barren ashes.
>
> ("O Delhi!" *Trapfalls in the Sky* 37)

If the poet is terse and emphatic in the above poem, in a similar frame of mind, he talks of another destructive quality of human mind and heart in "Felling a Tree" when he describes with subdued passion and hurt feeling the massacring of a tree. In a way, it is tribute to the helpless nature 'who' despite man's killing instinct, stays silent and defenseless to bear 'humiliation' that 'is lethal/when the victim has no weapons for defence/when you have to carry your own cross/and you are your own pyre,/ fuel, flame and ashes.' And finally, he relates the incident as if he has personally experienced the pains of a falling tree when he says:

> Now that it's done
> you may cart the body away in its full glory
> or in splinters
> like the dead man's bones, collected in a sack,
> for immersion in some confluence
> of love and hate.
>
> ("Felling a Tree," *Woolgathering* 39)

A cursory reading of "Returning Home" reveals appallingly monotonous and loveless killing of self while shrewdly involved in discharging obligations of life. There is inherent fear, diffidence and lurking guilt as various images unfold a person's inner predicament. It is a constant tossing between failure and probable achievement. One's sensibilities are in for a great shock as:

> We unlock the doors
> to antediluvian passages
> cluttered with dented skulls.

A radically amputated inner self, it appears, waits for in uncomfortable silence while the undefined anguish trickles in tiny drops. A chilly relationship permits no words while the fear of another curse of absolute stillness discourages as someone:

> Draw aside these curtains softly
> for the first ray
> from the old sun
> may decided the next eclipse.

In utter horror to the "I," it seems 'Under these sofas/now rat-nibbled/lie buried our instant reconciliations/gift-wrapped for the party' he finds vainness in living. The words are indicative of a life barren, wasted, vacant and futile; and he knows it is a movement to nowhere from an unknown start. The condition of sofa shows the mental and physical bankruptcy. The retreat to the kitchen is a usual armoury of a woman to avoid a near compromise in a life of unspoken faithlessness. But then to achieve a semblance of rapprochement the effort must continue, for finally, the poet observes:

> The backyard
> telescopes the house into perspective
> illumining the meanings of
> twisted syllables spoken indoors.
> Here in the open privacies
> the old gods counsel compromise.

("Returning Home," *Cobwebs in the Sun* 28-29)

In marital relations cacophonous notes creep in but sagacity, goodwill and mutual understanding can ensure a lasting relationship in spite of pleasant bitterness.

Kumar exhibits superb craftsmanship in building a structure of high sounding words which not only stun the reader by absolutely fresh images depicting truth but these many times function as a mirror to reflect contemporary reality. In "A Nightmare" the poet works on many images which speak of an utterly distraught mind where even thoughts of twinkling stars and glowing chandeliers of dreams and richness are insufficient as these soon turn into 'dark forebodings.' The poet is upset the way even religious matters are handled which do no good to mankind but on a slightest pretext dictates of the religious men bring disharmony in the society. To maintain individual beliefs is difficult, for one may be asked to repudiate. Here the word 'fatwa' carries many meanings:

> Beads of dread stood on
> My forehead. And on waking,
> I let out a cry
> like a tribal's wail
> across a ravaged cornfield.
>
> ("A Nightmare," *Losing My Way* 15)

The poet speaks of cold indifference towards life when he draws a parallel between the lean man's shedding tears on a mud grave and the quiet shrugging off a dog's bark by a stray donkey. Both the images paint life in absolute grouchiness and desolation.

> I have faltered
> between two truths.
>
> Let the waters carry away the ashes
> Swiftly past the antique bridge
> Not swing back to smudge
> The rock that has known many a corpse.
>
> ("Detachment," *Woodpeckers* 42)

Life has many shades and meanings. At times it is full of substance and at another moment it is all a jugglery of words and emotions concretised into little sentences impregnated with meaning. But in the long run man finds that it is futility and triviality that stare blankly. "A Poets' Meet" speaks of great ideas and principles while the characters mounting the podium, appear farcical and stupid. They define feelings of love, the concept of life and the conduct of man adding new but sarcastic dimensions. For example, man is defined by a woman-poet as:

> Trust not the man, she crooned,
> who breezes in with strawberries
> in his hands, and lisps like a
> gentle breaker on the beach.
>
> ("A Poets' Meet," *Losing My Way* 57)

It is total meaninglessness that devours a man so blindly engaged in multifarious adventures.

One thing is quite apparent that the poet is deeply worried about the destiny of man. He is realistic, touches many aspects of modern life with urban sensibility and philosophic bent of mind and in the process, slowly moves towards spiritualism but suddenly turns back. Perhaps it is dilemma of a modern man. Atma Ram rightly says that 'The poet writes in a forceful and original style. As a scholar-poet, he has an easy access to various disciplines. His experience has been multifaceted and multinational.' (*Indian Poetry and Fiction in English 62*)

Kumar's mastery over images is marvelous. He mostly writes short verses and most of the time he conveys message through images. In a few poems he scathingly talks of contemporary sufferings and sadistic callousness of those in authority. One finds that he is neither fully attached to the Indian culture and traditions nor is unbiased to the Western bent of mind. In between the thought and the emotional content, the poet tries to bring about reconciliation with a rare objectivity. To me it appears, most of the poets of that period, who had urban background, were inclined towards Western thoughts and habits but to find roots they often turned to the origin and that makes the difference. If such poets had the impact of T.S. Eliot and others, it is natural if one also analysis the tremendous influence of stunning material progress around in various wings of life. On the other hand, in poetic and intellectual range, one finds flashes of Ageya, Bharati, Shamsher Bahadur Singh and Narendra Mohan who were giving expressions to contemporary issues man was confronting at that time of history when scientific, industrial and technological growth was entering India with immense velocity. Here I believe that the poets may use any language but surprisingly the depth and scope of feelings and thoughts at the experiential level almost remains unaffected. Deeply rooted in Indian culture and ethos, poets like Rizvi, Chambial (with a number of rural images), R.K. Singh and Manas Bakshi are poets of urban sensibilities and undoubtedly their poetry is in the tradition of Kumar. To a great degree P.C.K. Prem, like Chambial, is not an exception. In short, Kumar's poetry provokes but he scrupulously avoids instructive approach while the poet's varied perception of life in intensity, astonishes the lovers of poetry.

Works Cited

Gopal, N. R. & Suman Sachar. *Indian English Poetry and Fiction.* New Delhi: Atlantic Publishers and Distributors (P) Ltd., 2000. Print.

Kumar, Shiv K. *Articulate Silences.* Calcutta: A Writers Workshop Publications, 1970. Print.

_____ *Cobwebs in the Sun.* New Delhi: Tata McGraw-Hill Publishing Co, 1974. Print.

_____ *Losing My Way.* New Delhi: Atlantic Publishers And Distributors (P) Ltd, 2008. Print.

_____ *Subterfuges.* Delhi: Oxford University Press, 1976. Print.

_____ *Trapfalls in the Sky.* Madras: Macmillan Indian Limited, 1986. Print.

_____ *Woodpeckers.* London: Sidgwick & Jackson, 1979. Print.

_____ *Woolgathering.* Bangalore: Disha Books, An imprint of Orient Longman Limited, 1998. Print.

Ram, Dr Atma. *Indian Poetry and Fiction in English.* New Delhi: Bahri Publications, 1991. Print.

Rizvi, I.H. & N.F. Rizvi. *Origin, Development and History of Indian English Poetry.* Bareilly: Prakash Book Depot, 2008. Print.

9

The East-West Fusion in Shiv K. Kumar's Poetry

—Anshu Bhardwaj

Many of the Indo-Anglian poets who assumed the role of making the ethos and culture of India interesting to the West through imaginative literature, and whose poetry truly represents Indian life and culture presented as poetic exponent of the spirit of the East to the West, have won universal recognition. They have tried to invite ideas from the Western culture in their poetry, and the presence of two cultures has given a wider perspective to their work. In this regard Balachandra Rajan writes:

> ...the presence of two cultures in one's mind forms a wider and therefore saner basis on which to originate the quest for identity, and ...the discordance between these two cultures can be creative as well as merely confusing. Perhaps one can go further and suggest that the man with mixed allegiances is contemporary Everyman.[1]

According to Dr. Mulk Raj Anand, India's contribution to the west was its rich humanism with strengthened the spiritual life. India's contact with the Western civilisation produced people like Kitsamy who with an Oxford education, and long years spent in England had become completely Westernised. We can find a rich crop of Indian poets who are writing poetry in English. Even though they write in English, they are deeply rooted in their native culture. They have acquired Western knowledge and have developed an enthusiasm for it. Derozio may be said to represent the first echo in India of western ideas that had begun to take root in Indian soil. He made a small start in the right direction to give expression to Indian ethos through the medium of English. That's why, his poems have the flavour of English romantic poetry, but they express Indian nationality thought and reveal his sense of patriotism. In this reference we may remember:

> Between East and West the cultural wind blows both ways, though a hasty present-day inspection might suggest that it blew mainly eastward. The wind from the East is quieter, older, less immediately detectable; it penetrates and mingles, and its note is deep. Today the student from the Orient may find himself to some degree at home in western though for the elements of his own culture that are mixed in it.[2]

Shiv K. Kumar is one of the most widely circulated and anthologised poets of Indian Writing in English today who have gained ground even in the West. He has travelled abroad considerably enough to get a feel of the different cultures of the world. In fact, the assimilation of Indian culture into the west also began around the Post-Independence Period. He himself underlines this aspect of post-colonial Indian English poetry in the following words:

> Another recurring theme in most contemporary Indian Poetry in English is East-West cultural encounter. This perhaps relates to the fact that several of our poets have had their education abroad-at Oxford, Cambridge, Leeds or some American University. So they often tend to write like expatriates or exiles while living in the west and look back nostalgically on their western experience when they return home.[3]

American influence has become more significant in his poetry. The West is a deep and vital influence in the shaping of his sensibility. Kumar spent the formative years of his life abroad and developed a keen interest in literature and was well read in English poets. He writes like a Western thinker and neither extols the Western lifestyle of America nor does he look at India with horror or denigration because of its 'deadly combination of finicky sanitation and consciousness disinfected by protracted escapes into the affluent.' He embodies a truly Indian sensibility with great delicacy. He has also been abroad for considerable lengths of time. He did his doctorate at Cambridge and taught in England and the USA. He nostalgically recalls the scenes of Cambridge when he was there.

> Beyond the campus precincts
> argent bulls chase mottled butterflies
> into the livid horizon.
> Freedom bares its sallow fangs
> for the primal assault.[4]

His Western education enables him to look at things and persons from a rational, even ironical, angle and he laughs scornfully at the priests and the pundits alike. The irony is his forte which sometimes becomes devastating and consuming: he does not spare even himself. The ironic tone reflects Kumar's rebellion, and his presentation has a cold, ruthless detachment. In his "Broken Columns" a teacher preaches that Indian 'degeneracy', not 'British might' brought about colonialism. But the teacher's vision of regeneration is undercut by the butter milk on his moustache. His father begins to suspect him of libidinous interests in women and orders him to go to a high priest who beckons him into a dark chamber of the Shiva temple and begins sensually caressing his neck.

In fact, his work reflects a perennial interaction between what he appears to see as the respective values of the Indian and the Western cultures. Keki N. Daruwalla writes that Kumar's poetry:

> floats between ironic counterpoints and its tension comes from the Indian environment he writes in with an outlook moulded by years of living in the West.[5]

We know that Kumar's sensibility about Indianness has always been questioned or variously interpreted. G.S. Amur says that 'there can be no commitment other than to his own art'[6] and goes on to state that, Kumar's sensibility, like his poetic mode is a shifting:

> though not disorganised, sensibility, Indian in the Western cultural context...and Western in the Indian context.[7]

However, in his attempt to sing of Indian life, Kumar appears to have been tempted to make his expression picturesque, with the result that his poetry makes Indian altogether a land of romance and mystery. The truth about India is complex, and certainly anyone who has not felt the romance and mystery of India is a Philistine. But there are other facts of India which need to be seen to make one's vision of the country reasonably faithful. His poems like 'A Hindoo to his Cow', 'My Mother's Lover', 'Indian Women', 'Rickshaw Wallah', 'A Mango Vendor', 'Kali', 'Crematorium in Adikmet, Hyderabad', 'Khajuraho', 'Shimla Hills', 'Farewell to Tis Hazari Courts', 'Lord Venkateswara's Temple', 'At the Ghats of Banaras', 'Karma', 'O Delhi!'and 'An Indian Mother's Advice to her Daughter Before her Marriage' are on decorative Indian themes are surrounded by a halo of romance. His fifth collection of poetry has three parts: On Native Grounds, Under Alien Skies and Genesis. The first part expresses his Indian experiences and the second part presents his alien experiences mainly in New York and London and the last section is inspired by the First Book of the Old Testament. In this way his collection can present a very beautiful blend of the East and the West cultures. On the one hand it provides many echoes of classical Indian writers like Kalidasa and Vatsyayana and on the other hand it also provides the echoes of the Western poets like Yeats and Eliot in the poem "Baptism of Fire". Kumar shows adolescent love, encroached upon by the sacred thread ceremony. He uses his sharp mind and beautifully presents how the sacrificial fire reminds the young novice of the fire of passion lit by the touch of his girl's:

> nascent breasts under the mango tree—
> and the earth spine on a
> bull's horns for a new gyre.[8]

Kumar gives a new shape to his writing with the encounter of East and West. The West has shaken him and his stay in the west has been useful for him. A large number of poems have been written about Indian life but he writes surprisingly little about his experiences abroad. Although he claims to look at both Indian and Western cultures from the perspective of an alien, he writes mostly about India with an anger which takes the form of cosmic satire. When a person has two landscapes-First where he was born and the other where he has achieved, he cannot escape himself from the influence of those persons who came in his contact. These influences give a new shape to his personality and writing. In this way Kumar's writing has influences of both cultures—Eastern and Western. We can find the shadows of Western writers and poets like Shakespeare, Lawrence, Yeats, Eliot and many other writers and poets in his writing.

Kumar keeps Shakespeare's views in his mind and tries to write something on him. For this purpose he takes his two great tragedies '*Othello*' and '*Hamlet*' as his subject in his poem "Shakespeare Seminar: Fall 1981." In this poem he presents a Professor of literature who lectures on *Othello* and *Hamlet* at an American University and invites the students to interpret Shakespeare in the purely cerebral manner. In plainer words, he never hesitates to debunk and satirise this intellectual scholar:

> Let's now move on from the Ecclesiastical
> law in 'The Prince of Denmark' a la Rocellus
> Sheridan Guerney to some problems of Judgment
> and feeting in The Moore of Venice
> a la Professor Jane Adamson.[9]

Further the poem explains the beautiful expression of sexuality when the Professor saw the young beautiful girl named Sheila sitting with her boy friend whose hand slithers like serpent on her nape. During the lecturing on 'Othello' he, in imagination, is almost sleeping with the object of his carnal desire and before talking to her on external, verbal plane he is still imaging a cuckoo bird, mating on the cornice. He also imagines of the frozen meat in a department store meat consisting of legs, thighs and breast:

...But should I feel jaundiced
if the cuckoo mates under a cornice
in a grocery store, above the frozen meats—
legs, thighs and breasts?[10]

Sheila is busy with her lover and ignores the Professor's lecture. At last, he advises her to come next week to his class intuitively. In this way Kumar wants to participate in the full blooded experience of Shakespearean plays. He can do it easily only after reading or seeing them acted on the stage, not through a scholarly interpretation of them. Thus, Shakespearean plays do not need any kind of interpretation Shakespeare's writings always impress Kumar and Kumar has tried to acquire his wisdom.

Kumar's Western education enabled him to make the new myth of the man-woman relationship. He regards this relationship as a uniquely precious thing in man's life. Like Lawrence he openly and frankly writes about this relationship and never hesitates to break up the norms and traditions of society in relation to sex only to achieve sublimation in the language of body that can be achieved through sex. 'He is essentially a Lawrentian with a strong belief in the authenticity of physical experience.'[11] True love demands complete surrender to the lover. The lover and the beloved cross all the limits and think to make complete surrender as Lawrence's Birkin thinks in "Women in Love". Kumar also shows this relationship in his poem "Cerebral Love" where the lover is always ready to surrender to the beloved and in "The Sun Temple, Konark" where gods and goddesses appear in various sexual postures in figures of stones. These stones show the sexual relationship between man and woman with frankness and openness. In fact, there lies a great mystery behind these stones which he tries to get through the language of body. In "A Letter to Sharad" he sees:

...two faces
mirrored in my mind's pool,
both floating in concentric circles
yet each drawn to its own moon.
One face to carry to bed

when the blood leaps in the veins
like a terrier snapping at the leash.
the moment for two bodies to spark off
each other.[12]

In his poem "A Stray Bitch Abandons her Litter at Dusk" he refers to "the body's urge to seek redemption through touch."[13] A man denies the body but sex comes into full play. If someone tries to institutionalise any kind of regimentations, Kumar reacts very sharply and that is where the satirical vein comes over him. In "Nude Before God" when Ram Krishna was sixteen, a love letter from Sheila was caught in the history book, by his father. His father sent him to a priest at the Arya Samaj Temple where the boy was told to keep away from women because:

where a woman's body creases
at the core of existence
a sewer runs through the dark
foliage.[14]

Kumar has tried to depict Lawrentic cult in his writing. Lawrence 's writing is a presentation of Western culture but Kumar expresses his western ideas within his native ideas. In this way Kumar' s writing is a beautiful fusion of East and West.

Kumar's poems echo Eliot's views and images. The use of city images like 'garbage can', 'murky streets', 'steel spines of sky scrapers', the 'snake pit' etc. remind us of Eliot's London as a city of broken images as described in "The Burial of the Dead". Similarly, the night club with 'tobacco joss-sticks' in 'Buddha at a Night Club' reproduces the ecstasy of taking 'air in a tobacco-trance' in Eliot's "Portrait of a Lady". 'Similarly Kumar was also impressed with the manner of Yeatsean images. The images of 'cross' and 'tattered shirt' in "Rickshaw-wallah" in Articulate Silences revive in our memory W.B. Yeats's 'a tattered coat':

Pulling his cross
on bellyful of questions,

with obesity belching complacency
on the cushioned seat behind,
he computes the patches
on the street's tattered shirt.[15]

Kumar has great love for Urdu language and always longed for writing a 'ghazal' or a 'nazam' in English. His love for Urdu brought him close to Faiz and he also translated Faiz's poems into English. Kumar has also tried to capture the rhythmic perfection of the Urdu couplet in his poetry as the poem "And Death Shall Speak With Many Voices" expresses:

Soft mallet strokes
on the navel,
thrumming past the heart
to seize the throat
by its soprano chords.[16]

Kumar has tried to capture the essence and music of Faiz in his poetry through the translation of Faiz's poems into English. In this reference Yousuf Kamal who has translated Kumar's award winning collection of poems "Trapfalls in the Sky" into Urdu, says:

> Kumar 's translation-with parallel Urdu text, is...the most outstanding and definitive of all the translations that have appeared so far by such poets and scholars as Agha Shahid Ali, Daud Kamal, Bill Kiernan etc...While these translators have been able to render mainly the thematic content, Kumar has succeeded in capturing both the essence and music of Faiz.[17]

Thus Kumar has Eastern influence within Western influence. His western approach comes from the flesh and eastern approach comes from the meditation. In this way Kumar's poetry has a fine fusion of East-West culture. He passed a long life there but he never forgot Indian culture. Whatever he saw there, he felt as an Indian. This is the main reason that we find the best kind of East-West fusion in his love poetry. His abroad life developed a deep awareness about India and its past in him. His poems show his love towards India. When he returns from abroad and puts steps in India, he gets satisfaction as he says:

I fly back to my roost
over the Gateway to India.[18]

Again he says in the next poem, "I carry my bride home."[19]

"Broken Columns" gains five more sections in the later edition of Kumar's poems entitled *Woodpeckers*. Sections eight and nine sum up his experience in England and ten, eleven and twelve detail his impressive of his motherland after his sojourn abroad; hence the metaphor of the bird:

...that stretches its wing
beyond the water's brink
often lands on some insidious rock.[20]

In contrast to the poet's firsthand experience and minute observation of the Western life-style, there are typically Indian poems like 'Indian Women', 'Fisherman', 'Kovalam Beach', 'Transcendental Meditation', 'A Hindoo to his Cow', 'A Temple atop a Hill', 'Lord Krishna to Arjuna', 'Lake Gandipet, Hyderabad', 'Kali', 'Cabaret Dancer', 'The Sun Temple, Konarak' and 'Moongasing' in which permeates the total Indian sensibility of the poet. In contrast to the dinosaur's entrails vulture's ribs and pavements hurling stones that Kumar finds in the West, the Indian scene is often portrayed with a tranquillising case and love. In "Coromandel Beach" the poet quietly watches:

clusters of blank eyes
caught in ringlets of sizzling
egg-beaten foam advance
in parabolas, ellipses, arcs,
then splinter sideways into puny rills
under their own weight.[21]

Instead of splashing local colour indiscriminately to attract foreign clientele to hunt for Indian exotica, he localises these Indian poems with great delicacy and meticulousness so as to give them a sense of precision, inwardness and authenticity.

"Pilgrimage" and "Lord Venkateswara's Temple" have a firm faith though, as the poet, wrily puts it:

> ...the gods had trapped me
> into belief.

The poem "Rickshaw Wallah" is written on Indian people with a deep understanding which betrays a sort of emotional involvement in their lives. He draws the pathos of Rickshaw-puller and the person who is sitting comfortably on the cushioned seat behind:

> Beyond the municipal precincts,
> is a slummed roost,
> the mother-hen is gagging
> her chicks 'full-throated cries
> for a few grains of rice—
> their last supper.[22]

Such an expression is bound to provoke "a bellyful of question" in rickshaw-puller, the poet and the reader alike. But questions are no substitute for food. Pity for the poor and the weak who suffer. Kumar satirises on Indian politicians who are 'vasectomised of all genital urges/for love and beauty.'[23] In "An Old Dry Well" he describes snakes creeping on old dry well. The snakes are the symbols of Indian women. The Indian women become restless in the absence of their husbands and begin to wait the snakes creep to and fro in the search of water. His western education makes him laugh scornfully at the priests and pundits who baptised him before the fire. It is a tradition that a child has to sit before the fire with unholy thoughts and his doom is visualised in the flame of fire. The whole ritual is very ironical. When the child is bound with the first knot of Damytatta with the words that this may help him in achieving "nirvana" and then the pundit instructs "Datta" that the young man should put a spoonful of ghee into the fire, the Youngman remains busy thinking of:

> ...all the mangoes in Sheila's back-
> yard till every tree cries out:
> 'let go!'[24]

The third time the priest utters 'Dayadhavam' which means to have sympathy with others in adversity but the young man thinks of sunbathe on the beach with alligators. Thus the poet points out the contrast between the priest and the young man because in the priest's opinion the ritual is full of meaning but for the young man it is all meaningless. In brief, he wants to suggest that when the ritual has been arranged free, knots in the sacred thread appear a burning binding that is an unbearable condition for the young man. What he feels has been presented there. It is true that Kumar got frustration in his married life as he felt a stranger in his own house in New York and his house appeared like 'a garbage can' but in his own country also he felt sorrow in his married life. He expresses his personal experiences of married life in poems in which he writes about the scenes of sorrow in married life:

> with the broken homes
> splintered all around...
> I open each morning my neighbour's Times
> Whisked away from his door
> before he stirs.[25]

and in "Twenty-fifth Wedding Anniversary" he says:

> There's the first knock at the door—
> they have started to pour in,
> each wearing his own anniversary on his painted face,
> poised to wish us many returns of the day—
> or the night eternal discord?[26]

These poems are based on his personal experience. The experience may be common, but it is given totally new dimension through its association with a diverse and opposite experience as in the poem "A Woman Labourer Breast-feeding her child, during Lunch-break" about the woman labourer breast feeding her child. This work of the lady is imbued with a luminescence that sets it apart in relief against the gray grind of her wok. It is an etching that can only be carved by an eye trained to observe the irony of contrast present in commonplace things. The image of the woman labourer is allowed to merge subtly with that of the Madonna and the child.

As a poet of city Kumar presents the city of Delhi, the capital of India, in the poem "O Delhi!" in which he describes the time of partition. It pulls one back from the artificiality of western sensibility to authentic Indian realism. A caravan of exiles took shelter on its Kingsway known as refugee colony. A refugee has also joined caravan:

> An aeon ago, I joined a caravan of exiles,
> Snail-paced across a continent
> to pitch my tent on your outskirts—Kingsway.[27]

The ghazals of Ghalib and Zauq were sung by the people in Delhi. In other words, the whole city of Delhi was coloured by the ghazals of Ghalib. This is famous as the young city whose:

> ...streets and alleyways were like the contours
> of a virgin's tarso-taut and accented.[28]

It is now grown into 'an old matron with aging udders and plastic dentures.' Time takes its toll of all things of cities, of passion of men and women. The first part of 'Delhi' raises its past rulers from the time of the Khaljis to the British and stresses on our importance. Here the sun appears on the Himalayas as an ominous skull. The second part is related to the experience of exile and Indian language (Tamil) has been transferred into an alien language and it presents a scene of the ruins of the city because there is created a linguistic tension for the poet that is evident in the concluding unit. At last, the poet has decided to learn to be simple and natural.

"Cleansing Ganga" is a poem based on Indian culture. It is pious and scared and full of mysteries. But Kumar says that now the Ganga is defiled by the people in the name of rituals and dogmas—the superstitious belief predominant in Hindu society. The piousness of Ganga is compared to the innocence of childhood. When he was a child, he was innocent and pious with crudities of life like mother's breast-milk. Everybody becomes chaste in his childhood because there is no logic in his mind:

> At nativity all creatures are chaste, like breast-milk –
> the downy chick, pecking its way out
> of the shell's prison,
> the littlun calf, gravitating on tottering
> legs to its mother's udders
> and the undiapered babe, thumped
> and thrashed into primal consciousness.[29]

When he grows up, the society makes him corrupt. In the same way the river Ganga is sacred but the society makes it unholy, impious in the name of rituals and dogmas by throwing ashes and bones and faded flowers as offerings to the dead. He says that the priests and pundits who chant mantras on the bank of Ganga, excite the people for the superstitious beliefs. They are like hungry crocodiles who wait for their prey. In this way they cheat the people by mounting pressure of religion on their minds. Now the question of cleansing Ganga comes before us. The scientists have tried to purify its water chemically or through a scientific process. But there is no result. He says that this work should be left for the little fishes and the water will be naturally cleaned. It needs not undergo any cleansing and consequently it remains pure like the waters of other confluences. The water is so clean, pure and fresh that a bride can see her face:

> The moon will recapture in the river's mirrors
> the sharp lineaments of her own face
> flushed like of bride's.[30]

Bride is the symbol of virginity-pure as Ganga. He has used the Hindu myth about Abhimanyu's birth to adore the purity of conscience at the parental state. Ironically he is deeply attached with the outside world which is crowded with people of 'chameleon moods'[31] practicing cruelty, gender discrimination and other sins. These poems are based on Indian culture that show Kumar's Indian sensibility.

Kumar's Indianness seems to intermingle on the theme of religion and death. Death is one of the most Indian characteristics of his sensibility. He has written many poems on death such as "An Encounter with Death", "My Mother's

Death Anniversary," "Crematorium in Adikment, Hyderabad", "And Death Shall With Many Voices", "At the Ghats of Benaras", "A Dead Bird on an Electric Pole", "Suicide", "To a Friend Who Died of cancer, Bequeathing his Body to Research", "Death of a Dog", "Self-obituary", "Death of a Poet" and "The Death of My Father". Death is certain and imminent so he desires to publish certain lines of obituary in some local newspapers for appeasement of his soul as it is not inseparable from body after his death:

> Give me a line or two
> in some local paper
> ever in fine print.[32]

After his father's death he scrapes his bones as a Hindu does:

> How is it that as I scrap up your bones,
> flowers as the Hindus call them,
> I hear a chant fluting through them –
> Om![33]

Kumar's association with the west is expressed in his rational outlook and critical approach to the human predicament. In his work irony is one of the major techniques to debunk and reconstruct. It operates upon several levels in his verse and fiction. His poetry is the fusion of Eastern and Western culture but lacks an integrated perspective. The two American poems are his comments on American life. These poems are full of moral and spiritual dirt that he feels in "A Letter From New York" and "Walking Down the Avenue of the Americas". In the poem "A Letter From New York" the poet sends a letter from New York to his friend who lives in India. In the letter the poet describes the features of American family life. Divorce is a minor matter for the men and women because they are after money and comfortable life. They have no love, affection, faith and intuition that can attach them together. While in India the women consider their husbands gods and are always ready to sacrifice themselves for the sake of their husbands. Here the poet writes about the condition of the manhole on the ninth floor where he lives and finds a broke family. In other words, he speaks disparagingly of broken American families and the lack of sexual relationship:

> Here I live in a garbage can
> and the pile grows bigger each week
> with the broken homes
> splintered all around.[34]

The image of the 'garbage can' expresses the irony of the West to east:

> They wouldn't believe it here
> that the Ganges' water can work
> miracles like Lourdes;
> in spite of the carloads of dead men's ashes
> and bones and the pundits' shit—
> daily offerings to the Mother River![35]

Besides The poet contrasts the East and the West in the concluding lines of the poem:

> Nothing is there but emptiness:
> Incidentally, there are no beggars
> at Grand Central or Broadway
> no cripples on wheel barrows
> no lepers with patches of scraped skin.
> Only eyes, eyes, eyes
> starting at lamp–posts.[36]

As an Indian Kumar's every step is in a quest of home; he can never remain contended with external glamour and opulence of New York where 'only eyes, eyes, eyes/starting at lamp–posts'. He also calls his apartment 'an inverted manhole' that conditions all his reflexes. So he sometimes feels tired of the noise and pollution of New York where the people are running after money. They want to have comfortable life and have materialistic achievements in their possessions. There is a large crowd of such people who are mad for material advancement. In such environment the poet wishes to get peace. He remembers the Buddha. For example: it is believed in India that if you feel some trouble in your body or mind, remembers God and He will help you. But there is no peace there:

En route to perdition
I sometimes stop at Grand Central to piss.
Where else can one ease one's nerves
to feel the Buddha's peace.[37]

About his life in New York he once said:

> In view of my extensive travelling in the west, I seem to be constantly returning to the theme of cultural interaction. I feel, unconsciously, I guess, that with me contrast is almost a mode of perception. It is this awareness that compels me to capture my days in New York as a kind of life-in-death.[38]

The characters of Kumar's writing reveal both eastern and western attitude and find themselves caught in the flux of changing values and assaulted simultaneously by the conflicting values of the East and the West. A close study of his poetry explores the complex and mysterious facts of life and death, Karma (deeds) and moksh (salvation), myth and religion, art and philosophy, sex and psychology and offers to the world of a philosophy of *nirvana* which is deeply embedded in the existential philosophy of pain and suffering.

Kumar's success is the result of the great experiences of Indian life as well as Western life. As an Indian what he felt, he expressed with western frankness. Temporarily relegated to a corner of the mind, he gives place to an entirely new personality, a new self, which is already heady within their own cultural tradition. Kumar's contact with the alien culture is like his contact with an alien woman who fulfils his long cherished desire to see the world abroad. As the other world is full of dreams and attractions so he (protagonist) may go astray. So an alien woman guides him and makes him familiar with an alien culture and helps him gain a novel experience at the foreign country. He need not go there but the eyes of his mind can see the foreign life as naturally as it comes in dream. Thus the experience of the foreign culture is the result of the development and growth of his mind. His poetry describes the things all around him—both at home and abroad. In relation to the east-west encounter in Kumar's poetry, S. S. Dulai makes a pertinent comment in the following lines:

> The West is a deep and vital influence in the shaping of Kumar's sensibility. Having intermittently lived for years, as a student or a teacher, in England, the USA, and Australia, Kumar has had a close lifelong contact with the western civilisation. This added to over two hundred years of western influence on Indian culture itself gives Kumar's writing its characteristic significance. His work reflects a perennial interaction between what he appears to see as the respective values of the Indian and Western cultures. Almost constantly, his work is held in a tension between opposite modes of thought and behavior associated, generally and in Kumar, with the two cultures. On the one hand are the primarily empirical thinking bordering on agnosticism and a lax sexual behaviour commonly perceived as western in origin. On the other hand are the primacy of intuition, faith, restraint and endurance usually considered the typical Eastern values. In his treatment of life in the west, Kumar presents a generally unflattering picture of it. His eye alights mainly on the outer squalor and harshness and an inner loneliness of the spirit that confront him as striking facts of human existence on both sides of the Atlantic despite material affluence. 'Litterbox', 'Walking Down the Avenue of the Americans', and 'A Letter From New York' portray in scathing terms the deprivation and the ugliness that Kumar sees and the suffocation of the soul that he experiences in New York. Here one lives in an "inverted manhole" or "a garbage can", "with broken homes/ splintered all around". "The white of the black maid's eyeballs/is the only clean thing here. . ." "One works for a boss whose grin shows "all the cavities/of his soul". There are tell-tale signs of racial discrimination. There "are no beggars", "cripples", or "lepers", asking for aims, "only eyes, eyes, eyes/staring at lamp—posts".[39]

Kumar sees the life in the West but thinks of his own country and returns home. In this way the encounter of both Eastern and Western ideas develops a new vision that distinguishes his work from the other poets and gives a new shape and sensibility to his poetry.

References

1. Balachandra Rajan, "Identity and Nationality" in *Commonwealth Literature*, ed. John Press (London: Heinemann Educational Books, 1965) 108.

2. Amalendu Bose, *Times Literary Supplement* 26 Dec.58, 751.
3. Shiv K. Kumar, *Contemporary Indian Literature in English* (in Collaboration with Indian Institute of Advanced Study, Shimla), (New Delhi: Manohar Publications, 1992) 5
4. Shiv K. Kumar, "Broken Columns VIII," *Woodpeckers* (London: Sidgwick & Jackson, 1979) 9.
5. Keki N. Daruwalla, *Two Decades of Indian Poetry 1960-1980* (New Delhi: Vikas Publishing House Pvt. Ltd., 1980) 110.
6. G.S. Amur, "The Same Route as My Ancestors Took—A Study of the Indian Sensibility Shiv K. Kumar's Works," *Indian Political Novel and Other Essays*, ed. O. P. Mathur (Allahabad: Kitab Mahal, 1995) 148.
7. G.S. Amur, "Poetry as Subterfuges: An Introduction to Shiv K. Kumar's Poetry," *Aspects of Indian Writing in English*, ed. M.K. Naik (Delhi: Macmillan, 1979) 136.
8. Shiv K. Kumar "Baptism of Fire," *Trapfalls in the Sky* (Madras: Macmillan, 1986) 21.
9. Shiv K. Kumar, "Shakespeare Seminar: Fall 1981," *Trapfalls in the Sky* (Madras: Macmillan, 1986) 64.
10. Shiv K. Kumar, "Shakespeare Seminar: Fall 1981," *Trapfalls in the Sky* (Madras: Macmillan, 1986) 65.
11. G. S. Amur, "Poetry as Subterfuges: An Introduction to Shiv K. Kumar's Poetry," *Aspects of Indian Writing In English*, ed. M. K. Naik (Delhi: Macmillan, 1979) 129.
12. Shiv K. Kumar, "An Indian Mango Vendor," *Cobwebs in the Sun* (New Delhi: Tata McGraw-Hill, 1974) 30.
13. Shiv K. Kumar, "A Letter to Sharad," *Thus Spake the Buddha* (New Delhi: Universal Book & Stationary Publishers' Distributors, 2002) 46.
14. Shiv K. Kumar, "A Stray Bitch Abandons her Litter at Dusk," *Woolgathering* (Mumbai: Disha Books, 1998) 37.
15. Shiv K. Kumar, "Broken Columns VIII," *Woodpeckers*, (London: Sidgwick & Jackson, 1979) 8.
16. Shiv K. Kumar, "Rickshaw-Wallah," *Articulate Silences* (Calcutta: Writers' Workshop, 1970) 22.
17. Shiv K. Kumar, "And Death Shall Speak With Many Voices," *Cobwebs in the Sun*, New Delhi: Tata McGraw-Hill, 1974) 6.
18. Yousuf Kamal, "Faiz Resurrected," *The Hindustan Times*, July 1, 1995.
19. Shiv K. Kumar, "Broken Columns X," *Woodpeckers*, (London: Sidgwick & Jackson, 1979)14.
20. Shiv K. Kumar, "Broken Columns XI," *Woodpeckers*, (London: Sidgwick & Jackson, 1979)15.

21. Shiv K. Kumar, "Broken Columns XI," *Woodpeckers*, (London: Sidgwick & Jackson, 1979)14
22. Shiv K. Kumar, "Coromandel Beach," *Subterfuges* (New Delhi: Oxford University Press, 1976) 41.
23. Shiv K. Kumar, "Rickshaw-Wallah," *Articulate Silences*, (Calcutta: Writers' Workshop, 1970) 22.
24. Shiv K. Kumar, "Epitaph on an Indian Politician," *Articulate Silences*, (Calcutta: Writers' Workshop, 1970) 25.
25. Shiv K. Kumar, "Baptism of fire," *Trapfalls in the Sky*, (Madras: Macmillan, 1986) 22.
26. Shiv K. Kumar, "A Letter From New York," *Subterfuges*, (New Delhi: Oxford University Press, 1976) 17-18.
27. Shiv K. Kumar, "Twenty-fifth Wedding Anniversary," *Woolgathering*, (Mumbai: Disha Books, 1998) 60.
28. Shiv K. Kumar, "O Delhi," *Trapfalls in the Sky*, (Madras: Macmillan, 1986) 36.
29. Ibid.
30. Shiv K. Kumar, "Cleansing Ganga," *Trapfalls in the Sky*, (Madras: Macmillan, 1986) 35.
31. Shiv K. Kumar, "Cleansing Ganga," *Trapfalls in the Sky*, (Madras: Macmillan, 1986) 35.
32. Shiv K. Kumar, "I was Old Before My Birth," *Thus Spake the Buddha*, (New Delhi: Universal Book & Stationary Publishers' Distributors, 2002) 6.
33. Shiv K. Kumar, "Self-obituary," *Trapfalls in the Sky*, (Madras: Macmillan, 1986) 31.
34. Shiv K. Kumar, "The Death of My Father," Woolgathering, (Mumbai: Disha Books, 1998) 13.
35. Shiv K. Kumar, "A Letter from New York," *Subterfuges*, (New Delhi: Oxford University Press, 1976) 17.
36. Shiv K. Kumar, "A Letter from New York," *Subterfuges*, (New Delhi: Oxford University Press, 1976) 17.
37. Shiv K. Kumar, "A Letter from New York," *Subterfuges*, (New Delhi: Oxford University Press, 1976) 19.
38. Shiv K. Kumar, "A Letter from New York," *Subterfuges*, (New Delhi: Oxford University Press, 1976) 18.
39. Shiv K. Kumar, *Ten Twentieth-Century Indian Poets*, ed. R. Parthasarathy (New Delhi: Oxford University Press, 1979), 53.
40. Surjit S. Dulai, "Shiv K. Kumar's Writing," *Journal of South Asian Literature* (Summer, Fall, 1990),

10

Searching Peace and Harmony in an Age of Terror: A Study of Pronab Kumar Majumder's *Passage to Peace*

—P.C.K. Prem

Pronab Kumar Majumder has been writing poetry for a long time. Born in 1941, he has written a number of books in Bengali and English. He has published eleven collections of poetry. A former bureaucrat, Majumder is a man of immense zeal and unparallel creative energy and has been editing an International Poetry Journal *Bridge-in-Making* for the last twenty years. His most significant creative works include: *Life and Eternity* (1997), *In the Ruins of Time* (2000), *Where Time is Dead* (2005), *Time Never Returns to Console* (2007), *My India: Through the Corridors of Time* (2008) and *Passage to Peace* (a collection of poems-2009). Other collections of poems are: *Dialogue with Time, Replies of Time and Creating-Killing Cosmic Time*. He is a widely anthologised poet and has won several literary awards for his unique contribution to Indian English Literature, especially Poetry.

Passage to Peace is the latest collection of poems devoted to the cause of peace and harmony in an age of widespread violence and terrorism. The first cursory glance at the poems reveals a poet immensely dedicated to world peace and humanism. Like a true human being Majumder is wedded to uphold the cardinal principle of harmony and is a staunch protagonist of peace while the concept of 'time' and 'death' continues to provoke him to find meaning in life. The idea of 'time' is mysteriously prone to varied interpretation; and 'death' defies all cogent definitions but still the poet attempts to define these concepts. Such probing into the mysteries of life reminds a discerning reader of ancient Vedic concept of life and death. Interestingly, if the reader is quite vigilant and conscious of the poet's inner turmoil and outer demeanour, he'll immediately get an inkling of poet's deep anxiety about the contemporary world. The collection contains 72 lyrics exhibiting concern for social obligations, the poet wishes to discharge and in the process he awakens us to rise to the occasion and help making the world a better place to live.

Not only that the poet is a responsible citizen deeply and painfully aware of the sufferings of the people but he is also committed to the cause of nation's prosperity and unity which are possible only if peace is maintained and violence of any kind is abhorred. Delving deep into the thought pattern of this intellectual poet, one frequently encounters words like: fears, social anxiety, peace, harmony, violence, time, terror, trust, distrust, love, hate, hope, history and future. These words appear repeatedly in changed contexts and convey hidden meanings of poet's ceaseless appeals to human heart to live in peace while exhorting man to abjure violent acts and thoughts. Before going into poet's contemporary worries, it is imperative that the thematic-content is probed indepth to arrive at the message poet wishes to convey.

In the first poem "Peace not for a Price" the poet unequivocally opines that no dispute can be settled with the use of arms and only love of truth brings victory. An inefficient State beleaguered with social ailments gives birth to terrorism and erroneous concepts breed violence, he believes. He forcefully avers that 'peace-Lovers are mightier than one beast' and bluntly tells that 'It is no heroic to use gun/To awaken specter of violence and misery.' ("What is Heroic,"2).

> No one can have the right to kill another
> Whatever be the pretest, caste, religion culture
> Greatest sin is to disdain your neighbour
> Fancying terror is just another adventure.
>
> ("What are for All," *Passage to Peace* 3)

In the above verse, the poet gives the message of brotherhood, universal peace and says brusquely that none howsoever powerful can have full sway over the natural treasures available for the benefit of humanity. Terrorism is a blot on man's life and acts of carnage need discouragement. Man ought to learn togetherness from nature living in harmony whether these are birds, petals, flowers or roses. It is a perennial truth man hears since ages from great seers and sages. It does recall Vedic truths. To inflict injury is an act of terrorism, the poet appears to say. "Blessings of Earth" must be enjoyed by all and there, an advocate of Environmental Crusade stands up to give a call of safety, amity and peace.

The poet observes:

> A safe life and living free from anxiety
> Some people are making the earth too much dirty
> Change in Presidency or Premiership hardly change
> Critical social global ambience
> Mindset of unholy rivalry and avenge
> Every time occupy uppermost eminence.
>
> ("Social Orphan," *Passage to Peace* 5)

The poet tells of a harsh truth where he subjects those in authority to scrutiny. Despite pledges and firm commitments, nothing concrete emerges which helps people live a harmonious life; and the gravity in universal ambivalence stays on to make lives miserable. Surprisingly, the poet turns to the concept of a 'global village' where hopes of permanent peace might become a reality but it would need a little bit of sacrifice from each; and with concerted efforts the fears of war can be eliminated totally. War thrives on because some people wish to subjugate others, he reiterates. The poet is also awakened to the on-going determined efforts being made at different summits of world leaders where fears, anxieties and uncertainties are openly expressed and appeals are made to the conscience of people to strive hard so as to usher into an era of peace. Such social, political and historical perspectives influence the poet. Majumder is not alone in this peace mission and if he frequently comes back to the thesis of peace and harmony, it is the poet's mindset where he can't hide feelings of anguish.

And if he says that all should "have a single stand/Live and let others live be the social mode" ("For a fear-free Society" 7) it is from the core of heart and it is apparent that he is worried about the destiny of man. Obsessed with fears of terrorism, the poet visualises a situation where continuous blasts cause anxiety and panic which finally wake up animal in man, to herald a journey back to hamlets. Though exaggerated, the poet's concerns are genuine. Agonising social consciousness and prayers for peace persuade the poet in Majumder to create and recreate scenes of despair and fear so that man understands that the monster-terror will not make lives happy. He woefully recalls an excruciating calamity in three verses namely "Tale of Mumbai Hotel", "Fearful Eyes" and "Mumbai Massacre" when Mumbai was a target of terrorists' bullets. As if it is not enough, he tries to fathom the remnants elsewhere of such brutal acts when he observes:

> Perhaps it is easier to deal with a hungry tiger
> Than a terrorist, an aristocrat killer
> Who has single option of killing civilians
> Innocent and unconcerned with politics of politicians.
>
> ("Theatre of Massacre," p.12)

This obliqueness makes a disquieting impact on the sensibility; and constitutes a depressing commentary on the State of affairs—a modern reality of devalued living. Recurrence of the theme of terrorism is awful and is a warning—a wake-up call to insensitive human beings, occupied in accumulating equipment of anxiety that ultimately leads to crippling of intellect and peace. It is a mad race to reach nowhere and children are busy in vexatious preoccupations, dull routine and fruitless pursuits where:

> Only they know they must be runners
> Though in the process joy of life they miss.
>
> ("Anxious Children," 15)

Anxiety in life is responsible for many sufferings and truly the poet avers that man is the perpetrator; and he also knows to eliminate a deadly invisible enemy. Majumder owes immense gratitude to mother Earth. Man is born on earth and she takes care of man's needs. So it is man's responsibility to take care of everything gifted to him.

The poet does not specify what precisely he hints at but one can infer that he is an upholder of pollution free quality of life. In "Hostage" the theme of terrorism occurs again to disturb the poet and a global village close to the poet's heart, is an answer to prevalent terrorism the violence, he suggests.

Hours of fear and anxiety overshadowing joys of peaceful inhabitants of Hotel Taj had lengthened into uncertainty. "Shrine of Peace" is an argument he offers to think over the idea of a global village, leading to an era of humanism. This thought current continues in a short lyric "Change of Planet". The poet's quest for law continues and he truly wishes an end to killing, violence and arson.

In temples even, dead bodies scatter around and the poet tells bluntly that the 'terrorists wild' strikes hard even the 'authority of almighty.' The theme of terror and peace is close to the poet's heart, and this contemporary anguish raises its head time and again. Majumder appears a messenger of peace and exhorts in plain words:

> Let our religion be mission of peace
> Let the whole of peoples be missionary of peace
> Violence hatred killings let us impeach
> Not a single day now should we miss.
>
> ("Another Sunrise," 24)

Again he takes the 'Flags of Peace' high and talks of a 'global village' where new religion and peace shall act as temple priests. Search for a holy light where birds sing and murky hands do not exist, continues.

He is an inveterate optimist:

> You peace, I say really I miss
> I say 'Om Shanti' 'Om Shanti' to reach
> Let you flourish at the end
> Of this dark murky old night
>
> ("Holy Light," 32)

Despite longings for a holy light, the poet is troubled by the assault of anxiety when he visualises a "Home of Fear" where guns and grenades shatter peace. As a stranger in a transitory world he moves to an 'awful civilisation' where dreadful worries rip off moments of love and happiness. Life is like tilling a barren and rocky stretch sans water yet bases need strengthening. To this extent the poet is right. But to think of a global village in a world of sectarian and fissiparous tendencies is an impossibility as eclipse of sensibilities is a certainty where religion is sold in little fragments by babas and saints of religious sects patronised by the authorities. The poet, in search of bliss and heaven for injured humanity is disturbed:

> Violence can be defeated by use of force
> Peace can not be ordained by a magic call
>
> ("Not a Gain Windfall," 39)

The poet speaks of a belief and hope when he says:

> Then only can be built my dream house of peace
> lit by thousand stars of hopes and light
> 'How long away is the destination to reach
> I am a robust optimist, violence around in spite
>
> ("House of Peace," 40)

To strengthen belief in peace and love, he even goes back to history and relates horrifying events of war ("Quit and Quest" and "Memories Ineffaceable") to remind that in peace alone are hidden the secrets of life and dreams of a blissful future.

In the background, the poet is aware of terror striking population killing people irrespective of age and gender, creed or class when he says:

> This is the first and primary duty indeed
> To Combat terrorism and apprehend terrorists
> It is also to find how is born this creed
> It is the job of you and me, not the priests.
>
> ("Who Are the Terrorists," 47)

An iniquitous terrorist exists everywhere who keeps hostages and befriends fanaticism but the will of the people can defeat it provided it stands up to establish a global village, a dream project of the poet—like many others, an utopian thought for which he writes profusely. But alas, it is unrealistic. If one is pragmatic, true and genuine, obstacles in the way to peace can be brushed aside, the poet perhaps ignores. But still determination makes the path easy:

> Humans' problem is how to achieve peace
> It is easier to chisel a God out of stones
> And to seek his intended bliss
> But not easy to carve out peace out of human bones.
>
> ("Human's Peace," 53)

He is deeply worried about the future when he observes:

> What are we going to leave for children in anxiety
> Is it really impossible that safety we can guarantee.
>
> ("Safety can't We Guarantee," 46)

For the poet the world as a global village fortifies secular and catholic outlook and to aspire for peace is mankind's objective. Undoubtedly, there is consistent avowal for the cause of peace and harmony but fears pollute the environment. Not precisely a contradiction but here the poet is realistic when he observes tellingly:

> Speed is the creed of advancing civilisation
> You can't avoid anxiety in a speeding carriage
> When every moment progress is given go-ahead
> Peace and anxiety how can have a comfortable marriage.
>
> ("Uncomfortable Marriage," 61)

He gives vent to feelings of eternal dilemma a man confronts and if solutions are not found, future life of man will definitely be filled with fears and violence, he seems to say. The poet like a prophet wishes peace and then if he repeatedly drives man to the significance and meaning of peace, it is like neta log who often, either on podiums or in public meetings frequently exhort people to live quietly abjuring violence.

The poet's movement from point to point is enrichment and strengthening of earlier argument. He thinks like a philosopher that poverty does exist with peace but it rarely finds a friend in plenty. As is the human nature, crises unite even bitter enemies but in pleasure and comforts, disruptive tendencies play havoc.

One is amazed at the obsession, the poet displays while putting up a strong opposition to the demons of fears, anxieties, hatred and terrorism and here he gives a clarion call to all to unite and fight against the evil forces that bring disharmony.

> Hatred is a burden one has to carry
> Love is blood that flows to flourish
> Shun hatred which is mother of violence
> Love and peace always mutually nourish.
>
> ("How to Shun Violence," 67)

In another poem "Dilemma" 68, he observes:

> May be inner forces create peace in you
> But how can you remain peaceful if your
> Neighbour and neighborhood are aflame
> Something pure is peace, but absent is something pure.

If the poet reverts to the themes of peace and violence, it is a deep rooted desire to see that the world becomes a safe place. If progress in life has made man prosperous, it has not contributed to love and non-violence but has consequently led man to more violence defeating efforts of peace seekers.

He makes a fervent appeal when says:

> Violence and anxieties are by-products
> of the neck-to-neck race for progress
> Flames of violence are but constructs
> Of mindless reckless unholy horse race.
>
> ("Conquest of Man," 70)

The poet is aware of the efforts made to establish peace on earth and somewhere, in the inner recesses of mind, he is not ignorant of various international forums and bodies particularly the United Nations Organisation, making arduous efforts to reach amicable solutions to the world problems which create disturbance and lead to acts of terrorism at many levels whether these originate from religious thoughts or have roots in social, economic or political structure.

To understand the poet's true message, one must go deep into the oft repeated words mentioned elsewhere and the poet's frequent delving deep into thoughts of anxiety and fears. At the basis lies the phantom of violence and hatred that permits not a moment's peace. It is individual anguish given universal touch. The poet appears working at many levels and whatever happens at the conscious, unconscious and subconscious mind inspires him to look at a problem from various angles resulting in myriads of impressions. He is unable to restrain feelings and thoughts which subsequently force various reactions converging on a single theme-content.

To give a positive message to humanity is a dominant aspect of Majumder's poetry. As a teacher, he believes that creative writings must conform to an ideal life and he appears to 'master his perspective' quite competently, if one recalls the words of Virginia Woolf. Majumder unquestionably, treats poetic themes with all the 'truth and seriousness' (to quote Mathew Arnold).

If there is any dissonant note or irritant, it must be corrected with an ethical and moral touch about which Mathew Arnold and Dryden talked centuries back while dwelling on the theme of creative writing, particularly the function and value of poetry.

Briefly, a mention of two other anthologies with almost similar theme-content and emotional treatment is pertinent here. In *Creating-Killing Cosmic Time* and *Where Time is Dead* if the poet is concerned about time, life, mystery of time and its links to life, life's sufferings, anguish, fate and destination of human life, it is again a search for eternal peace, love and faith in human life and here one does find unique streaks of *Passage to Peace*. Mysteries of birth, rebirth and death, nature and consequent destruction paint a dismal picture but if a man learns living in harmony with nature and its objects, he can definitely make this world worth living. If frequent theme of *Passage to Peace* is understood keeping in mind the poet's philosophy of *Creating-Killing Cosmic Time* or where he stipulates "Time's Death", his message is evident. Whatever takes place within in its multifaceted dimensions is the area which the sensitive mind of the poet seriously tries to comprehend in deeply religious consciousness. If he handles social themes with apparent clarity and felicity, down deep these are complex issues and the solutions offered have ethical connotations making poems not only repetitive but a little ambiguous.

Only a few poets in Indian English Poetry have touched upon the theme of peace so exhaustively. Incessant search for peace is a perennial prayer of every peace-loving human being. In the wake of continual physical sufferings and fears of insecurity born out of fanatic terrorism and sporadic incidents of battles and battle cries in different parts of the world, peace and harmony are threatened. Peace has been a subject with many poets but the way Majumder has dwelt upon the theme speaks of terrible craze and passion, he cherishes. To him, the thought's application is a guarantee of everlasting peace on earth and man has a bright future only if peace and harmony are ensured and to the poet it is not a utopian ideal. If human values have a definite imprint on life, the world would be a better place to live in. The poet in Majumder stands tall in the company of Krishan Srinivas, S. Rangaswami, Rabindranath Menon, Aju Mukhopadhyay and Raghupathi to name a few who are equally occupied with man's inner turmoil and behold the world with socially relevant perspectives.

Perhaps somewhere, the poet is making earnest attempts to seek harmony amidst struggling thoughts; and emotions appear preeminently occupied with finding cogently parallel meanings for peace, time, death and birth. At this stage, he is conceptual and indefinite and while reconciling the contradictory thought currents he turns a little cryptic.

Works Cited

Majumder, Pronab Kumar. *Creating-Killing Cosmic Time.* Kolkata: Writers Workshop, 2002. Print.

_____ *Passage to Peace.* Kolkata: Bridge-in-Making Publication, 2009. Print.

_____ *Where Time is Dead.* Kolkata: Writers Workshop, 2005. Print.

11

Time—The Dominant Theme of Pronab Kumar Majumder's Poetry

—Kurt F. Svatek

At the first moment it seems to be a simple question even for each schoolchild: What is time? We all know what time is. It's the ticking of a clock, the flow of sand in an hourglass, the whine of an alarm, the calendar on the wall. And since we all agree about how those things work, time can seem as solid as a rock. The concept of time is self-evident. The year consists of a certain number of months and days, a day of hours, an hour of minutes and seconds.

Time is passing non-stop, but we cannot say what exactly happens when time passes. And so suddenly there is a moment when we first encounter the paradoxes that lie just behind our everyday understanding of time. In fact, it's a lot squishier. We need a leap day to keep the calendars in the line with seasons, and even so, time will eventually get away from us.

'If you feel there aren't enough hours in a day, just wait,' said Max Tegmark, a cosmologist at Massachusetts Institute of Technology. He continued: 'In a few hundred million years, tidal friction will have slowed Earth's rotation to make the day 25 hours long.' The passing time is indeed closely connected to the concept of space. According to the general theory of relativity, space or the universe emerged in the Big Bang some 14 billion years ago. Before the big Bang, there was no space or time. Kari Enquist, professor of cosmology: 'In the theory of relativity, the concept of time begins with the Big Bang the same way as parallels of latitude begin at the North Pole. You cannot go further north than the North Pole.'

Time is a component of the measuring system used to sequence events, to compare the durations of events and the intervals between them, and to quantify the motions of objects. Time has been a major subject of religion, philosophy, and science, but defining it in a non-controversial manner applicable to all fields of study has consistently eluded the greatest scholars.

One of the most peculiar qualities of time is the fact that is measured by motion and it also becomes evident through motion. Motion alters time. Einstein in his special theory of relativity postulated the constancy and finiteness of the light for all observers. He showed that this postulate, together with a reasonable definition for what it means for two events to be simultaneous, requires that distances appear compressed and time intervals appear lengthened for events associated with objects in motion to an inertial observer.

Pronab Kumar Majumder in Sparkles of Time (Poem 8):

> Time is measured by light-year
> Interference is existence of light
> Light and Time darkness tear.

In physics and other sciences time is considered one of the few fundamental quantities. To physicists, time is defined by quantum mechanics. A photon with energy h (Planck's constant) behaves as though it were oscillating once per second. Modern atomic clocks are based on this.

Time direction is something else. It is based on information, which sits uneasily in the world of physics. But, any quantum system must have an arrow of time.

Among prominent philosophers, there are two distinct viewpoints on time. One view is that time is part of the fundamental structure of the universe, a dimension in which events occur in sequence. Time travel, in this view, becomes a possibility as other 'times' persist like frames of a film strip, spread out across the time line. Sir Isaac Newton subscribed to this realist view, and hence it is sometimes referred to as Newtonian time.

The opposing view is that time does not refer to any kind of "container" that events and objects 'move through', nor to any entity that 'flows', but that it is instead part of a fundamental intellectual structure within which humans sequence and compare events. This second view, in the tradition of Gottfried Leibniz and Immanuel Kant, holds that time is neither an event nor a thing, and thus is not itself measurable nor can it be travelled. Kant described time as an a priori intuition that allows us to comprehend sense experience.

In Existentialism, time is considered fundamental to the question of being, in particular by the philosopher Martin Heidegger.

Henri Bergson believed that time was neither a real homogeneous medium nor a mental construct; bur possesses what he referred to as Duration. Duration, in Bergson's view, was creativity and memory as an essential component of reality.

The earliest recorded philosophy of time was expounded by the ancient Egyptian thinker Ptahhotep (about 2600 BC), who said: 'Do not lesson the time of following desire, for the wasting of time is an abomination to the spirit.' The *Vedas*, dating back to the late second millennium BC, describe ancient Hindu cosmology, in which the universe goes through repeated cycles of creation, destruction and rebirth. Ancient Greek philosophers believed that the universe had an infinite past with no beginning. Antiphon the Sophist: 'Time is not a reality, but a concept or a measure.' Parmenides went further, maintaining that time, motion, and change were illusions, leading to the paradoxes of his follower Zeno.

Other ancient cultures such as Incan, Mayan, Hopi, and other Native American Tribes, plus the Babylonian, Buddhist, Jainist have also a concept of a wheel of time, that regards time as cyclical and quantic consisting of repeating ages that happen to every being of the universe between birth and extinction.

Medieval philosophers and theologians developed the concept of the universe having a finite past with a beginning. This view was inspired by the creation event shared by the three Abrahamic religions: Judaism, Christianity and Islam. The most sophisticated medieval arguments against an infinite past were developed by the early Muslim philosopher Al-Kindi, the Jewish philosopher Saadia Gaon, and the Muslim theologian Al-Gazali. In general, the Judaeo-Christian concept, based and the Bible, is that time is linear, with a beginning, the act of creation by God. The Christian view assumes also an end, the eschaton, expected to happen when Christ returns to earth in the Second Coming to judge the living and the dead. The Christian view is that God is uncreated and eternal so that He and the supernatural world are outside time and exist in eternity. *Christian Science* defines time as 'error' or illusion. But in everything Christian view may not be so different from the scientific view. Physics tells us that all moments exist equally; at once it's only our consciousness that distinguishes the present from the past or future. Or as Max Tegmark says: 'If live were a movie, physical reality would be the entire DVD: Future and past frames exist just as much as the present one.'

The Greek language has two terms for the word time: *chronos* and *kairos*. The Reverent Jacqueline Lewis, senior minister at Middle Collegiate Church in New York says that while we may be most familiar with *chronos,* the clock time, we should also be aware of *kairos*, or God's time. It's what the theologian C.S. Lewis called 'God's unbounded now', where now is both this moment—right now—and what stretches into eternity.

In Book 11 of St. Augustine's *Confession*, he ruminates on the nature of time, asking: 'What then is time? If no one asks me, I know. If I wish to explain it to one who asked me, I know not.'

All this is the background to ask what sort of thing time is for a poet, for the retired Special Secretary to the government of West Bengal, for Pronab Kumar Majumder?

In all his books time is the major theme of the author. We can see it citing some of his book titles: *Dialogue with Time, Replies of Time, In the Ruins of Time, Creating Killing Cosmic Time, My India: Through Corridor of Time, Sparkles of Time, Life and Eternity, Where Time is Dead, On Time Un Time, Time Never Returns to Console...*

By metaphorical personification the author looked at time from different perspectives, different angles and settings of everyday life and cosmic eternity as though time stands sentinel in its creating and killing activities through ages.

Time is a flowing river
Demolishes all on one side
Builds the other.

Sparkles of Time (Poem 2)

The whole cosmic world is bound to time. One day even the sun will be reduced to a compact white dwarf because nothing in the universe, living or non-living can escape or avoid the bliss and bane of time. Time is carriage and human lives are carried passengers. Time never carries the dead and drops in its timeless journey. Time is dead in a dead person because a dead person is outside the influence of time. Time is only active in something alive. Every event of our life is time-bound and activity of time stops when one is dead. There are the points of contact with modern science.

Silent both life and Time
In activity Time is prime
Time does not touch dead.

(Poem 7)

In the 50th number of the magazine *Bridge-in-Making* he published a poem called: Bridge-in Making. Here the first two stanzas:

Time rolls down into look-back past
Having done multiple journey-dice cast
Man and his life gradually recede to the background
Every phenomenon of life has a slot time-bound

Time posts milestones at regular interval
To announce its unsung arrival
all the posts are not equally aglow
Yet its journey Time never does slow
...

About it the gerontologist Michael West, who teaches at the University of California said: 'Time has little impact on biology. From a gerontologist's standpoint biological time is not wear-

and tear, it's a genetic program. It's sort of like a time bomb. The cells are programmed to last just long enough for us to rear children, and no longer.'

David Sinclair, director of the Paul F. Glenn Laboratories for the Molecular Biology of Aging: 'Sooner or later, nearly everyone becomes aware that time is running out. We quickly learn to suppress these disturbing thoughts. Those who don't learn this act of self-defence require a pharmacopoeia of pharmaceuticals to get through each day.' But Deepak Chopra warned of the dangers of a hectic lifestyle. 'People who feel that they are "running out of time" have speeded up their biological clocks. They have faster heart rates and jittery platelets with high levels of adrenaline. When they drop dead from a premature heart attack, they have literally run out of time.'

So sometimes we just need a little practical help dealing with the alarm clock, flight schedule or calendar. But David Allen is warning: 'Time management is a foolish idea. You don't manazge time. Have you ever mismanaged five minutes and come up with six? Or four-and-a-half? Time just is. Our actions are what we manage during time.'

But length of live is for Majumder not the length of time. A person may live outside life though alive. A man may live hundred years but time may not touch him. Thus time and life are co-related. We are under impact and influence of time, so are all cosmic phenomena. Whether time was ever birthed and will end someday is an enigma. Time was born with the Big Bang which ushered in the universe and time may end with the possible Big Crunch, which may destroy the universe. But on the last these opinions differ under the modern scientists.

Sparkles of Time (Poems 3 and 4):

Time began in Bib bang
In which no music rang
Ever since a listless runner.

When everything will be dead
In a big crunch raid
Buried will be Time.

Pronab Kumar Majumder considers poetry as versified thoughts motioned by emotions, passions, compassions, imaginations, experiences of life and experiences with the life. Poetry is mirrored sometimes by present events around, sometimes by rewinding the past, sometimes projecting the future and sometimes imagining something yet unknown, like cosmic world.

He says: 'A poet may capture flash of a moment and create a poem. Suppose one is standing eastward in a vast meadow at dawn break when a round and purple fireball is leaping up the horizon. The sun is rising. It is an ecstatic beauty, heavenly bliss. Immediately a poem is born in the consciousness of that one who may be a poet.'

Poetry may or may not be narration or description of events. It may be realisation and perspiration of poets unloaded on receptacles of lines of poems which are really works of wordsmith. Since poetry is emotional, passionate, compassionate response to any and every phenomenon of life and time. Those phenomena are his inspirations of writing poetry. He cannot and he did not want to ignore the circumstances he is: He wrote for example the poem "The Waiting Child" by imagination that a child was waiting on the door for her parents who were lost in the battleground of Baghdad.

Another poem, "Non-descript Woman," was written after he noticed a group whores waiting in dim light expecting possible clients.

"Where Time is dead", also the title of one of his collections, he wrote watching the eternal stillness on the face of his dead mother.

"Flew Away the Bard" is a tribute-poem to the poet Amrita Pritam, which was included as the last poem in his anthology *Time Never Returns to Console and Other Poems.*

But as each other poet Pronab Kumar Majumder is inspired of many other ways too. Par example by his own nation in the book *My India: Through Corridor of Time*. Regarding from Europe to India the poems introduce to India in a very particularly way, and each traveller from other countries should read this book before departure as a poetical travel guide to India. He will see India in a very specific light, full of warmth and love, full of poetry without shutting one's exes to the glory history and also the hard times, without shutting one's ears to the melody of the past and the modern times, and without shutting one's heart to the dreams on the one hand and the daily life of people of the other hand—always integrated in the generic term: time.

Therefore it's no accident that the author got his inspiration also from the centuries-old and 'timeless' Japanese poetry forms: Haiku and Tanka.

Haiku began in Japan during the seventeeth century. Haiku are short, imagistic poems about the things that make people feel connected to nature. In Japanese, haiku traditionally have seven short sounds divided into three lines of a 5/7/5 syllable pattern, with the middle line longer than the first and third lines. In Japan people of all ages and walks of life write haiku and people all over the world are writing haiku in many different languages.

Most, though not all, haiku reflect nature or one of the four seasons. The words of haiku should evoke emotions felt by the poet in the heart of the reader, and should not merely describe these emotions.

When we write haiku in English we use also three lines but the 5/7/5 pattern suits some languages better than others. English and Japanese are so different, that we cannot get the same rhythmical effect as in Japanese. It's quality not quantity that counts. So it's better to compose haiku rather freely. The best maxim is probably: 'Just as many syllables as are enough,' because effective power of poetic device in language comes from simplicity, elegance and concentration of mind.

Pronab Kumar Majumder gave his book *Sparkles of Times* the subtitle: haiku-like poems. So the poems need not to be exclusively natural poems but could be compared with the Japanese Senryu or the European aphorism because of their strong message.

Time is fruit hanging high
Standing below life ups hand
Sometimes failing heaves sigh.

(Poem 15), Sparkles of Times

When one is living outside
Is really rejected by inside
Only hanging onto Time is not life.

(Poem 14), Sparkles of Times

When one forgets Time
One is reduced to a dime
Time is pulsation of life.

(Poem 19), Sparkles of Times

Tanka means short poem in Japanese and is written using 31 Japanese syllables in five phrases in a 5/7/5/7/7 syllable sequence, because it sounds rhythmical.

Tanka has a history of more than 1300 years, but it has been modernised and many Japanese people today enjoy reading and writing tanka.

When we write tanka in English we use five lines with about 20 English syllables because this shortness is very close to Japanese tanka. But we can also use more syllables, maybe up to 30. They are also presented with no capitalisation at the beginning of lines and with minimal punctuation.

However, English and Japanese are different. Even we try to use the 5/7/5/7/7 pattern in English, we cannot get the same rhythmical effect as in Japanese. So it's better to compose the tanka rather freely.

Compared to haiku, we can use more words in tanka and we can express our feelings and emotions more directly. Tanka expresses the intense spontaneous feeling of the poet, and is in many ways much easier for the Western mind to relate to than haiku.

The romantic tradition is very strong in tanka, dating from early times right down to the present day. Some of the best-known tanka poets were the women of ancient Japan, whose poems reflected longing in their socially confined lives. Tanka was also a means of communicating between lovers, and the ability to write a moving tanka was an important part of ensuring the success of a love affair. So abundant and rich is the romantic tradition that tanka could well be labelled the poetry of love. While tanka is so much more than this, it is still one of the most powerful means for expressing the sentiments of the various forms of romantic love.

After romance, family is one of the major themes of tanka. But tanka are also about real moments in our lives using the outside world to reflect our deeper feelings.

Pronab Kumar Majumder's poetry book *My India: Through Corridor of Time* has the subtitle: tanka-like poems. So he could compose the tanka rather freely—and this with great deal of sensitivity.

Time an uncut thread from the past
Which is sometimes obscured by dust
But corridor of Time never collapse –
My nation is passenger of Time with dignity
Against any threat will not surrender sovereignty.

(Poem 4)

In Sparkles of Times Majumder writes:

Possible is a society
In love and amity
And mutual trust.

It is trust
That is must
For del social or political.

Absence of trust
On mutual trust
Co-existence comes illusionary.

(Poems 174, 175, 177)

So we come full circle. The author wants to carry forward justice, to disseminate truth, and to steer people onto the right road, to expose darkness and corruption, to castigate evils, so as to purify the society from a new angle and to promote the advancement of human civilisation. Going through his books the poems mirror all these excellent framed by the shimmering rainbow of time.

The last words are reserved to Pronab Kumar Majumder:

When Time and life are compatible
Anything and everything is accessible
It is a victory of duel.

(Poem 16, Sparkles of Times)

12

Minor Themes Vis-a-vis Time in Pronab Kumar Majumder's Poetry

—Swagata Ray, R.K. Singh and M. Mojibur Rahman

Pronab Kumar Majumder's poetry is unique for his distinct theme, approach and philosophy. In fact he shares some of his themes and philosophy with a few other contemporary poets such as Bibhu Padhi, Niranjan Mohanty, A.K. Ramanujan and R. Parthasarathy. But his reflective style, as he demonstrates in dealing with subjects like Time, Life, Philosophy, Nature, War and Peace, offers a different perspective which entails self-introspection against certain personal issues and social understanding.

Majumder has been concerned with subjects of violence, interpersonal relationships, natural calamities, etc. almost like a philosopher to understand practical challenges and their attributes. He explores these 'with a consciousness which recognises the physical experiences 'with mediating ease' and tells of the memories that are 'more outspoken/than human tongue and temperament.'[1]

The poet wears a mask to unravel the 'eternal ringings/of the bell that keeps tolling' though he hardly reflects on meaningless death or purposeless life. In fact as a poet of Time, he exposes his philosophic vision against personal self experiences, against 'the mortal world time.'

Time

The theme of Time has been an important theme with all the poets of all ages. Shakespeare, through Jaques, says that it was nine one hour before and it will be eleven one hour after. So we ripe every hour and get rotten, and like ripe fruits we fall down. Andrew Marvell also presents the fact that in front of Time, human life and love is ephemeral:

> But at my back, I always hear
> Time's winged chariot hurrying near
> And yonder all before us lie
> Deserts of vast eternity.[2]

William Wordsworth and T.S. Eliot have written poems on Time. Rabindranath Tagore has also written poems on Time. As he says:

> Have you not heard his silent steps? He comes, comes, ever comes. Every moment and every age, every day and every night he comes, comes, ever comes, ...[3]

Several new millennium poets, such as Krishna Srinivas, Maha Nand Sharma, S.L. Peeran, and Rabindranath Menon have also written poems on Time. R.K. Singh has defined Time in his own way:

> I can't understand
> their mystic heaven or thrills
> housed in awareness
>
> time's intricacies
> or sources of plastic mist
> through mythical depths
> ...
> I stand on the edge
> Of earth's physicality [4]

Pronab Kumar Majumder, too, conscious about Time as omnipotent, discovers:

> The cosmic world is dictated by Time
> Every bit of it is Time relative.[5]

In his reasoning, whatever belongs to Time—life, mind, thought, nature, various quotidian experiences, whatever—is fragmentary. It is not whole. Rather, it is the result of various causes and results. One needs to understand all these to be holistic, that is, life which is full of love, affection, and care; mind which is attentive and not lost in the pursuit of pleasure; and thought which is not controlled by materialist movement. The poet's search for the 'whole' can be articulated with an understanding of the 'parts'.

All his thinking—his thoughts—are enclosed by Time. He might try here and there to soar above or beyond (Time), but essentially he remains confined to the quotidian time and mechanical, rather than spiritual, which is Timeless. His consciousness is wrapped in hundreds of remembrances and recognitions that are simply egoistic and self-centred.

The poet's observation of himself appears superficial, as Time, life, nature, etc. are part of the 'cumulative memory' which does not allow anything deeper to set in. Nothing extraordinary seems to enlighten or experience. Majumder may appear to seek something permanent or everlasting in the sense of Time, but the verses reveal that everything he mentions – events, situations, issues, or even reflections—is in transient, in a flux. He fails to offer something beyond the measure of time, or the known, or which does not operate through thought or the response of memory. Time engages him to explore the world around him and it breeds dissatisfaction. It doesn't move beyond the superficial wrangles of the mind. He fails to experience the quietude of the mind, so essential for any spiritual experience.

Life

In almost all of his collections, Majumder tries to define Life in consonance with Time. He says Life is not merely passing days. Life has its own image, its own identity:

> Life not some passing days
> Life has an image
> Life is an entity
> Having some identity ... [6]

The struggle and pain of Life reminds us that we are living our life. To quote him:

While walking along
The rugged ascent
Of a mountain path
Pricking pains reminded me
For living a life [7]

He seems to explore himself in experiences and relationships that lead him to a sort of 'conditioning' vis-à-vis environmental influences and beliefs that obstruct the understanding of reality. He seems to suffer fear of what is, and seeks comfort in Time, exposing ideas, reflections, experiences, knowledge, and concerns that indicate his own inner insufficiency. That is why he realises that it is more tough to live than to die:

Every moment I am struggling to live
For I know quite well, well enough
It is more difficult to live than to die [8]

What is known through the mind, which functions within the domain of time—pain, trouble, disappointment, ambition, failure, achievement, fulfilment, frustration, or simply, facts of daily life—is, truly speaking, the result of Time.

The poet also seeks to highlight that Time is beyond human reach. On the one hand, it creates everything, and on the other, it destroys. If one utilises it, one gets reward from it and if one misses the opportunity, it never returns to give one another chance. Time is omnipotent and life has to follow its path. Human beings are trapped within Time and with the passage of Time, one has to decay.

Though Majumder tries to define Life and its experiences with respect to Death, sometimes he sounds hopeful of a better life. Then, he uses Death as a metaphor: the death of ignorance, old and worn-out thoughts, leading to a new birth, a better and prosperous Life.

Love

Apart from the themes of Time and Life, Majumder's poetry includes some other themes such as Love, Mind, Ecology, Society, Personal experiences, and others. But he views these *within* Time, that is, these operate in time, physically as well as psychologically. It is immaterial that he may sometimes echo higher values or a different way of life.

Love, for example, is treated at personal level as an emotional feeling which has overwhelming effect on individuals. The eyes of the beloved inspire him to write poetry. When words struggle for proper position, or when paper and pen lose their contact, the poet finds the whole poem in the eyes of his beloved:

> When the empty page before me
> Does not pull the light of the pen
> I am persuaded to feel then
> In your eyes the poem I seek do I see. [9]

The fascinating touch of the fingers of his beloved makes him feel as if he is a 'stranger'. He feels that time has stopped when he looks at her:

> My body I feel a stranger in your arms
> How bewitching is your touching finger's charm
> On yours when I fix my searching eyes
> Time seems to have stopped flowing tides. [10]

The poet says that if one wants to show too much possession over Love, then Love sickens and will lose its lustre and warmth:

> I want to possess by keeping the possession away
> I want to dream possession with pleasure everyday [11]

She is pretty and adorable as if she is an epitome of the 'goddess of beauty':

> You are incarnation of goddess beauty
> A being of wonder a cuty [12]

The intensity and truth of his love can be seen in his eyes:

> My words may not reach you
> In mirror of mind you may view [13]

It is the eyes which express each and everything hidden in the mind and heart. He presents the view that where words fail, eyes succeed:

> Eyes do hold
> All words untold [14]

He sounds sensuous as he feels to swim in the eyes of his beloved because her dark eyelashes are his 'sheltering petals'. Her brown nipples awake all his sensations and cuts him off from all around:

> Your brown nipples
> Stirred my blood my neighbourhood [15]

He is baffled and asks why with the music of violin love grows in him, why the sensation arises with the touch of someone. But he can philosophise:

> Love needs no seed for culmination
> It is a feel born of imagination.[16]

Majumder says that the place between the lips of his beloved is the most secured place where he can stay:

> Between your lips is the place
> I land, I live in safety ... [17]

To him, a lover is a person who sacrifices everything for the sake of love. He never needs any crown. Instead, he feels free in love with his beloved, who is simple and sober:

> ...
> He feels free in love with
> Flowers, fountains, bird and breeze
> And surely with his loveable woman
> Who is placid and without pomp. [18]

One can find a 'silken touch' in the love poems of Majumder. Here he evinces a romantic sensibility, just as he understands that mind too is not free of time. Recalling (or imagining) love, he is engaged in a self-centred movement of thought within the domain of time and resultantly, he is caught in the web of fears, anxiety, likes and dislikes, and what is and what is not.

Mind: Fear, Confusion, Dream, Memory, Loneliness

Krishnamurthy says that fear, confusion, desire, memory all are the products of the mind. Mind is not without past, present or future. The mind is crowded with worries and concerns of everyday life, ambitions, fears, anxieties, pettiness, etc. It is so full that it is far from what is timeless. There is so much disturbance that it is not quiet or peaceful. It suffers blockages and hindrances, seeking to discover something 'new', or truth, reality, or freedom. It creates confusion through the process of thinking.

In a poem "Change of Planet", the poet tries to identify his present position with what he had once. He says that when he turns towards his home he finds nothing familiar. Everything appears to have changed. He cannot recognise the planet or the place where everything has become unfamiliar to him:

> ...
> I remember yet having a home
> Sometime somewhere on this planet,
> ...
> I come across only grey land
> Have I changed the planet? [19]

He is caught in his own thoughts. He can't break away from memory or time to find something new. Possibly because his mind is not quiet? Or, he cannot feel the spirit, or the eternal?

Memory

In "Where Is The Cradle?", Majumder reminisces about his childhood days and says:

> Where is the cradle?
> In which I slept I wept once?[20]

The same feeling of the poet can be noticed in other poems like "Lost Childhood" and "Courtyard". The poet's reminiscence of his childhood days makes him nostalgic:

Presently my busyness keeps me engrossed
The courtyard died under weight of high-rise
countenance graying days are embossed
What might be a childhood I wonder I surmise.[21]

The poet says that a letter from distant relative shakes the memory which is hidden in the unconscious mind. He says: "A letter we expect always to sustain furthermore."[22]

In another poem "Light and Shade" in *Life and Eternity*, the poet describes a room which was once replete with people. But today there lives no one. He finds only stale footprints, rubber slippers and few other things which were once in use. In another poem "Yesternight", the poet reminisces and calculates what he has lost in these years.

In another poem "Photograph", the poet's eyes are struck on a photograph which stirs his memory personally and touchingly:

...
I poured all my kisses
I stored thru my life
Upon the cheeks of
The hundred years old
Young and fresh girl.[23]

Confusion

The Mind is not free from the past, nor can it see the truth; it cannot unburden the known, the ego, the self, or the beliefs, rituals, values, and norms. It is filled with everyday challenges, tensions etc, and stays confused. In a poem "Confusion" in *Dialogue With Time*, the poet reveals his state of confusion. The fear in his mind makes him unable to find a way out from a closed room. In another poem "Echoes", he says that his confusion is darkening his days, making him unable to return to his home, and due to this he is wandering aimlessly:

Confusion darkens the day
Mist enshrouds my way home
Should I be wandering
On the paths of the earth

Aimlessly, reaching nowhere?
Hearing echoes only in the void. [24]

His attempts in various poems arouse memories of actual experiences that are not devoid of confusion and conflicts of daily life. Obviously, at times he is not likely to be clear or precise.

Fear

Confusion leads to 'fear'. The greatest of human being's fear is "Death". As the poet says:

Fear is fear losing them we endear of
Another selfish fear is fear of losing mortal body sheer [25]

A fear of rejection in the poet's heart is presented in the poem "Hand". The poet says that he has 'singed' his hand in the Sun, purified it by dipping it into the river. Till he has a fear whether his earnest effort will be successful or he will be rejected:

...
All this I did in quiet earnest
All, I thought best
But do you still need a hand now?
Do I need yet to be faithful? [26]

The fear of safety, security, loss of everything etc. can be seen in his other poems also.

Loneliness

Just as the confusion leads to fear, fear leads to the development of the feeling of loneliness in the poet. The poet says, nothing of this world is ours, be it a river, tree or anything. The place where we live in is not ours. This feeling of possession of nothing makes him feel alone in this world. In a crowd also the poet feels lonely. He says that with the passage of time everything is disappearing:

Slowly but surely
A crematorium is growing

Enshrouding all my senses
And I hear the silence
Of nightfall in the solitary crematorium.[27]

Dream

Majumder says that only dreaming will not bring success. It is the will to do something that fulfils the dream:

What you can dream
You can mostly do
It all depends upon
The will to do the same ... [28]

His desire of doing good for the society, and making life comfortable and secure is projected through poems of dreams.

Ecology or Landscape

The poet portrays a picture of evening landscape by using human images to describe it. In the following two poems the poet describes an evening scenario by using human imagery:

Evening dresses like a smiling damsel
Sun dips in depth like a burnt old man
Skies splash crimson red as vomited blood
As though ancient earth dying purple pale [29]

and,

Sometimes an evening becomes audible
It's different from usual wan face
Of an olden woman vomiting
Stale blood continually
Before vanishing in the abyss.[30]

In poems like "Kanyakumari" and "Sagar Mela", Majumder describes the whole landscape very artistically. In *Time Never Returns To Console and Other Poems,* the poet's keen observations of natural environment and landscape can be seen.

Personal Poems

The personal poems of Majumder are generally introspective in nature. The time he has spent as a bureaucrat is full of such incidents which has left a great impact on his personal as well as poetic life. He always introspects. He always tries to find out the answer to such questions as why he is here, why he is doing these things and such other questions. He is always in confusion what to do and what not to do. And in this situation no one hears his yearnings. In a poem "My Yearning".[31]

Society

Majumder's concern for society is also visible in his poems. In a poem "Non-descript women", the poet describes those women who are engaged in the profession of prostitution. It disturbs the poet to note that they come into the streets in darkness, waiting for their customers in a row. There is no one to hear their woes, no one comes forward to raise voice for their better lives:

> The oldest human profession is yet aglow with busyness
> The animal in man never shuns him despite wisdom resources.[32]

In another poem "Call Centre Woman", the poet highlights the general condition of women working in the Call Centres. In "A Societal Crime", the poet describes the cause of abandoning an infant anywhere. The same theme has been dealt by I.K. Sharma. Majumder is upset to read in newspapers or watch on television the reports of "abandoned infants". He says that two adolescents when come in contact with each other, the momentary pleasure leads to birth of a baby and to hide it, they leave infant anywhere. He writes:

> Conjugation for a fun brought her a child
> A societal crime most viled
> I leaps of shame in her piled
> In a bush the abandoned child isled [33]

Majumder is also aware of the contemporary social changes. In *Time Never Returns To Console*, the poet, for example, writes about wedding, in the poem "Wedding":

> It is supposed to be a relationship of mutual trust
> Love and surrender to each other for which a thrust

Of inner bond and binding and feeling essential
Thus an equation of "made for each other"
becomes substantial [34]

Poetry

The poet's love for Poetry is clearly visible in the poems written on poetry itself. He says that when his suffering is 'worded away', his loneliness speaks. He is fascinated by beauty. When morning blossoms in smiles, it constitutes poetry for him. He says that poetry has neither introduction nor any conclusion. In "The Poet And His Pen" [35], the poet says that a poet has storm in his pen and when he starts writing or composing, all might of the pen settle in the mother's lap like a baby.

Miscellaneous

Majumder has written many other poems too. His poems on Science and Technology, Religion, Humanity highlight his anxiety about the changing moral ethics. In poems like "Whom Should I Go To?" and "What Cuts Both Ways", the poet talks about the change in human nature. Everywhere corruption has spread its hands to grab human values. He says that the sword cuts everything but it can never cut itself; sin can blemish but it can never blemish itself; fire can burn everything but it can never burn itself. To quote him:

But a man is not invincible anyway
For, a man only, is the killer and the killed.
He beautified his dreams and deeds
And it is he who ravished beauty wholly.[36]

The poet says that with the advancement of technology people become more brutal and cruel. New technologies should be used for developmental work and not for the purpose of destruction.

A clear influence of Time can be noticed in the poems centred round Love, Mind and Society. With the passage of time, love loses its lustre and warmth. Living life in a limited span of time fills the mind with tension and worries which lead to confusion, fear, loneliness, etc. Losing their moral values people move towards anarchy.

Conclusion

To sum up, Majumder's poetry has a lot of variety. The poet demonstrates his proficiency in handling each and every aspect of present-day life and society even as he is excessively preoccupied with Time which is not without excluding mind, life, nature, love or memory. But, he seems to confuse his individual time, which is experiential, with universal and local time, and as a result, he exhibits inner restlessness, even as he may succeed in expressing flashes of self-knowledge or his own being. His meditative wandering may reflect his watchfulness in worldly affairs and relationships, yet it demonstrates his restive spirit rather than stillness of the mind.

He explores his own state of being, as well as the state of the world without, and gets attached to it and keeps repeating it, be it time, mind, life, or nature.

References

1. R.K. Singh, "The Poet—Editor—Administrator: Mr. Pronab Kumar Majumder," *Metverse Muse* (11, Jan-June 2001) 105.
2. Andrew Marvell, "To His Coy Mistress." *The Winged Word: An Anthology of Poems for Degree Course,* Ed. David Green (Chennai: Macmillan, 2001).
3. Rabindranath Tagore, "Silent Steps," Ed. A Board of Editors, *An Anthology of Indian English Poetry* (Hyderabad: Orient Longman, 2001) 10.
4. R.K. Singh, "Eyeless Jagannath." Eds. P. Raja and Rita Nath Keshari, *Busy Bee Book of Contemporary Indian English Poetry* (Pondicherry: Busy Bee Book, 2007) 338.
5. Pronab Kumar Majumder, "Me A Slave of Time," *Time Never Returns To Console and Other Poems* (Calcutta: Writers Workshop, 2007) 16.
6. Pronab Kumar Majumder, "Time," *ONTime UNTime* (Kolkata: Bridge-In-Making, 2007) 7.
7. Pronab Kumar Majumder, "Hyphen," *Life And Eternity* (Calcutta: Writers Workshop, 1997) 10.
8. Pronab Kumar Majumder, "Hyphen," *Life And Eternity* (Calcutta: Writers Workshop, 1997) 27.
9. Pronab Kumar Majumder, "Poem In Eyes," *Time Never Returns To Console and Other Poems* (Calcutta: Writers Workshop, 2007) 95.

10. Pronab Kumar Majumder, "Secure Arms," *Time Never Returns To Console and Other Poems* (Calcutta: Writers Workshop, 2007) 96.
11. Pronab Kumar Majumder, "Secure Arms," *Time Never Returns To Console and Other Poems* (Calcutta: Writers Workshop, 2007) 96.
12. Pronab Kumar Majumder, "Love," *ONTime UNTime* (Kolkata: Bridge- In- Making, 2007) 33.
13. Pronab Kumar Majumder, "Love," *ONTime UNTime* (Kolkata: Bridge- In- Making, 2007) 34.
14. Pronab Kumar Majumder, "Love," *ONTime UNTime* (Kolkata: Bridge- In- Making, 2007) 35.
15. Pronab Kumar Majumder, "Spring," *Dialogue With Time* (Calcutta: Writers Workshop, 1993) 20.
16. Pronab Kumar Majumder, "Birth of Love," *Where Time Is Dead* (Calcutta: Writers Workshop, 200) 49.
17. Pronab Kumar Majumder, "For A Hapless," *Replies of Time* (Aligarh: Skylark Publication, 1996) 49.
18. Pronab Kumar Majumder, "A Lover," *Dialogue With Time* (Calcutta: Writers Workshop, 1993) 69.
19. Pronab Kumar Majumder, "Change of Planet," *Replies of Time* (Aligarh: Skylark Publication, 1996) 7.
20. Pronab Kumar Majumder, "Where Is The Cradle?" *Replies of Time* (Aligarh: Skylark Publication, 1996) 29.
21. Pronab Kumar Majumder, "Courtyard," *In The Ruins of Time* (Calcutta: Writers Workshop, 2000) 72.
22. Pronab Kumar Majumder, "A Letter," *Dialogue With Time* (Calcutta: Writers Workshop, 1993) 26.
23. Pronab Kumar Majumder, "Photograph," *In The Ruins of Time* (Calcutta: Writers Workshop, 2000) 65.
24. Pronab Kumar Majumder, "Confusion," *Dialogue With Time* (Calcutta: Writers Workshop, 1993) 9.
25. Pronab Kumar Majumder, "Fear," *Where Time Is Dead* (Calcutta: Writers Workshop, 2005) 69.
26. Pronab Kumar Majumder, "Hand" *Dialogue With Time* (Calcutta: Writers Workshop, 1993) 14.
27. Pronab Kumar Majumder, "Crematorium," *Life and Eternity* (Calcutta: Writers Workshop, 1997) 55.
28. Pronab Kumar Majumder, "Dreams," *Creating Killing Cosmic Time* (Calcutta: Writers Workshop, 2002) 27.
29. Pronab Kumar Majumder, "Evening Landscape," *Time Never Returns To Console and Other Poems* (Calcutta: Writers Workshop, 2007) 81.
30. Pronab Kumar Majumder, "Audible Evening," *Replies of Time* (Aligarh: Skylark Publication, 1996) 54.

31. Pronab Kumar Majumder, "My Yearning," *Dialogue With Time* (Calcutta: Writers Workshop, 1993) 45.
32. Pronab Kumar Majumder, "Non-descript Women," *Where Time Is Dead* (Calcutta: Writers Workshop, 2005) 29.
33. Pronab Kumar Majumder, "A Societal Crime," *Time Never Returns To Console*
34. (Calcutta: Writers Workshop, 2007) 92.
35. Pronab Kumar Majumder, "Wedding," *Time Never Returns To Console*
36. (Calcutta: Writers Workshop, 2007) 89.
37. Pronab Kumar Majumder, "The Poet And His Pen," *Replies of Time* (Aligarh: Skylark Publication, 1996) 31.
38. Pronab Kumar Majumder, "What Cuts Both Ways," *Replies of Time* (Aligarh: Skylark Publication, 1996) 27.

13

Pronab Kumar Majumder: An Adept in Love Poems

—Aju Mukhopadhyay

After studying a good number of poems by Pronab Kumar Majumder I find that he is not at all a poet of Time but a poet with a burning romantic heart, with a longing and taste for true love, even beyond the sphere of the physical, but impatient with the time which is prone to snatch his ebbing life:

> I am in a hurry
> The whistle of the carriage for me
> Is blowing impatiently.
>
> ("Bewilderment with thc replies," *CKCT 71*)

Pronab Kumar Majumder, up to 9 September 2009, had published 13 books of poems in English besides seven in Bangla, written six One Act plays, one short novel and edited two anthologies of poems in English. He is an editor of a literary magazine, *Bridge-in-Making*, which still improves in spite of his graying age. He has been variously honoured and awarded by several national and international institutions.

But I was not feeling happy to write eloquently about his poems even with half a dozen of his books before me. Ten of his books with different themes are tagged to time yet I was not satisfied with his conception of time for it is truly divine, beyond the conception of man. But the question is, if he is not a real poet he could not have written so many, could not continue to produce more. And knowing that many have written critique on his poems I did not feel inclined to read to be guided for I know that I may be satisfied only when I have a tryst with real poetry. And I searched them out, mostly in his "Creating-Killing Cosmic Time" and some in "Time Never Returns to Console."

Beginning with time, we find the poet analysing it in his preface to '*My India Through the Corridor of Time*.' "Time is dead in a dead person, i.e., a dead one is outside the influence of "Time." "Time" is active in something alive.... Whether Time was ever birthed and will end someday were enigma. Modern great scientist Stephen W Hawking evolved the theory that 'time' was born with the 'Big Bang' which ushered in the universe and "Time" may end with the possible 'Big Crunch' which may destroy the universe." *MITCT* was published in 2008 but Pronab wrote the following lines in *Sparkles of Time*, published in 2007.

> Time began in Bigbang
> In which no music rang
> Ever since a listless runner
>
> ("Time and Life," *SOT* 1)

and

> When everything will be dead
> In a Big Crunch raid
> Buried will be Time
>
> ("Time and Life," *SOT* 1)

He writes 'Time does not touch a dead' (SOT 2) and 'Graveyard of Time is history' ("History," *MITCT* 9) but writes to emend in the same page, 'Time gone not really dead/That is where history is made.'

Let us see his look at Time further; to begin with two contradictory observations are:

> There can't be a beauty indifferent of time
> With time's care beauty has to rhyme
>
> ("Beauty in Time's Care," *TNRTC* 22)

and

Nature's beauty is silent solitary lonesome
They stand sentinel overtime fulsome

("Beauty: Human; Nature," *TNRTC* 34)

His observation that, 'Body clock records passing time punctually,' and 'Every today is the father of Tomorrow/Past has offerings for the future to borrow' in 'Never-will-be' and 'Course of civilisation' (Both in *CKCT* 22 and 82) are pithy but temporal.

When he writes:

Thus we enjoy our childhood
At old age when comes back old image

("Return of Memories," *TNRTC* 23)

or

And again memories write
Memoirs for a little more survival.

("Memories," *CKCT* 75)

he is in a happy mood accepting Time's benevolence but he becomes stern at times, rejecting such things.

Memories are necessary burdens
Life never repeats
Time and sound
Do not return

("No Revisitations," *CKCT* 44)

When he humbly writes,

In the flowing life my identity is immaterial
Life is depth of sea not waves superficial

("Life Not Waves Superficial," *TNRTC* 26)

we understand that he has moved from the temporary to the eternal aspect of time. We can not catch it even with body clock. It is beyond. Memory, though related to time, is a different thing. About his ideas of flower's perishing in time it may be said that flower's freshness and decay depends on changing weather; effect of nature on a flower is inherent in flower's nature. Some flowers get decayed in plants within hours of its blooming but some buds bloom in flower vase, though cut from the plant. We have seen, poet himself agrees, that history is not time's graveyard. Apparently it seems that 'Time does not touch the dead' because a living being only feels the touch of time but going deep into its longer range we find that time lifts up some dead and makes them immortal like Shakespeare and Rabindranath Tagore, as the poet writes.

Time has two aspects, temporary and eternal. Worldly and beyond. While something of it is universally acceptable, the total range of it is baffling to humanity. It is in fact related to consciousness. We shall try to comprehend time to the extent possible.

Neither a big bang was able to give birth to it, nor could a big crunch crush it. Time is every imperial. Stephen Hawking's *A Brief History of Time* is a good read. Neither he is emphatic about big bang nor about black hole. A chapter is titled, 'Black hole ain't so Black.' Let us now hear him talk about big bang: 'Throughout the 1970s I had been mainly studying Black holes but in 1981 my interest in questions about the origin and fate of the universe was reawakened when I attended a conference on Cosmology organised by the Jesuits in the Vatican. At the end of the conference the participants were granted an audience with the Pope. He told us that it was all right to study the evolution of the universe after the big bang, but we should not enquire into the big bang itself because that was the moment of creation and therefore the work of God. I was glad then that he did not know the subject of the talk I had just given at the conference—the possibility that space and time was finite but had no boundary, which means that it had no beginning, no moment of creation. I had no desire to share the fate Galileo...."[1]

Even in the chapter titled, "Conclusion" he could not come to any satisfactory conclusion. The scientist could not but admit the existence of God, though obliquely. He wrote, "But if the universe is completely self-contained, with no singularities or boundaries, and completely described by a unified theory, that has profound implications for the role of God as creator."[2]

But it is usually revolting for a scientist to admit God on whose existence he has no faith. Expressing his dream that a unified, complete theory would bring satisfaction to all, he concludes by putting a volley of questions to God himself without addressing him.

'Why does the universe go to all the bother of existing? Is the unified theory so completing that it brings about its own existence? Or does it need a creator, and, if so, does he have any other effect on the universe? And who created him?' [3]

Stephen has referred to large number of scientists and few others like philosophers in his book but all from the western world. Though he has not named any, I must believe that he has the awareness about the great Rishis and astronomers of India who too knew things scientific even before the western scientists. He has frankly admitted that 'Any physical theory is always provisional, in the sense that it is only a hypothesis: You can never prove it.'[4] He has admitted that Newton, Einstein and he himself committed mistakes.

Scientific theories and speculations of philosophers change but Time stands on its solid ground in both static and dynamic modes. It has to be comprehended at the right level.

Paramahansa Yogananda quoted from an article published in East West (Los Angeles) in February 1934:

> "The very ancient brahmagupta, one of the Jyotish works, is an astronomical treatise dealing with such matters as the . . . earth's daily axial revolution, the presence of fixed stars in the Milky Way, the law of gravitation, and other scientific facts which did not dawn in the western world until the time of Copernicus and Newton."[5]

He has referred to division of time into equinoctial cycles further divided into ascending and descending Arc, called Yugas: Kali, Dwapara, Treta and Satya, corresponding to the Greek ideas of Iron, Bronze, Silver and Golden Ages. The life span of the whole universe was calculated in terms of millions of solar years. But none of us will live to see through such calculations. It has been said that our solar time and eternity are not the same.

Referring to the *Upanishads* Sri Aurobindo writes that Brahman is one without a second, one and all like Tao is to ancient Chinese sage: 'The Lord of beings is that which is conscious in the conscious being, but he is also the conscious in the inconscient things, the One who is master and in control of the many that are passive in the hands of Force-Nature. He is the Timeless and Time; he is Space and all that is in space; he is Causality and the cause and effect: He is the thinker and his thought, the warrior and his courage, the gambler and his dice-throw. . . . The Brahman alone is, and because of It all are, for all are Brahman; this Reality is the reality of everything that we see in Self and Nature.'[6]

This age old Indian philosophy and faith on God and Time; temporal and eternal, answers the volley of questions raised by Stephen Hawking.

I have spoken at some length about the 'Time Poems' of Pronab Kumar Majumder as most of his poetry books are tagged to Time, to see his concept of time and its use in poems. But he has other books of poems too and though tagged to time, all the poems do not belong to that category. In some books there are sub-categories like 'philosophy', 'love', 'landscape', 'child', 'peace', 'desire', 'dream' and so many.

My India: Through Corridor of Time is a book that glorify India in five line verses. These are very simple lines, sometimes didactic, sometimes puerile, supported by patriotic feelings fuelled by idealism. When he writes, 'My India is great' in 'Nation' No.13 (*MITCT* 5), we instantly remember Rajiv Gandhi's well publicised slogan, "Mera Bharat Mahan".

> Some inspiring lines in the book are,
> National Flag the highest pride
> National anthem the inspiring guide
>
> ("Nation" No. 16 *MITCT* 6)

or

> Holding head high we proclaim
> We are a nation sovereign
>
> ("Sovereignty" No. 19 *MITCT* 7)

but

> India's strength is solidarity
> Of both geography and humanity
> ("Territorial Identity and Integrity" No.37 *MITCT* 13)

or

> In a void no myth is born
> With no field there will be no corn.
> ("Literature, Myths Epics" No.37 *MITCT* 18)

do not impress much; rhymed only.

Passage to Peace is perhaps the latest book of poems published by Pronab in September 2009. All the poems consist of four or five quatrains. Here he finds trouble all around, especially terror and terrorism. He finds not his peace, feels disturbed. But he never relents to find peace in dreams.

While

> Peace cannot be hawked for sale
> Peace cannot be bought for a price-
> ("Peace Not For A Price," *PTP* 1)

may have a taunt directed towards the international peace hawkers, but lines like

> All and every storm sometimes calms
> May be ruins and rubbles will be dumps .
> It is a challenging job to clear all debris
> Below which quietly lies our cherished peace
> ("Cherished Peace," *PTP* 63)

depicts a strange wishfulness or extreme satire.

Though not involved deeply in any movement, the poet is aware of his surrounding: Nature and Ecology, things mechanical under the cyber age and nuclear rage:

> "Computer is superstar/World in fear of blockbuster/Is ruled by push-bottom power" ("Cyber Age," SOT 46). And

"In this cyberage . . ./Words of love unlearned in lifetime remain untold" ("Wedding" *TNRTC* 89) or "Don't disturb the earth by nuclear fission fusion" ("Volcanic Eruptions," *CKCT* 66) or "Pokhran was never for succour/But chosen for rehearsal nuclear" ("Desert Song," *CKCT* 68) or "Possibilities of green grasses everyday die" ("What Earth Grows Now," *TNRTC* 39) or "Human encroachments everyday/upon fields and forests . . . . A mad craze for taking possession/Of skies" ("Suicidal Adventure," *CKCT* 57) and such warnings as "Only concrete culture can't feed you give you air . . . you don't know fate of your self-killing mirth" ("Greens At Stake," (*TNRTC* 38) tells us enough of his concern for what is happening all around us. He knows that together with friendly hand science has extended its other demoniac, poisonous hands too towards mankind. He knows that man spoils the silent beauty and benevolence of nature, provoking it to take revenge.

Jibanananda Das, a Kolkata poet of extraordinary calibre, one among the remarkable Bengali poets after Tagore, wrote that Kolkata one day would be *Tillotama*, a mythological virgin of incomparable beauty, made by the divine artisan, Vishwakarma. In short, a paragon of beauty. The old Calcuttans love it to the core in spite of suffocating in its jaws. Poet Pronab Kumar Majumder, a man of Kolkata from his childhood, has penned some poems focusing some aspects of its life which may be similar to life in other mega cities.

Crowd gone berserk after year-wide
Suffocation crunch of everydayness.
Yes, this is the last night of three-night-long
Durga Puja

("Third night," *CKCT* 86)

In "An Afternoon Park in Kolkata Today" he has focused on a pathetic scene in a park of a mega Indian city, which usually goes unnoticed.

What this leftover little vacant space miss is playing
minors
Who are engaged in and out day and night for Exam
result-fruits

(*TNRTC* 106)

True it is that large number of little magazines or non-commercial literary magazines are published from Bengal, particularly Kolkata. Many of them meet with untimely death, many continue till the lifetime of the editors. But most of them are not blessed by establishments, commercial media or big bosses in the field. Many editors and writers connected with them die unheard, unworshipped. Some come out, what is called successfully, leaving that life of literary practice in the long run. In "Little Mag Editors," Pronab writes to celebrate their work.

> The editors are at work till late night with unsung dedication
> May be for their selfless single handed work they get scant recognition
>
> (*TNRTC* 103)

I must say that ordinary city dwellers know little about other birds than crows and sparrows (now rare). Crows are well known to Pronab. In many of his poems crows appear-peeps or caws boldly in public. He writes in "Calcutta crow":

> Calcutta's necessary evil is the black neighbour
> Unnoticed he works as unpaid scavenger.
>
> (*CKCT* 72)

as if telling it, using an oxymoron, an evil benefactor, showing his love for the neighbour.

Even as he observes his surroundings, nature and humans, Pronab Kumar Majumder keeps himself aware of the flow of time, affecting his mind, life and body throughout the span of his living time.

Though his references are not so replete with ardent love for God, as an Indian, living with its tradition, the poet has intrinsic faith in God, with which he tries to remain on the safe side, consoling himself that everything is for the good; whatever the best shall happen. It must be that studying and translating Tagore, the poet has imbibed some of his sublime ideas. But the following two lines remind us of a song by Kazi Nazrul Islam.

This earth is but your toy
Playing so many games in whims
("Source of Light," *CKCT* 14)

In "God's Entity" he writes, "God is colourless/Formless boundless" (*CKCT* 46).

In "Discovery of the Self" he says, 'You are the God the power/Unbeaten the super/Discover yourself in stupor' (*TNRTC* 68). In 'The undying mind' he feels that mind is not aged with life's age, it has every right to see all beauties 'Mind an identity separated from old age' (*CKCT* 40), he feels. 'I am amid the sun-down hour facing the west/Yet I believe the future will deliver its best' ('Sun-down Poetry' *TNRTC* 58). He consoles himself writing further that his works will survive even after him. He writes, 'Manuscripts never burn/As the Times do not/ . . . . Flames failed to consume Time/And Time's fire-proof products' ("Manuscripts Never Burn" *TNRTC* 62), but his mind and heart vacillates. In another poem, "Book Worm," he writes:

After I am dead who will take care
Of books of poems authored by me . . .
In any case worms and times won't spare
(*TNRTC* 21)

Something gnaws at his heart. Knowing the soul, its undying state and eternal journey, he is bewildered at his own dichotomous state:

The day I pass everyday
Not knowing it is but brief stay
Of the eternal journey of the soul
In search of the ultimate goal . . . .
The day passes through dark alley of blinding glow
Crowds of mob stirs swiftly proceeds slow
. . . I don't know
Where the journey is going to go
("Pardon? Would They Seek?" *TNRTC* 73)

It pricks him that
Admittedly superior is the mouse
I still don't have a house
("A House" *CKCT* 73)

Now begins my journey with the poet in his world of love. His "Faces of Love" is a book full of witty and humorous observations and pithy sayings on love. Not all are exactly quatrains in rhyming patterns but mostly rhymed, they all are four lined poems:

Love is a transparent glass
Not to be touched with finger
She is a beauty plus
So long observed from afar

(No.83, *FLO* 21)

Love is never immortal
As believed as a myth
Truly nothing remains with
Everything passes through oblivion-portal

(No.122, *FLO* 31)

In spite of his 'lived life' the poet denies accepting a position of non-observer, as we have seen. He wants to see at least all beauties to his heart's content.

On yours when I fix my searching eyes
Time seems to have stopped flowing tides

("Secure Arms," *TNRTC* 96)

In "Peerless Countenance" the poet writes his feeling about his love:

Beauty is flames that do not burn . . .
Her eyes unsoiled like the autumn skies
Her reticence eloquent like a mountain peak
With her the whole of earthly beauty vies

(*CKCT* 76)

Eyes again in "Poem in Eyes":

But I long to have elongated pleasure of waiting
For the poem to swim in your eyes before coming to writing

(*TNRTC* 95)

I am graying I know for sure
Only do I crave for her view holy pure
Thousand autumns afar yet the allure

And in the same poem "For Her," the graying poet hopes with trepidation her return:

Is it she returning in steps silent slow?
("For Her," *CKCT* 77)

It is like "The Blind Wife" who never gives up hope of return of her unknown lover who she never met

It's winter, not far off
Is spring, he is sure
To be back as he promised,
(*CKCT* 80)

she murmurs. The idea of Spring coming after the Winter echoes Shelley's strong wish. In the "Lost Ring" 'She' has been idealised as a ring which the poet has lost in the ocean but strongly feels, may be after his life:

I shall be carried
To the abyss
Where she is
(*CKCT* 71)

Though he is in a dilemma as to how to answer billions of replies received at the fag end of his life, of the billions of letters he wrote at the beginning, as in his poem 'Bewilderment with the replies' (*CKCT* 71), as he is chased by the Time; 'I am in a hurry,' he says but he is not in a mood to give up, as we see elsewhere.

To a romantic and adventurous heart there is an answer, as in "A Dilapidated Poet," a woman poet like a dilapidated building that has crumbled to the ground, lost everything but her boy friend living on the other side of the ocean, who has only one last thing in life to do:

It was a love poem that she could write better
("A Dilapidated Poet," *TNRTC* 107)

like poet Pronab Kumar Majumder who knows to write Love Poems better.

The haiku like "Sparkles of Time" and tanka like "My India: Through the Corridor of Time" have poems resembling haiku and tanka in three and five lines but in essence and spirit they are different. Haiku and Tanka, the Japanese short verses have become very popular across countries, they are being developed further. The traditional ones have syllabic count besides other characteristics of haiku and tanka. Others are light footed, subtle and beauty simplified, focusing momentary images without any rigidity in forms. They usually have three and five lines in their bodies.

Not in these books but fine haiku I find, penned automatically without considering them as such, in some poems like "Nocturnal Phenomena", a page with six haiku. One of them is

Across the sleeping meadow
Sway a long shadow
Of a man with a lantern
(No. 5, *TNRTC* 81)

See the imagery in another poem titled, "A Journey Unending" has four unrhymed quatrains, almost tanka in quality if divided in five lines. Of the four line stanzas one is:

Last flicker of the sun burning in the west
Long shadows gripping the unspeakable village
Chirping of returning birds stirred awhile
Gradually the village enters undiscovered dark.
(*CKCT* 78)

This is what for the present I have to say about the contents of six referred books of poems by Pronab Kumar Majumder. But there remains some other things to mention, going back to the preface.

In his preface to *My India: Through the Corridor of Time* the poet has defined poetry as 'Versified thoughts motioned by emotions, passions, confessions, imaginations, experiences of life and experiences with the life.' I may add, motioned by ethics, morality, awareness, straightforwardness, etc. But in my opinion all of them make a rational utterance of forcibly rhymed or unrhymed prosaic pieces, if not dross. Many of the poems in the volumes are reproduction of rational thoughts, sometimes forcibly rhymed. Some of his unrhymed poems are beautiful though most of his poems are rhymed and some of them are spontaneously, nicely rhymed. His language is simple, straightforward and without any ambiguity, sometimes sprinkled with some Indian words.

I feel that poetry is something beyond the creation of rational mind, rhymed or not, something intuitive, romantic, touching all emotions, but above them, tending towards the impossible. True poetry is inspired utterance. It is, at least a portion of it, is realisable by the resonant heart of the reader. And that is what has happened in his love poems, pulsating with emotion. Pronab Majumder has superseded his "Versified Thoughts" in them. He has excelled in his love poems otherwise I could have difficulties in finding him.

Notes

1. Stephen Hawking, *A Brief History of Time* (Great Britain: Bantam Books, 1989) 122.
2. Stephen Hawking, *A Brief History of Time* (Great Britain: Bantam Books, 1989) 184
3. Stephen Hawking, *A Brief History of Time* (Great Britain: Bantam Books, 1989) 184
4. Stephen Hawking, *A Brief History of Time* (Great Britain: Bantam Books, 1989) 11.
5. Paramahansa Yogananda, *Autobiography* of a Yogi (Mumbai; Jaico Publishing Edition, 1997) 168.
6. Sri Aurobindo, *The Life Divine* (Pondicherry: SABCL, Sri Aurobindo Ashram, 1970 Vol. 18) 324-25

Works Cited

Majumder, Pronab Kumar. *Creating-Killing Cosmic Time* (CKCT). Kolkata: Writers Workshop-Redbird Book. 2002. Print.

Faces of Love (FOL). Kolkata: Bridge-in-Making Publication, 2008. Print.

My India Through the Corridor of Time (MITCT). Kolkata: Bridge-in-Making Publication, 2008. Print.

Passage to Peace (PTP). Kolkata: Bridge-in-Making Publication, 2009. Print.

Sparkles of Time (SOT). Kolkata: Bridge-in-Making Publication, 2007. Print.

Time Never Returns to Console (TNRTC). Kolkata: Writers Workshop-Redbird Book, 2007. Print.

14

Critical Perspectives on Prof. Syed Ameeruddin's Poetry

—Binayendra Chowdhuri

Commonwealth Literature first paved its way with English fiction, subsequently, poetry followed its path and good number of Indian poets with their laudable creative craftsmanship distinguished themselves in the field of contemporary world poetry. Naturally, a young generation of Indian poets took the lead. Among them the names of Sarojini Naidu, Toru Dutt, Aurobindo Ghose Harindra Nath Chattopadhya, and Nissim Ezekiel are worth mentioning. In this process, Dr. Krishna Srinivas founded the World Poetry Society and launched an English international monthly as its Editor from Chennai in 1960. An epoch-making era ushered in and a large number of young Indian poets joined and facilitated their access to international readership. Of late, the prominent Indian poet Arun Kumar Mehrotra of Allahabad University was nominated to the post of Professor of Poetry at the University of Oxford. It can be safely concluded that Indian poetry in English has attained maturity and adulthood. In this context, the relentless efforts of P. Lal of Kolkata and his Writer's Workshop can also be mentioned. Mr. Lal founded his publication department in 1950 to inspire the Indian writing in English and a large number of Indo-Anglican poets and writers benefited themselves from the Writer's Workshop and the world poetry society to publish their creative activities.

Prof. (Dr.) Syed Ameeruddin, Head of the Post-Graduate & Research Department of English, University of Madras, is the worthy inheritor and promoter of this legacy. He has distinguished himself as a poet writing in English and critically acclaimed in India and abroad. He is gifted with creativity perpetuated by heavenly bliss, and has been described as a conglomeration of metaphysical—the surreal and existential. His ecstatic creative craftsmanship placed him as one of the brilliant stars among the galaxy of Indo-Anglican poets and world poetry.

Visioned Summits is a collection of twenty-one brilliant and beautiful poems wreathed together in a single lively, lovely and long creeper climbing upwards and reflecting the realities around it including the classical values of the society and the life. The poet is a creator, he creates as he witnesses, feels, and experiences, and ultimately his perception translates those subjects, objects and characters to form poetry with his powerful rhetoric language, Dr. Syed Ameeruddin has distinguished himself as a great poet in the field of contemporary English poetry.

"*Eloquent Serenade*" is the first poem in the book *Visioned Summits* which has been- composed in an epic dimension with the poet himself as the central character depicting elaborately the imagery and happening in the course of a long journey. So, the poet unveils the poem:

> Fifty summers I have crossed
> Across the hurricane of ravens
> Through empty daybreaks
> *And crumbling sunsets,*
> (*Visioned Summits* 23)

A note of pessimism and dejection reverberate in the poet's mind in view of the present gloomy and crumbled civilisation as well as the untimely demise of his beloved. An inherent psychic suffering has been causing deep agony in his heart. He is restless and feeling uneasy, and in this uncertain state of mind, he says:

> Yesterday, you parted with me
> With an unrelenting wound

Leaving me to an unsure season
Where the wind sings broken melodies.
(*Visioned Summits* 23)

The poet is very touchy and sensitive. He cannot bear the loss, his melancholy note and voice sings:

A lover and a wanderer, I am
I must return to strange lands,
(*Visioned Summits* 23)

He cannot control his grief and like a high fevered patient, he utters:

No, I will not die in your memories
Nor see my face through
The mangled sunlight in your eyes.
(*Visioned Summits* 24)

At this stage, it may be concluded that the poet has made up his mind to forget his beloved, and so, he tells the readers that they would not come face to face again. Therefore, he resolves to walk in the land of 'Alphabetic anarchy...' he sings:

I will walk
Into the alphabetic anarchy of stars
Marching into the nebulous night
Ahead, into the azure eyes of futurity.
(*Visioned Summits* 24)

The poet has used a very beautiful metaphorical phrase 'Alphabetic anarchy' which denotes that he expresses his earnest desire to make a safe journey in the land of world poetry but 'Cyclone centers his mind' (25) and loneliness makes his normal life topsy turvy and that is the reason why in the midst of vast crowd, he feels himself lonely. It is a psychological trauma caused due to the sad and untimely departure of his life partner. At this juncture, he feels that gipsy river races through his veins, the rhapsodic silence sighs in his eyes, and therefore, he affirms,

I have always been alone amidst the multitude
A nowhere man with a longsong satchel.
I have raged against the volcanoes
I have silenced the scissoring storms
And found its silence was a symphony.

(*Visioned Summits* 25)

The grief-stricken heart of the poet expresses his deep feelings in the above lines and moisten the eyes of the readers also. His insight and feelings create a communicable verbal forms, and the use of metaphorical epithet like 'Rhapsodic silence' creates touchy emotions. His superb talent exhibits his mastermind craftsmanship and vividity in the poem which has the quality of an epic poem. His existential crisis is surrealistic. He has been very sensitively and courageously facing the present moments of his life. So, he has silenced the scissoring storms and also found out 'a symphony' which will prove to be a harmonious, enlivening and refreshing energy. This made him to continue in his march in quest for the 'SELF'—his identity.

In his long journey, he finds the horrified horizons of the present day life where:

'Buddha's bodhi—bewilders
Gurunanak's compassion—crumbles
Gandhi's ahimsa—gurgles—

(*Visioned Summits* 271)

Further, he says:

In the frensied endeavours
Of determining an abode
For Ram and Rahim—The one and only Reality
—Ishwar—Allah Tere Nam'.

(*Visioned Summits* 27)

Thus the poet experiences that the ultimate truth is, all human beings are alike irrespective of their caste, creed, religion, faith, and this disparity is in practice; this can only vanish from their minds when the humanity realises the truth behind it. The real truth is that all religions have given different names to the

Supreme Power. They are artificial. Although different faiths have given different names to the Almighty yet the real truth is that the Almighty is one and only one, and when humanity will realise this truth, this anarchy will vanish. So, the poet is disturbed with these whirlwinds of darkness, the flash of culture of human bomb, aka Bombay blast, Ayodhya devastation, Somalian, Bosnian bereavements and many such untoward incidents, occurring now and then—here and there—all over the globe. All such terrible and horrible incidents make him nonplussed and his anguish enhances with these cords:

> In the dark the death scorches me
> The fevered soul discovers its own secret
> In the tattered lull that surrounds me.
> The thought of death is terrible.
>
> (*Visioned Summits* 27)

His dear one's death has upset his present existence and he has been expressing his anguish using phrases like 'unrelenting wounds', 'fevered soul', 'tattered lull', in different stages of the poetry and 'death is terrible' reveals the agony, intense anguish which is no less than being in an inferno. So, considering the present situation, he says,

> 'When I die, I am redeemed' (*Visioned Summits* 34)

i.e., he will continue to live with his creations through the ages to come to eternity. Naturally, death cannot touch his 'SELF', (ibid.35/36)

Since his mind is facing this crisis of trauma, he cannot stay in a particular place and that is why he says:

> I am a wanderer, I am a nowhere man.
> Gypsy river runs through my bones.
> I walk with the thunder,
> And share Us magnificent pride.
> 1 am a wanderer. 1 have a goal. A purple purpose.
>
> (*Visioned Summits* 35-36)

He has to move on and on, and will not look back. This make him remember the oft-quoted lines of Robert Frost, "And miles to go before I sleep." Here he ruminates the reminiscences of the memories 'love times' spent with his beloved but says:

I have long buried the memories
Of fractured sunsets
And long forgotten lovetimes.

(*Visioned Summits* 36)

His secret grief of humanity and existence has overwhelmed him, and the picture of the slum dwellers with their miseries and poverty sadden him. He says, "The horror of opaque living" he has encountered during the course of his journey and lately he "accepted the reality as we have to accept the different seasons throughout the year by rotation." Therefore, he admits that poverty is like the season and so he writes:

'I understood the calmness of rivers
And compassion of storms.

(*Visioned Summits* 41)

So, he determines to serve mankind and says:

I worshiped the God to console
The guilt of my wavering mind
I served mankind to pamper my seeping self

(*Visioned Summits* 43)

Here in the form of introspection, he tells,

I have to voyage, I have to march,
I have to discover the secrets of my self.

(*Visioned Summits* 47)

In the "Vicissitudes of Life" he introspects in a pessimistic mode. He opens the poem with:

Within me a harrowing dark
An eclipsed heart, a sedative soul

(*Visioned Summits* 50)

Here the poet is in the state of perplexity and he considers himself as a 'splintered mirror' and his memory is blown to pieces with these changing thoughts. He says.

I close my eyes
To watch the controversy of hurts
My iconoclast mission
My surrealistic vision...
World calls me mad

But, the poet immediately thereafter affirms,

'But these are all garbs I have worn'

The poet aptly realises that all these peripheries of life are due to his loneliness and so he says.

My reality is my loneliness
My quest is my self
(*Visioned Summits* 52)

Here he comes face to face with Reality and so he affirms:

Reality trembles in my eyes
When I think of violent
I have experienced on this savage wasteland.
(*Visioned Summits* 56)

Here, too, his loneliness reminds him that he is a stranger, a nowhere man with a long song to keep his creative intellectuals, but in spite of all these, he is determined to march ahead alone in the shadow of ravines.

The next poem in this series is 'My India' in which the he has portrayed the past and ancient glory of India in a marvellous manner where he says:

The lifting lure of *Vedas, Upanishad*?
The whispering radiance of
Yogis, Munis, Rishis—
Soulfilling breeze of the benign Bodhi,
Mellowing, sobering,
Sustaining melodies of *Ramayana*,
Awe inspiring, harmonising
Drum beats of *Mahabharata*.
(*Visioned Summits* 59)

But the poet is very much disappointed to the real picture of the country and so with a heavy heart he questions.

India, where all your grandeur gone?
What happened to your symphonic
Spiritualism of here and hereafter.

(*Visioned Summits* 60)

These revelations exhibit real love and a spirit of patriotism that the poet is possessing in his heart for the country. In this regard, we can remember the oft-quoted line of *The Discovery of India,* where Pandit Jawaharlal Nehru has said of India, "She is a myth and a vision of her own." And the same thought of expression can be found in the famous poem and song of D.L. Roy where he says, "Swapna diya tairi se je smriti diya ghera." In fact the cultural spiritual and intellectual values of India include the tunes of Bhakti singers, harmonic notes of Sufi saints, teachings of Guru Nanak, Kabir's song of symbolism—bliss and bond of unity, harmonic songs of Sufi saints and Vaishnavs, teachings of Ramakrishna, Vivekananda. The present India is suffering from a grievous collapse due to political and social degeneration, spurts, terrorism, hatred tongues of the young generation and as such kindness, compassion, truth, service to humanity have evaporated from society. So, to the poet, the world is a:

Savage wasteland
Of hypocritical hybrids and tiny shams
Towards a strange and unknown destiny.

(*Visioned Summits* 57)

This wasteland is full of deceitful people and they all are engaged in cheat and exploitation with the result the nation is advancing towards a strange and unknown land.

The poem 'Whispers of Beyond'—he again says,

Today I am alone
Like an alabaster soaring into nothingness
Telescoping the purple moments we spent
On the sand dunes of memory.

(*Visioned Summits* 71)

Here, the word 'alabaster' is a simile but creates an ambiguity since alabaster is a white statue made of several varieties of carbonate or sulphate of lime. The statue is an inanimate object, how can it sour? Probably, it is in poet's imagination or the poet intends to refer to the sea bird 'Albatros' that flies over the vast ocean quite alone and soars from there. S.T. Coleridge has described about this bird in his poem "He Prayeth Well...."

The poet has very aptly compared his loneliness with this sea bird who, while flying so high, might be soaring and telescoping the purple moments the poet spent with his beloved to ruminate the lost sweet memories. But the poet also reminds that the time has changed, and so, the sand-dunes might have concretised the abstract memory. Thus in course of his long journey he realises:

> With frozen whispers of beyond
> The beyond of the diminishing life-line of lights
> I drown in miraged rhapsodies.
> AII your memories a fabricated shadow
> Hanging on the ornamental borders of illusion,
> Like a spectrum returning to its broken prism.
>
> (*Visioned Summits* 73)

The poet has drawn a very beautiful imagery[7] illusion that transformms into unreal ecstasies of involvement. So, life remains to the poet:

> Life, a criss-cross crisis
> A midst dwindling destinies
> Delirious dreams And diabolic disillusions.
>
> (*Visioned Summits* 75)

Reaching at this stage of his journey, the poet feels that "Deliverance—is an opposite idea to living.... A dialectic of existence and evangelic..."

The poet in the poem "Ambiguity" confessing and above line asks himself, 'Then, what is Nirvana?' Actually, 'Nirvana' means complete emancipation of the individual which can otherwise be said ' Supreme Bliss'. Therefore, the poet ends the poem with the words 'meaning in ambiguity' (77) which suggests that both the words Deliverance and Nirvana are theoretical hypothesis and so, ambiguous in terms of reality. In the poem "Wounded Dawn" the poet expresses his anguish as his pain is sharpening when he witnesses the sufferings of humanity, death and destruction happening everywhere now and then. The poet concludes the poem, 'Tears terminate to volcanic upsurge/Man in flames—in flames Man/Smoke explosion, annihilation.'

In spite of all these contradictory ideas in the mind, the poet is serious in his journey. He says, 'It all started in right earnestness/After being convinced of tales, mystic, real and unreal' (*Visioned Summits* 82).

However, he continues his pilgrimage and comes across with the stories of the Purana, yogis of yore on Bhakti and divinity with other fables of Moses, Mount Sinai., Buddha and Bodhi Trees, Mohammed in a solitary cave at Mecca, Jesus at Jerusalem, Krishna's *upadesh* at Kurukshetra and many more such enchanting episodes that occurred in the different faiths from time to time. All hunt his psyche and coax him to write. He feels the faiths float on the cosmic ocean of light but fails to understand their enigma of the heart of emotion. So, he throws into the air the garb of worldliness to seek a home serene on his new voyage (p.53). The home serene is practically in imagination where every human being dreams to reach. To reach this home of eternal bliss (salvation), one has to cross mountains, rivers, valleys and other physical hurdles, and here, in the poem, the poet ultimately attains the final path and discovers that it is the most wonderful place. At this stage, he realises the truth of life—all other lives are unreal, a mirage, whereas the human life is the only reality. He aptly remarks, "Be alive to now, here and around" (*Visioned Summits* 86). He also realises the 'Tandava' and the dark cyclone in the mind also vanishes. He feel the sweetness of serenity of home. Home is the place where the heart of human being belongs and there only the symphonies of the heart are discovered. Here the poet has been very much influenced by the sermons of the *Bhagavad Gita*, where Sri Krishna says to his dearest disciple Arjuna, to be 'Stitpragya', that, is 'equipoise' ... it is the stage of life when no pain, no joy exhilarates the human being and one attains 'oneness' with the physical and spiritual existence. The poet says, 'I have come to terms with shadows/to face stores and joys in equipoise' (*Visioned Summits* 92). In the *Gita*, Sri Kṛishna says, 'Sukh...Dukha same kritva lamalaman jaya jayo! ....' (2/08)

"Pilgrimage", is the poem where the poet has attained the state of serenity and calmness of mind, and a part of his journey is at the end but the he restarts with the poem "Back Again":

> We are back again
> With flames of flamingos
> To the pulsating pavilions
> Of our petalic love times.
>
> (*Visioned Summits*: 88)

Since he is a wanderer, he walks with the storms and breath its immutable pride. Here, his madness returns afresh again at the thunder on the mountain ranges and faces both storms and joys in a balanced mind. The present world is materialistic and the modern life is running after gold and mirth. Hatred and jealousy overpower the sentiments and emotions of human being. Man has become mechanical. At this stage Dr. Syed is influenced by the great epic poet of the modern age, T.S.Eliot and this kind of picture has been portrayed by Eliot in his poem the "The Waste Land".

The poet, in order to restore harmony to the world of disharmony, dreams anew in his poem "New Dawn". He sings with new energy:

> In the blazing inanes of life
> I shall bring to the Universe
> A vibrating tideless song
> Which will replace
> The parched serenade.
>
> (*Visioned Summits* 113)

His earlier pessimistic thoughts and ideas have given birth to a sound optimistic beginning and so he intends to put an end to the 'parched serenade' of lamenting and weeping mankind. With new vigour and energy affirms:

I am yet to explore
The frontiers of longest pilgrimage
Of life's vast vicissitudes.

(*Visioned Summits* 149)

Prior to reaching the Summits, the poet hears the sound of the footsteps of the Almighty—the master of the Universe. He, in the penultimate poem "His Footfall Rings" narrates his mystical feelings—his inclination and enlightenment and spiritualism. He gives us a message that God blesses all human beings:

'His footfall rings!
From mystic steep
Of soul's chambers,
From lovely strings
Of chanting Hope
His footfall rings!
His footfall rings!

(*Visioned Summits* 146)

So, hearing the footfall rings, the poet says, I am yet to explore/ The frontiers of longest pilgrimage.

And this is the concluding superb poem Visioned Summits. He concludes that the spiritual journey is long, tiresome and there are many hurdles on the way. But on reaching here, one realises the realities of life—the Supreme Truth. Now he believes that the journey of life actually commences after death and that journey continues till Eternity. This is the Upanishadaic philosophical truth. The seers of the *Upanishads* attained the light after coming out through the darting dark: 'Vedahametang Purushang Mahantam Aditya Barnag Tamas Parahastata' Reaching this stage of his journey, the poet Dr. Ameeruddin has been greatly influenced by the innovative thoughts and ideas of the great Upanishadic Nature. Poet Rabindranath Tagore, who himself claims his descent from Vaishnavite bards of the medieval Bengal, owes his inspiration to the *Upanishads*. He believed that the whole world is pervaded by Brahman—the only one Creator- and the Destroyer of the Universe. So, the single credo of the

Upanishads is 'Sarvang Khaling Brahma'. He lives everywhere. Poet Dr. Syed has also totally absorbed himself with this credo, and so, he illustrates that the kingdom of God is not outside but it is within us. His spiritual vision also resembles the mysticism of William Blake. In this way, his 'Mahaprasthan' comes to an end and he visualises.

Thus, I Visioned
Summits of illuminated peaks
Of benign Nirvana
Aham Brahma, Anal Hag
And touched a moment eternal
Breathing the divine light of bliss
The Sat-Chit-Ananda !

(*Visioned Summits* 156-157)

Poet Dr. Ameeruddin's "Serenade" carries ironic tides since it is an undeclared postdated supplement and it reminds "The Wasteland" and love song of Alfred Prufrock by the great epic poet of the modern age T.S.Eliot. In the love song of Alfred J. Prufrock it has been cited that Prufrock was growing old and prematurely lost his virility. Poet Dr. Syed also expresses his personal tragedy and he is aware of crossing fifty summers. In regard to "Absolute Reality" both Dr. Syed and Prufrock evade the answer and the same essence can be smelt, 'Oh, do not ask, what is it', here the poet also feels that he cannot digest and accept the confusion of the present-day society. He says, "I moved and marched/and mangled in the jungle." It has been observed that in the two poems the Prufrock poem closes with a reference to the sea-storm whereas "Eloquent Serenade" concludes with a positive note—a realistic approach.

Incidentally, it is also seen that "The Wasteland" concludes *with* the vibrating notes of the *Upanishad*: 'Datta, dayadhyam, damyata/Shanti, Shanti, Shanti', It means—Give, Sympathise, Control—Peace, Peace, Peace. Poet Eliot is the unrivalled master of symbolism and allusions whereas poet Dr. Ameeruddin's style and attitude are alliterative. His poetry is out and out philosophical and mystic in nature.

Dr. Ranchana Mehrotra has rightly said, 'Dr. Syed Ameeruddin's mysticism is a relation of the present.... His poetry illustrates the truth that the kingdom of God is not outside. It is within us....He is a poet of joy and peace.... His ecstatic and lovely poems make him a fascinating poet of today.'

While concluding the discussion, it may be said that *Visioned Summits* is full of melodramatic poems enlightened with introspection as well as realistic spiritualism of life. Dr. Syed is a versatile genius with an outstanding knowledge of different faiths and scriptures and is at home in their applications. The book is a pride of possession of the present commentator to whom the great soul and the world poet Dr. Syed Ameeruddin has very kindly resented.

15

Quest for Self: The Poetry of Syed Ameeruddin

—D.C. Chambial

Since man began to differentiate between body and soul, he began to enquire about the mystic phenomenon of soul and what happens to it after the ephemeral existence, in the form of body, vanishes in the ultimate end known as death. Various writers, through the ages, have responded differently to death and self. Burns calls death 'the poor man's dearest friend-/The kindest and the best.' John Donne does not consider death mighty and strong and warns him, 'Death be not proud though some have called thee/Mighty and dreadful.' 'We do not die of death:/We die of vertigo,' philosophises Archibald Macleish; and Shakespeare consider 'death,/The undiscovered country from whose bourn/No traveller returns.' *The Old Testament* proclaims about this mundane existence: 'For dust thou art, and unto dust shalt thou return.' About this eternal truth, the Gita preaches. One who is born must die.... Besides the knowledge of death, man has also ever delved deep into the deeps of vast ocean of knowledge to fathom and pick up pearls about the knowledge of self: If 'Proper study of mankind is Man' for Alexander Pope, then Thales exhorts men: 'Know thyself.' Edgar A. Guest says, 'I want to be fit for myself to know.'

Syed Ameeruddin is already a well-known signature in the domain of Indian English poetry with *Visioned Summits* and *Visions of Deliverance* besides being the founder president of International Academy of World Poetry. *National Herald* (Delhi) claims that "His poetry can, at best be described as a conglomeration of the metaphysical, the surreal and existential." And *The Hindu* holds that the poems in *Visioned Summits* are about 'the search for ultimate meaning in life' and *Deccan Herald* (Bangalore) finds that 'The divine light of bliss overwhelms him.' *The New Indian Express* comments that 'The poet, in a blissful state of spiritual enlightenment yearns for peace on earth.' Krishna Srinivas thinks that 'Ameeruddin is Primarily a poet of social, metaphysical, spiritual and humanitarian concerns and philosophical encounters to unravel the seeming realities of life' ('Opinions' 177-78). The objective, in the background of the said observations about his poetry, of this paper is to study his poetry for quest of self as demonstrated in his poetry for finding "ultimate meaning" in the present manifest life. A critical study of his poems, in *Visioned Summits*, will be taken to explicate the thesis of the paper.

Soul or self can best be interpreted as immaterial aspect or essence of a person, conjoined with the body during life and separable at death. Soul and self become identical in philosophical and literary studies. Most of the religions embrace the idea of the dual nature of soul, but Buddhism rejects and terms it misleading. Different world religions have varied views about soul/self:

> The ancient Egypt conceived of a dual soul, one surviving death but remaining near the body, while the other proceeded to the realm of the dead. The early Hebrews did not consider soul as distinct from the body, but later Jewish writers perceived the two as separate. Christian theology adopted the Greek concept of an immortal soul, adding the notion that God created the soul and infused it in the body at conception. In Islam the soul is believed to come into existence at the same time as the body but is everlasting and subject to eternal bliss or torment after the death of the body. In HINDUISM each soul, or *ATMAN* was created at the beginning of time and imprisoned in the earthly body; at death the soul is said to pass to a new body according to the law of KARMA. Buddhism negates the idea of soul, asserting that any sense of an individual self is illusory (*Britannica* 101).

The poem 'Eloquent Serenade' opens with parting when the persona claims, 'Yesterday, you parted with me/With an unrelenting wound' (23) and the "wind sings broken melodies" (ibid.). The poem apparently sings his love to one who has gone away leaving him alone. He feels hurt: 'With an unrelenting wound.' His songs which he calls broken, because of his wails, are in the air. A note of inherent psychic suffering comes to the fore. And then the line, 'No, I will not die in your memories', suggests that the persona has decide to forget the beloved who has deserted him recently. He tells the readers that he will no more 'see my (his) face through/The mangled sunlight in your (her) eyes.' Or it may be his decision not to come face to face with the one who has left him. To undo this shock, he resolves to 'walk/Into the alphabetic anarchy'. The phrase 'alphabetic anarchy' suggests a journey into the world of poetry which lies before him but is in bedlam. He has not identified himself with anybody and any place and feels lonely. Even in the crowd, he feels lonely. He avers:

> I have always been alone amidst the multitude
> A nowhere man with a lonesong satchel.
> I have raged against the volcanoes
> I have silenced the scissoring storms
> And found its silence was a symphony. (25)

However, the phrase 'a lonesong satchel' is ambiguous. 'lonesong,' as an adjective qualifying the noun 'satchel', as the sense demands, should be lonesome. (The printing errors in the book certainly add to the critics'/readers' dilemma in clear interpretation.) It may be a portmanteau word coined by joining 'lone' and 'song' to suggest lonely song. Here the persona projects himself in the image of a lonely person moving in the crowd of people without finding any identity with any one, which makes him feel lonely. He, as a traveller 'Into the alphabetic anarchy,' is concerned only about his songs, that he thinks, he carries in his 'satchel.' In his solo voyage, he has encountered several 'volcanoes' and 'scissoring storms'—vicissitudes in his life. They have not deterred him from his onward march and search of his identity. These 'volcanoes,' that stood in his way to stop him, have only enraged him and the protagonist divulges that because of his resolute will he has overcome and 'silenced the scissoring storms.' He has found in this 'silence'—peace—'a symphony' that is life-giving, harmonious, enlivening and refreshing energy.

He is moving on all alone in agreement with Hinduism. He does not look for any companion. He comes across 'horrified horizons of our time'—faces 'the surreal' (33) experiences of contemporary life. He faces the reality which is bewildering and crumbling. He realises: 'Ram and Rahim—/The one and only one Reality.' The God is One and only One. All religions and different names given to the Supreme One are artificial and arbitrary catering to the handiness of the people who have devised them. The ultimate truth dawns upon him that all human beings are also alike as there is only one God, though different religions call Him with different names; different names do not make Him different. The truth is the essential unity of man—that all men irrespective of their religions/castes/creeds are primarily similar biologically—and God. All disparity of this world and anarchy will vanish as soon as humanity realises this truth. The protagonist's anguish finds voice in the following lines:

> In the dark the death scorches me
> The fevered soul discovers its own secret
> In the tattered lull that surrounds me.
> The thought of death is terrible. (33)

He interprets the present existence as dark. He is unable to bear the loss of his dear one's death that has left an 'unrelenting wound' (23) on his psyche. His 'fevered soul' finds its own hidden essence in the quietude that encircles him. This 'tattered lull' is nothing but the vacuity created by the death of his dear one. And, perhaps, the secret is that the very 'thought of death is terrible.' The word 'terrible' is the pivotal word which reveals the protagonist's agony. This anguish is so intense that his present existence, he feels, is no less than being in inferno. However, he has one solace that he is a poet and 'poet never dies.' He maintains: 'When I die, I am redeemed' (34). Under the present situation his fear of death has left him and he, even in his death, finds his salvation which will make him immortal as a poet: he will continue to live in his poems through the ages to come till eternity. Thus death cannot touch his poetic self transmuted into his poems.

His mind is not attached to any place. He is 'a wanderer' and 'a nowhere man' (35). 'Gypsy river runs through my (his) bones.' It is not in his nature to stick to one place. He is a wanderer so he has to move on and on. He is never to look back. He has a goal to achieve in his wanderings. He knows that his journey is long and he cannot stop until the goal is achieved. It reminds one of Robert Frost's line, 'And miles to go before I sleep' from his poem "Stopping by Woods." The 'memories of fractured sunsets'—loss of some hopes—and 'love times'—time spent with his beloved—no more haunt him. He has become indifferent to them. His 'secret grief of/Humanity and existence' (36) has overwhelmed him.

The poverty of the slum-dwellers saddens him. He has spent many years in search of his goal, which still remains unattained. In his wanderings, he has 'encountered ... the horror of opaque living' (39). The adjective "opaque" does not mean solid, thick or something that does not let light pass through it, but it connotes the hard/difficult life of the poverty-stricken people. 'However, my (his) quest continued' ((39), he declares. In order to find an answer to his pursuit, he visited godmen, mountains, seas and even sun (39-40), which metaphorically suggest every possible means to find an answer to his query but without any avail—but all were silent. None helped him find his answer/solution. Consequently he decided to explore the mystery of poverty-ridden humanity and 'accepted the reality,/As we accept the seasons' (41). One has no control over nature and seasons; one cannot have them by their choice, so he also accepted the reality that lay before him—the reality of this existence, the reality of the rich and the poor. Here his pessimism surfaces that poverty is natural like the seasons and nothing can be done to end it. He 'served mankind' to coddle his 'seeping self' (43). He has come to a pass where he sees only the 'faraway rain' which has bedimmed his goal—'nowhere goal'(47). Yet he tells himself: 'I have to discover the secret of myself' (47). He does not give in to despair and hardships that try to delude him from his objective.

The persona again admits: 'My reality is my loneliness/My quest is my self' in 'Vicissitudes of Life' (52). He considers this world a 'savage wasteland' while he comes face to face with reality—'Reality trembles in my eyes' (56) and his loneliness continues with his resolution to explore 'the wasteland/Of hypocritical hybrids and tiny shams,/Towards a strange and unknown destiny' (57). In this wasteland deceitful people and frauds abound which is nothing but mutual deception: all are engaged in deceiving one another. In "Whispers of Beyond", he sings:

> Today I am alone
> Like an alabaster soaring into nothingness
> Telescoping the purple moments we spent
> On the sand dunes of memory. (71)

With the help of a simile of an alabaster he reinforces the premise of loneliness and tries to capture the 'purple moments'—emotional moments—already spent. However, ambiguity again perplexes the clear thinking of the critic/ reader: for, 'alabaster' as a noun, is white stone used for making statues and other objects of decoration so how it can 'soar'. If the verb soar is taken as key-word then it must be albatross, a large white ocean bird, which flies alone 'Telescoping the purple moments' from the great height above the ocean where it flies. It suggests focusing on the highly emotional moments/times spent in the past—'sand dunes of memory'. These moments live only in the protagonist's memory. These are now fading: 'sand dunes' connote the changing nature of sand-dunes in desert and concretise the abstract 'memory' in this image. Thus, in his journey, he prepares himself to 'drown in the miraged rhapsodies' (73). These transform into unreal ecstasies of involvement. 'Life', remains for him, 'a criss-cross crisis' (75). For him 'Deliverance' is an opposing idea to living—'a dialectic/ Of existence' and 'Nirvana' is a philosophical hypothesis to find 'meaning in ambiguity' (77). It diametrically suggests that 'deliverance' and 'nirvana' are theoretical ideas which are true only theoretically and not pragmatically.

The march continues non-stop, as the protagonist admits: 'In all seriousness, I set on my pilgrimage/.../To seek a home serene' (83). This home serene is a place only imagined to be in heaven, if it exists, and not anywhere else. In his endeavour to find this home of eternal bliss (salvation), he has to cross mountains, valleys, rivers forests which reminds the readers of Raja Rao's story, "Companions," in which Moti Khan, the snake charmer, vows to find God and crosses such physical hurdles to reach Sheikh Chisti's Tomb at Fatehpur Sikri to find eternal peace. Like Moti Khan, our hero's courage and determination escorted him in his pilgrimage. Ultimately, the protagonist in the poem 'reached the final path' (85) and discovered that it was very 'wonderful ... to be a 'Human being' (85). This is the truth—the ultimate truth: all other lives imagined are unreal, 'mirage', while this human life is the only reality that none can escape. The poet aptly remarks: 'Be alive to now, here and around' (86). He also realises: 'I have come to terms with shadows/To face storms and joys in equipoise' (92). Thus he attains a state of 'equipoise' as propounded in the *Gita*: (*Bhagavad Gita* II 38). Equipoise is a state when neither any pain tortures nor joy exhilarates: one attains oneness with physical and spiritual existence. All shadows and illusions of this world stand banished.

The need of restoring harmony to the disharmonious world is paramount. He is keen to bring:

> to the Universe
> A vibrating tideless song
> which will replace
> The parched serenade. ...
> Heralding a—
> Resplendent new dawn. ("New Dawn" 113-14).

His earlier pessimism gives in to optimism. He now sounds optimistic; he talks of beginning a 'new dawn' which will put an end to 'parched serenade'—weeping humanity. However, he has not reached the end point of his journey, it is yet to come. He re-affirms: 'I am yet to explore/The frontiers of longest pilgrimage' (149): longest journey is the journey of life-after-death, which continues till eternity. It is everlasting. Life does not end with physical or biological death. It continues ever and ever .... He puts an end to the discussion by saying that 'Only those return to Eternity/Who on earth seek out eternity' (157). He hypothesizes, like the mystics of yore, that only such individuals, who in their physical life endeavour to and aspire for eternity/moksha/salvation, through their deeds and meditation, are able to enter that metaphysical domain of existence.

The poet, through his poetry, seeks to bring about a change from a life of suffering, as he has observed it around him, to a joyous life free from all prevalent incongruities and sorrows. Whatever an individual does, he does it for his happiness—physical and/or spiritual. In this respect, Dr Rachana Mehrotra pertinently comments: 'Dr. Syed craves for true spiritual happiness, which brings unity and harmony ...' (169).

Thus, the discussion can be bound up with the remark that the poet, Syed Ameeruddin, like any other contemplative individual on this earth, also thinks about his self and tries to know what lies beyond the bourns of ephemeral existence and how this existence, even after the termination of bodily life, can be made to exist eternally. He begins as a being attached to his love, but is shocked when she departs leaving him agonised. He decides to find Truth and begins his journey, visits so many places and persons to realise his goal but is disillusioned everywhere and, ad finem seeks to face sun and shade of this life in 'equipoise' and realises that 'human' life is the most important life where one can make or mar one's future life of attaining immortality. His mission is yet on and he admits that the end is far off, but before that end comes, he has to search the limits of 'longest journey' of life in order to know and quench his thirst of his quest for self. His poetry is out and out philosophical and mystical which endeavours to unravel the mysteries of present and future in the form of manifest, non-manifest and beyond manifest-life.

Works Cited

Ameeruddin, Syed. *Visioned Summits*. 2nd ed. Madras: International Poets Academy, 2005.Print. All references in the text are from this edition.

Britannica Ready Reference Encyclopedia. Vol. 9. New Delhi: Encyclopedia Britannica (India) Pvt. Ltd., 2005.Print.

Dictionary of Quotations. Delhi: Sahni Publications, 2005. Print.

16

A Critical Analysis of the Poetry of Prof. Syed Ameeruddln

—Har Prasad Sharma

Prof. Dr. Syed Ameeruddin occupies his position as one of the most significant poets in the galaxy of international poets. He scatters glittering pearls of his ideass thoughts and emotions in the republic of letters. His poetry attracts readers as much as the beauty of a pretty young girl. This is the magic of his poetry.

While everything is perishable in the world Prof. Ameeruddin rightly thinks about the immortality of a poet about which he writes so beautifully in the following lines:

> A Poet never dies, he goes on forever,
> No grave can bury him,
> No monument can confine him.
> A poet is for all times, and for all climes,...
>
> (*Visioned Summits* 34-55)

These thought currents about the immortality of a poet are true as steel indeed in the above stanza.

Dr. Syed Ameeruddin is as good as another Omar Khayyam of the present time who wrote *Rubayat* that packed with the thoughts of the existing realities of human life which made his work immortal in the field of poetry. So also Dr. Ameeruddin's poetry is full of wisdom, full of meaning and fully reformative for those who go astray in their difficult journey of life just to inform them that this life is to be led with joy and merriment and it is not so futile as it is comprehended by many people in the world. So he writes:

> There should be laughter and smile everywhere
> My hands should create the new language of love
> New alphabets of equality,
> New syllables of solace
> So that, fireflies may weave the manuscript
> Of man's rainbow dreams,.
>
> (*Visioned Summits* 41)

Dr. Syed is a mansion in the house of poetry. He writes romantic poems, philosophical poems, mystical poems, nature poems, man-making poems, war poems, spiritual poems, short poems, long poems and many poems of the like being a poet of rich experience which enlighten the brains of the people. Such poets are rare in the literary firmament today. His poetry is of a high order beyond a shadow of doubt that compels man to think that his life given by GOD is to pray to Him, so that, he is able to reach Him through prayers and through his noble deeds in his life. He writes poetry about Allah, about Rama, about Krishna and about Shiva which fills one's mind with the thought that one should ever contemplate upon God who is the ultimate reality and who is one without the second though He. is known by many names in each language of the World.

Here, I am going to critically evaluate his two recently published Masterpiece collection of poems: (1) *Visioned Summits* (1995) (2) *Visions of Deliverance* (2006) which contains very intellectually engrossing and emotionally captivating poems that offer a vast wealth of knowledge to readers to think over the existence of human life.

In his poem "Life's Enigma", he thinks once again of earthly things that are in existence falls into non-existence to prove this truth to the hilt that everything on earth is short-lived and nothing is permanent and so he writes thus contemplating upon the nothingness of life also as a philosopher:

> All existence
> Is being, becoming and withering.
>
> (*Visioned Summits* 123)

Then once again the poet looks puzzled and he seems unable to solve the mystery of life like endless thinkers and philosophers that, after all, what is for this human existence and what is its ultimate mission to live on earth, so he writes in a confused mood in this fashion:

What are we?
What are we?
Why are we ?
What is world to Universe?
(*Visioned Summits* 11)

Dr. Ameeruddin is a poet of distinction. He thinks about his own redemption in this manner which conveys two meanings at the same time.

First: he will get his redemption on earth after his death and second: he will also be redeemed from the old cage of his body

when his soul flies away from it. So he writes in his Collections of poems from *Visioned Summits:*

My redemption is here,
When I die, I am redeemed.
(*Visioned Summits* 11)

Dr. Ameeruddin is not an ordinary poet, he is extraordinary who makes a thorough study of each and every subject and then he writes what he feels about it. He is a right-thinking man who writes what is right of a thing after his right analysis of it. Once again, he talks about the enigma of life. How man comes and how he returns in different moods from this earth. That he oscillates between birth and death facing distress, misfortunes and death in the long run, so he writes like this, enveloped in despondency:

What is this enigma, after all
Bottoming and peaking encounters
Reaped distress and harboring longings
Haze and maze of birth, copulation, death.
(*Visioned Summits* 4)

Now in the following beautiful stanza with many and varied realities of human existence it is apparent that the poet has touched many branches of literature in his life. So he writes:

Existence is a cosmic drama
Where life and death
Are interlined in struggle
For a sustained sojourn in this world
To suffer the trauma of ego-weakness.

(*Visioned Summits* 120)

How true it is that man exists here to play a cosmical drama where struggle between life and death goes on during the short stay of his on earth to let him suffer for the weakness of his ego. For this reason *Deccan Herald* of Bangalore writes that '*We are part of the incarnate cosmos, part of the Earth*'. And *National Herald* of New Delhi writes of him that 'Dr. Syed's poetry is really an enigma, because it conjures up so many images, throws up so many ideas, sees life in so many different ways that each adjective merely confines him and is applicable only to one aspect'. Sometimes Dr. Syed seems plunged into the thought that the journey of life is not a sleeveless errand and therefore man should live life for the day and so he writes as an optimist:

Try to wake up
At every new-dawn
Like afresh
Dew drenched petal,
Live life for the day
And leave the rest to oblivion.

(*Visioned Summits* 123)

Longing for a new day and a new experience, though the poet is also aware of the fate of the world whose ultimate result is this:

But the ultimate
This is a world of fossilation
Decay and delusion.

(*Visioned Summits* 124)

Therefore *Deccan Herald* writes of him that, 'He feels the magnificent here and now of life in the flesh of ours alone and ours only for a time'. Professor Ameeruddin reveals in his poetry deep philosophy of life captivating thoughts, mind-pleasing imaginations and tales of love that seen in the following poem of love in which we find the beauty of Christina Rosetti's poetry.

When we sat face to face
We are like the waves
Gently marching towards the eye of the storm
When we close out eyes We descend
The crumbling staircase to oblivion
A new day breaks from visual rhapsody
A gesture. A whisper, A new dawn dances.

(*Visions of Deliverance* 49)

Dr. Syed is another Khaleel Gibran of the present day for he thinks like him and writes like him that we can see in this stanza of his:

Savage sunsets, broken daybreaks
Haunted memories down a strange lane
And mute wilderness of the mountains
All dissolve in transparent resplendent
Life sparkled again in the seed
In the breath, in the love and in the soul
A vibrant trance and a new dawn

(*Visioned Summits* 89)

Poet Dr. Ameeruddin is as good as Wordsworth whose one stanza of poem is as breathtaking in beauty:

Again, we are face to face in the vast
As the ocean of the night fills everything
Let us listen to the voice of the stars
And bathe naked in the
Silvery mist of the full moon ....

(*Visioned Summits* 91-92)

Dr. Syed creates newness, freshness, excellence, brilliance, fascination, uniqueness, wonder, truth, love and magic in his poetry which attract the attention of readers to read his work with gripping interest. And he has wonderful command over the English language that creates poetic beauty in his works as it should be. He is a world thinker who thinks about the welfare of mankind, who minks about "world peace and asks the warmongers to sheath their swords so peace may come once again under the sky. So, the *New Indian Express* writes: 'The poet, in a blissful state of spiritual enlightenment yearns for peace on earth.'

Dr. Syed writes like Alexander Pope in his masterpiece poem, "The Pomp of Gold", that while a man rolls in wealth how he's dead in sin, how he drowns in the sea of sorrow and how he loses freedom of the self which is so necessary for a human being to live on earth.

> Wealth hovers around
> A wealthy man
> Like a vulture hovers
> Over a carcass,
> Yesterday's freedom of
> The Sheppard is gone
> Today, he is a prisoner of
> Greed and mirth
> Engulfing himself into the realm of
> Restlessness, dismay, anguish and misery
> Yesterday's soaring of
> The singing bird is gone
> ....
> Today, he is a slave
> To the pomp officklish gold
> Virtue, love and delight, His erstwhile companions
> Freedom and fearlessness,
> His yesterday assets.
> Today, he is like
> A frightened lamb
> Among the wolves
> Amidst the frowning faces of
> Hatred of jealously.
> The thoughts of gold and glory
> are nothing but an eternal inferno.
> Then, what for
> These serpentine temptations of glitter?
>
> (*Visioned Summits* 95-97)

After knowing of the surrounding difficulties in the life of a greedy man who loves to hoard gold in his coffer the poet comes to the conclusion like this:

Wealth is good,
It is serves like a warming
Money is like water,
It flows towards the parching paths
And it enlivens the others
Who turn it upon his fellowman. ....

(*Visioned Summits* 98)

Dr. Syed is indeed a world poet who writes magnificent poetry with unvarnished truth that appeals to one and all with the result wherever he goes he is honoured and welcomed with open arms. What he writes about life and nirvana in his poem "Ambiguity" is worth noting:

Life, a criss-cross crisis.
Amidst dwindling destinies
Delirious dreams
And diabolic disillusions,
World, a frensied humdrum existence
Of banality and triviality
Of nauseating human experience

Of cerebral jigsaw puzzles
Of bated broth and
Spiritual destitution.
Reality, an elusive enigma
Between here and hereafter
A ravishing rainbow.
Between life and death
A hazy horizon
Between material and metaphysical,
Deliverance, dialectic
Of existence and evangelic
Poised on the horns of a dilemma,
The ambiguity and the ambivalence.
Then, what is Nirvana?
Reflecting on the smoky layers
Of gloom and solace
And seeing—
Meaning in ambiguity. .....

(*Visioned Summits* 75-77)

Dr. K. R. Srinivasa Iyengar writes of him, 'Since your first book of poems you have been active, and won a name for yourself in the field of Indian poetry in English.' Dr. Ameeruddin feels that there is nothing sweeter than, and better than one's home where calm and peace ever prevail, where people who discover harmony sounds agreeable to ears and have a strong feeling that their heart ever in essence resides only in their native place where they were born an brought up. That is why this is said, 'East or West Home is the Best'. So the poet writes these lines which are so accurate:

Home of course is sweet and serene
For those who discover symphonies of heart:
Home is a place where your heart belongs.

(*Visioned Summits* 86)

Dr. Syed is one of those high-ranking poets who ever writes chef oeuvre poem which will ever remain unscratched upon the wall of time for the welfare of the mankind.

W.H. Auden says that, "Man is history-making creature who can neither repeat his past nor leave it behind'. The poet has a wide knowledge of the past as well as of the present history of the world. Apparently he seems proud of the highest glory of India upon which he contemplates seriously and asks certain questions about it from India in a melancholy mood in this fashion in his poem "My India":

India, where all your grandeur gone!
What happened to—
The lilting lure of Vedas, Upanishads?
The whispering radiance of
Yogis, Muni's, Rishis—
Soul fitting breeze of the benign Bodhi,
Mellowing, sobering,
Sustaining melodies of Ramayana,
Awe inspiring, harmonising
Drum beats of Mahabharata,
He further asks about its past glory.
....
India, where all your grandeur gone!
What is this desolation

What has set in?
What clouds of gloom
Have cast these shadows?
What is this churning
Of the blinding dust?
What spider is weaving
This web of bewilderment?
What is this evil design
Of decimation-

(*Visioned Summits* 59)

He again asks how the transformation of time has now marred it; beauty and glory.

India, where all your grandeur gone!
What is this
Disease of imbecility?
What is this
New cult of blurred youth,
Where tongues of hatred
Licking each others brain;
Where sense of belonging
Is reaching its brink.
Who has cast
These shimmering shadows?
What is this sinister look
That has ceased
The smiles from innocent faces?

(*Visioned Summits* 60)

And yet the poet sadly asking broken hearted—INDIA, where has all your grandeur gone!

I know! I know!!
Some nasty finger has stuck
Into your dreaming eyes.
I know! I know!!
You are sobbing and bleeding,
With bruises of infidelity, inhumanity,
And frantic fervor of religious hatred,
With manifold harms and hurts
Inflicted by your misled
And miscreant children.

(*Visioned Summits* 60)

W.S. Gilbert writes about the power of love: 'Its love that makes the world goes round.' So Dr. Syed Ameeruddin writes something in his masterpiece poem entitled 'Turkey' about its love. A fragment runs as under:

You gave the world a visionary, Yunus Emre
Whose message capsule in verse-eternal
As love man, love Universe, love God
Love man as acme of all creations,
Love nature and visualise the
Divine radiance everywhere
And experience the bliss of God,
The Sat, Chit, Ananda.
Turkey! You symbolise the Essence
Of spiritual Beauty]
Man's life on earth a Visioned March
From Darkness to light;
From untruth to righteousness:
From Death to immortality.
"When love arrives, all reads and flaws are gone?

(*Visions of Deliverance* 110)

Hence there is a Greek proverb, 'The heart that loves is always young'. He has written another poem on love in his 'Love Time' in accordance with what Sebastian R.N. Chamfort thinks about love is tantalisingly depicted here by Dr. Syed which is really breath-taking and worthreading.

Tonight let me face my strange destiny.
The honeyed memories—
And patelled pleasures
Drifted to the shores—
Like the foamy waves,
Thus, we celebrated our togetherness—
The confluence of the swirling rivers—
The meeting of the distant sea
With the azure sky—at the horizon...
A sculptor's dream.
A statue of Ajanta..
Thus,
I smelt,
All the secret wine waves
Of your body

And swayed with them in every movement
And listened to the orchestra
Of sensual melody
In that trance of romantic rhapsody
Suddenly, you twisted tantalisingly
With the twists and wriggles—
Of a fitful snake—
And enclosed my body swarming.
I kissed you on the neck
And tickled your hard nipples in that
Honey splashing, nectar mood—
In your ecstasy, you possessed me.
Hard to yourself
To touch the dizzy zeniths—
Of exotic heights;
At that, I entered you as the evening sun
Enters into the dusky deep ocean,

(*Visions of Deliverance* 103)

Professor Ameeruddin is a glittering ornament to the literary circle who creates extraordinary beauty, diction, metaphor in his poems which are always flabbergasting. The structure of his each poem is perfect in construction from every point of literary view. As long as the clock of skin and bones a man wears on earth how deep attachment he has to his near and dear is utterly explicit from the poet's first poem of his poetry book 'A Prayer—For My Grandson....' Martha Graham writes in this connection that "The body says what words cannot". Therefore the poet writes in this way about his *'Grandson in a Prayer'* in love and amazement!

Who are you my Jitter angel....!
Your smile radiates divine sparkles
Your eyes twinkle
Like morning stars
Your chirpy mono-syllables
Scintillate Autumn birds
Your tangling toddle
Titillates peacock dance
Your forehead reflects
Twilighty dawn
Your slumber in the cradle
Symphonies serenity

Your looks tantalise
Eternal embers of veracity.

(*Visions of Deliverance* 25-26)

Dr. Syed knows what poetry is because he is at home in poetry writing craft. He works wonder in his poetry every time. That is why John Keats writes: 'Poetry should surprise by a fine excess and not be singularity it should strike the reader as a wording of his own highest thoughts, and appear almost a remembrance.' Hence, the poet writes in his poem "If I Were You......" a fragment is given below-

If I were you, I will be true
To haunting bliss that ever is
The shining bridge of longing glees
That roll their floods in heart's abyss
If I were you, I will be true
To dreamy heights our beaming lights
Fling raging love that flames rejoice
And throws for fires of our joys!

(*Visions of Deliverance* 161-162)

Therefore Wallace Stevens defines the character of a poet in this way—'The poet is the priest of the invisible.' And what should be his style of writing, writes Aristotle. 'A good style must, first of all, be clear. It must ... be appropriate', we find all these qualities in Dr. Syed's poetry undoubtedly.

Today man is crossing sword with Nature with the result he is facing its fury time and again for his own destruction which is a matter of deep distress and despondency. There is a Latin proverb: 'Nature is our Mother'. So William Penn writes, 'If we are happy if we studies nature more in natural things and acted according to nature, whose rules are few plain and most reasonable.' The learned poet warns the people of the world in his poem, "Mystery of the Divine" not to fight with Nature which is the mystery of the Divine.

Mankind can never forget
That day of delectable deluge
That hoary hour of myriad deaths.
Looking at this quietus quietude

Man's maneuvering ego
Torn to smithereens—of smoky screams—
Reflecting on the delirious—
Exuding explosions of nature
In mutilating meanderings
A sudden flux
Of tycoonic tidal waves—
In the avatar of Tsunami—
A overnight vicarious
Volcanic floods of fury
In the garb of a blazing infernos—
An unaware
Spiraling spin of the earth
In the form of quivering quacks—
An unexpected flashy floods

(*Visions of Deliverance* 118)

In the visage of criss-crossing cyclones
Or, the big bang of
An astounding asteroids..
AH this is a warning to mankind
To realise the reality
Of uncertainty and the unknown.
And the unraveling
Mute mystery of the Divine.

(*Visions of Deliverance* 119)

Dr. Syed is an embodiment of humanity, philanthropist and a torch of civilisation who writes the truth, as he sees it, in human life with frankness and fearlessness. Some critics who recall his poetry may raise an accusing finger at him consuming with envy that his poetry is sensual and obscene. But, the critics should know that romantic poetry is a part and parcel of world literature which is inevitable. Philosophical, psychological, mystical as we'll as poetry on other subjects is not read so much by readers throughout the world as the romantic poetry is read with tremendous interest and is highly appreciated. Poetry on man and woman-love is always fascinating, thrilling and enchanting for one and all everywhere. The statues in Khajuraho, in Madhya Pradesh, India, can be seen by such critics where man and women are exhibited in stark nakedness even in compromising positions.

Great writers of the world have written enough about them whose books are still famous in historical books. Samuel Taylor Coleridge writes about critics and book reviewers as it is 'Reviewers are usually people who would have been poets, historians, biographers, if they could, they have tried their talents at one or the other, and have failed. Therefore they turn critics'.

How true it there are lot of critics of this type who are not impartial in reviewing a poet's book. A critic must be impartial who should write merits and demerits about a book using a decent language so that truth is known to readers about the book. He should not be biased at all as a good critic. There are two kinds of critics. First, who are brave as a lion who tell the truth at the face of a living author about his work; and the second, who are timid as a hare who cast stones of a dead author to paint him as black as they can while he is not alive to defend himself or to give them a fitting reply

Dr. Krishna Srinivas, the world renowned poet and critic writes about Dr. Syed's masterpiece poem, "The Visions of Deliverance" .... Having traced the journey of the soul from the womb to womb, he goes beyond where the souls encounter 'twin tunnels' at the 'beacon light', the dark and despicable souls are 'crushed and crashed' in an 'abysmal sea of fire' and 'tortured to molten pieces'. He envisions these souls being punished, not in an everlasting fare, but 'in fumes' where they are;

> Drifted into layers within layers
> Of flames—multidimensional
> Till a space of timeless time.
> Till the souls are crystalled and crafted
> Molded and shaped—in molten lava
> To the pristine peaks of purity
> And then finally bathed
> In the mellowed flames of green
> And made to wait in repentance
> To receive the radiance
> To grace of eternal light
> To experience the eternity
> And the blissful—eternal bounty.
>
> (*Visions of Deliverance* 197-198)

Dr. Krishna further adds that having told us about the evil soul plight he goes into follow the other souls who enter the second tunnel. They are in ecstasy bathed in 'a spectacular panorama of light'. These souls have attained the ultimate enlightenment or what the poet call, 'Deliverance', The poet wakes up from his vision to discover it was dream. But what makes it so fascinating is the concept of the bad soul: being 'purified' and not as many people believe, in an everlasting hell, it is interesting to note that this is the same concept that is offered by writer like Melvin More in his "Where God Lives" and James Van Praagh in "Reaching to Heaven". In this respect I can put Dr. Syed on the place of Guru—"A Mellowed Mystic"—who has had a vision of the after life and of Deliverance, not only for himself but for all of us.

Dr. Syed Ameeruddin is a highbrow with a rich experience about the world and human life and he writes such powerful poetry which leaves an indelible impression upon the minds of reader. Truly speaking, his poetry contains several gospel truths that make his poetry immortal in the world literature and therefore it has a significant place in it—for all times to come to influence the universal sensibilities of mankind in general.

17

Syed Ameeruddin as a Didactic Poet

—S. Kumaran

Syed Ameeruddin is one of the eminent poets writing in English today. His works have been translated into several other languages and are critically acclaimed in India and abroad. He has published six collections of poems and three reputed anthologies on world poetry. This analysis attempts at identifying how he uses poetry as a medium to express his: perception and philosophy of life, views on relationship, concern for humanity, universal brotherhood, care for the universe, and the reflection of the present day world.

Ameeruddin's poems impress the readers through their vivacity and fusion of multifarious ideas. In "Eloquent Serenade," he reveals the pangs of love and separation, rationality of human life, religious meaninglessness, degeneration of culture, terrorism, power of poetry and his philosophy of life. In the beginning of the poem, the poet mourns that his companion in whom he had rested his confidence had abandoned him halfway and parted with him and left him 'with an unrelenting wound' (*Visioned Summits*) to face 'an unsure, season where the wind sings broken melodies' (*Visioned Summits*). The poet also questions the ongoing activities of the world and finds no rationality behind the actions. He wonders, 'What is this daggers of dark on a moonless night. What is this trailing of blood down the dale of shadows? What is this bleeding cry that shrouds the brooding hills' (*Visioned Summits*). The poet is disgusted with the religion of his time and exposes exploitation, violence and bloodshed in the name of religion.

In "Eloquent Serenade," he asserts that in our time, 'Buddha's bodhi,' Gurunanak's compassion,' (*Visioned Summits*) and 'Gandhi's ahimsa' (*Visioned Summits*) have lost their meaning and purpose as people 'in the frenzied endeavours of determining an abode for Ram and Rahim' (*Visioned Summits*) forget to realise the sameness of 'Ishwar-Allah-Tere Nam' (*Visioned Summits*). The poet is shocked to find the 'whirlwind of darkness' (*Visioned Summits*) that unveils the 'culture of human bomb and AK47S terminating many a shining stars to smithereen Bombay blast—Ayodhya devastation, Somalian shrieks, Bosnian bereavements, Godmen gossips, milk miracles Rathyatras, Padayatras' (*Visioned Summits*) that have changed the abode of peace, into a place of 'rivalry and ruthlessness' (*Visioned Summits*). Further, he mourns that the 'Himalayan valley, a paradise of purple peace has become a citadel for militant inferno'(*Visioned Summits*) and the people fight in the name of Gurunanak and Gurudwars and shed blood of their brethren and dispel love and humanity.

Through "Eloquent Serenade" the poet bemoans the birth of anarchy through the mushrooming of states, development of 'racism and religious bigotry, computerisation, globalisation, satellite communication, and interstellar transmission' (*Visioned Summits*). Further, he points out 'environmental holocaust, religious fundamentalism, ethnic and racial vandalism, political hegemony, national pride, economic disparity, social discrepancy, abnormality, obscenity, shallowness, sensuality, amorality, paranoid passions, devilish dareness' (*Visioned Summits*) as an 'echo of swan song' (*Visioned Summits*) for the oncoming deluge of humanity. Amidst these chaos of the present day world, the poet keeps his faith in the transforming power of his poetic enterprise and assures that he 'shall not be buried in these sullen graveyards' (*Visioned Summits*) as a poet never dies and he goes on forever. Moreover, grave can neither bury him nor a monument confine him as a poet is for 'all times, and for all climes' (*Visioned Summits*). Ameeruddin chides politicians for their 'pomp, power and glory' and also mocks at their neglect of 'the hunger of multitudes' (*Visioned Summits*). He juxtaposes the life of rich with that of poor and finds that 'the wealthy taste the delicacies of five stars and while away their time in liquor and pleasure' (*Visioned Summits*) where as the poor women are made to put their modesty to bid 'for a few tainted silver coins' (*Visioned Summits*).

The poet wants to find an answer for the chaos of the world and proceeds with his 'quest.' He goes to God and Godmen, mountains, seas, sun, and gets no answer. At last, he discovers the answer in the acceptance of reality as 'we accept the seasons' (*Visioned Summits*) and urges humans to act in their lives as if they are going to 'live forever' (*Visioned Summits*) and to live their life as if they 'are going to die tomorrow' (*Visioned Summits*).

Ameeruddin's insight into human life is really commendable. He shares his perception of life in "Vicissitudes of Life." He reveals his bereaved heart in the opening of the poem and points out his 'iconoclast mission, surrealistic vision, petallic love times, detached attachments, love and wanderings, existential encounters, rainbow dreams and dusky disappointments' (*Visioned Summits*). Owing to his multidimensional personality, he is called 'mad' by the world but he is aware of the impermanence of things. He avers that 'nothing is constant' and all seem 'time-bound trivialities' (*Visioned Summits*). Even his glory and dignity keep changing. He says that he was touched by the supreme power some time before and attained 'immutable pride' (*Visioned Summits*) and 'longed for beautiful dreams' (*Visioned Summits*) but 'today' he descends 'the crumbling staircase of oblivion leading towards the terrace of empty daybreak and shattered sunlight' (*Visioned Summits*). Further, he declares that he has always been alone as a stranger and 'shall march alone in the shadow of ravines exploring the wasteland of hypocritical hybrids and tiny shams, towards a strange and unknown destiny' (*Visioned Summits*). The poet discloses the complexities of life in "Ambiguity." He states that life is 'a crisis-cross crisis amidst dwindling destines,' 'delirious dreams and diabolic disillusions' (*Visioned Summits*). Life happens in the world which is a 'frenzied humdrum existence of banality and triviality' (*Visioned Summits*) and where reality is 'an elusive enigma between here and hereafter a ravishing rainbow between life and death'

(*Visioned Summits*). He realises Nirvana as the meaning in ambiguity.

In "Musings," the poet brings out his opinion of life. He avows that humans should 'never exchange the smile' of their heart for 'the lilting lures of the multitudes' (*Visioned Summits*). People should 'mingle with the broken hearts' (*Visioned Summits*) with 'trembling tear' (*Visioned Summits*) and they should prefer 'death in moments of tranquil delight to a lousy life in gloom and in despair' (*Visioned Summits*). Further, humans should 'aspire for an eternal craze for love and beauty to a life of smothered ambitions and hypocrisy' (*Visioned Summits*). Ameeruddin cautions that the worldly possession and wealth will only bring 'misery' and attests that 'life is a conglomeration of farewells and reunions, hope and fulfillments, peace and despair, and tears and laughter' (*Visioned Summits*). In "Jigsaw Puzzle Life," the poet urges the human community to stop their contemplation of 'creator and destroyer,' 'here and hereafter,' 'reality and duality,' 'virtue and sin' (*Visioned Summits*) and to leave them 'to the cynics, mystics and ascetics' (*Visioned Summits*). Finally, he urges the people to 'enjoy the lilting present dancing to the titillating tunes of today' and to forget 'the forlorn hopes of jigsaw puzzle life' (*Visioned Summits*).

In "Pilgrimage," the poet scrutinises the validity of pilgrimage and identifies staying at home as a human being is better than pilgrimage. He has started his pilgrimage after being convinced 'of tales, mystic, real and non-real, stories of puranas and yogis of yore on Bhakthi and divinity' (*Visioned Summits*). During his pilgrimage, he abstains himself from worldly pleasures and focuses only on his goal. The initial journey is quite interesting and he is 'unmindful of hardships to face' (*Visioned Summits*) as he is stubborn in his journey. Though he is disturbed often by the memories of carnal pleasures, he is determined to shun them away. Finally, he reaches his destination and finds his 'confusion confounded' (*Visioned Summits*). He fails to understand why he is there. Moreover, he also discovers how wonderful it would be, to be a human being. He ends saying, 'Home of course is sweet and serene for those who discover symphonies of heart' (*Visioned

Summits) and it is a place where one's heat belongs. In another poem, "Voyage," he reveals the purpose of his journey in this world. He feels that he has to march 'to discover the secrets' (*Visions of Deliverance*) of himself though the urge 'is a momentary crisis-cross which fades away' (*Visions of Deliverance*). He asserts that he is 'a wanderer' and has to travel a long distance as his path is 'winding' (*Visions of Deliverance*). He also considers 'cycling and recycling experiences' (*Visions of Deliverance*) and 'Haze and maze of birth, copulation, death' as enigma and 'all a syllabled ding-dong song....' (*Visions of Deliverance*).

The poet reveals life as a journey in "Life is a Journey." He uncovers life as a journey with different stages and the journey 'starts from one dark chamber to another with a cry from the womb, and with a tear at the tomb' (*The Dreadful Doom to Come*). It passes many stages that include Boyhood, Youth and Old age. Boyhood is the most interesting stage and it holds innocence and wild joy. Youth is the 'most fascinating stage' (*The Dreadful Doom to Come*) and it embraces 'romantic thoughts' (*The Dreadful Doom to Come*) and 'pulsating perceptions of sensations sweet' (*The Dreadful Doom to Come*). Old age is the dreariest stage with its 'horrified thoughts and throbbing gloom and shock of the dreadful destination' (*The Dreadful Doom to Come*). In "Visioned Summits," Ameeruddin identifies the ultimate reality at the end of his spiritual journey. After having faced all the odds of life, he experienced new hope and radiance in his attainment of divine ecstasy. He assures that 'the eye of the cyclone has centered' in his inner world 'to unravel the mystery that hovers around' (*Visioned Summits*) him. Through his perseverance, he 'visioned summits of illumined peaks of benign Nirvana Aham Brahman, Anal Haq, and touched a moment eternal breathing the divine light of bliss—The sat-chit-Ananda!' (*Visioned Summits*).

In "Transcient Time," the poet asserts that life belongs to those who 'try it, fill it with vitality and vibrancy of share joy, share sorrow and to spread the aroma of quietitude and loveliness to sparkle the fragile moment into a purple paradise' (*Visioned Summits*). The poet declares his inner urge to shed away the routine and irksome activities of day-to-day life and to attain liberation in "Irksome Everydayness." The heart of the poet 'shudders with tormenting tears' (*A Lover and A Wanderer*) to see his spirit 'caught amidst the cruel flames of irksome—everydayness' (*A Lover and A Wanderer*) and his mind experiences the 'terrible strokes, on its mental anvil' (*A Lover and A Wanderer*) to see his spirit 'engulfed in the devastating whirlwind of day to day, incessant agony' (*A Lover and A Wanderer*). He desperately yearns for the 'heaven of liberation' to 'experience the Bliss' (*A Lover and A Wanderer*).

The poet's attitude towards love and relationship is remarkable and thought provoking. The poet unveils his love for his better half in "My Beloved." He accentuates the fact that he has been alone without the comfort of his beloved who is also his 'spiritual companion' (*Visions of Deliverance*). He yearns for her and finds solace in the fond memories about her. He finds nature joining his quest for his beloved and expressing its concern for him. He invokes the moon to reflect the passion of his soul to his beloved and requests the stormy wind to convey his heart's rhythm to her. As he does not have her beside him, he sees 'only the fractured sun and the fissured moon, emptied oceans and dead seagulls,' (*Visions of Deliverance*) and 'fallen leaves and sterile lands' (*Visions of Deliverance*). In "Love Song," the poet reveals the power of love to elevate human souls to spiritual heights. He asks his beloved to allow him the strength to reach the 'spiritual heights from the scintillating sensuality' (*Visions of Deliverance*) of her body and to reach the 'inner temple' (*Visions of Deliverance*) of her soul. Further, the poet divulges his love for his loved one in "Your Eyes." He could find the 'future manuscript' (*Visions of Deliverance*) of his poems in the eyes of his loved one. The eyes threw 'floodlight' into his dark soul and also illumined his 'winding path' (*Visions of Deliverance*). He desires to continue living in the eyes of the loved one as 'sun never shines as bright' (*Visions of Deliverance*) as the eyes of the loved one.

The poet considers nature as a part of humans and cherishes his correspondence with it. He recollects the precious time he spent with his beloved in "Drumbeats of Dampatya" and glorifies marriage as a sacred bond. The beloved went to the poet 'like the winter breeze with whispers of summer dreams and tantalising-tender love times' (*Visions of Deliverance*) and he 'saw a sonorous Parvathi' (*Visions of Deliverance*) in her. The poet also accounts that the objects of nature showered all blessings upon her on her birthday and unveils his desire to create a heaven out of their 'mundane-marriage!' (*Visions of Deliverance*). Finally, he declares that heaven should be experienced in married life and 'in the zestful celebrations of humanity' (*Visions of Deliverance*). The poet analyses the bounties of Nature in "Ocean Rhapsody." He avers that 'Nature writes her poems in flowers and smiles her joys in glows of radiant sunset bowers that shine around Night's toes!' (*Visions of Deliverance*).

In "Birthday Song—For My Son," the poet expresses his love for his son Ameen. The poet says that only during the birthday of his son, the dreams he had about his son when he was born becomes a 'delectable reality' (*Visions of Deliverance*). In fact, he realises his 'existence' had got 'meaning' only in the birth of his son and he is also made a 'part of the galaxy' (*Visions of Deliverance*). He reveals his love for his grandson in "A Prayer—For My Grandson." He has much faith and expectation towards his grandson and considers him a 'spiritual family tree' and 'a sage in trance' (*Visions of Deliverance*). Further, the poet considers his grandson a 'new sun' (*Visions of Deliverance*) that emerged 'to reinvigorate' his 'murky mystic race' (*Visions of Deliverance*). The poet also points out the chaos of the present day world through this poem. The poet does not know 'what paragons of virtues' (*Visions of Deliverance*) or 'what examples of human code' (*Visions of Deliverance*) he can teach to his 'little angel' as he finds only 'gloom engulfed environ of growing global genocide and universal desolating frenzy with lilting lunacy and itching egos of hegemonic human hatred' (*Visions of Deliverance*). Moreover, he asserts that 'all the values of Moses, Jesus, Mohamed and Ram have ended in a dreadful fiasco' of the 'New Millennium' (*Visions of Deliverance*). The New Millennium holds 'volcanic human infernos of startled-shattered world trade fair peaks' (*Visions of Deliverance*) and 'human shrouds of shrieking smoky Gujarat' (*Visions of Deliverance*) instead 'of sanity and oneness of Man' (*Visions of Deliverance*). The poet finally urges his grandson not to 'be influenced by the mundane maladies' because his grandson is a 'wanderer with gipsy intricacies' (*Visions of Deliverance*) and 'a pilgrim with an infinite goal' (*Visions of Deliverance*) to propagate a mellowed message: 'Share Joy,' 'Share Sorrow,' and 'Share Nature' (*Visions of Deliverance*).

Ameeruddin is not bound to his boundary and feels the whole universe as his home. He also extends his love towards all beings. In "Turkey," he captures the greatness of Turkey. For him, Turkey symbolises 'the golden moments in human destiny' (*Visions of Deliverance*) and he considers magnificent Istanbul as the 'citadel of human civilisation' (*Visions of Deliverance*) and 'a testament to humanity bridging continent to continent' (*Visions of Deliverance*). Turkey gave to the world 'Yunus Emre whose message capsuled in verse-eternal as love man, love universe, love God, love man as Acme of all creations, love nature and visualise the divine radiance everywhere....' (*Visions of Deliverance*). The poet expresses his agony over the loss of lives due to Tsunami in "Mystery of the Divine." He says that he is 'crushed over the extinction of mute millions, wrapped and rolled to horrendous doom by horrific titanic tidal waves' (*Visions of Deliverance*) and asserts that 'Mankind can never forget that day of delectable deluge' (*Visions of Deliverance*). He further warns that Tsunami is 'a warning to mankind to realise the reality of uncertainty,' (*Visions of Deliverance*) and the 'unraveling mute mystery of the Divine' (*Visions of Deliverance*). In "Glaucoma—A Highway Robberer," the poet announces his awareness of Glaucoma, a 'diabolic devil of dark shadows' (*Visions of Deliverance*) and cautions humans to keep vigil over the disease as 'it's a highway robberer of the sight' (*Visions of Deliverance*). Further, he assures that the disease can be cured through 'an early detection,' 'a visual vigilance,' and 'a devote perseverance' (*Visions of Deliverance*).

Ameeruddin reveals the evils of acquiring riches in "The Pomp of Gold." He says wealth hovers around a wealthy man like a vulture hovers over a carcass and it also imprisons who possesses it by robbing the freedom of the person. Further, it engulfs the person 'into the realm of restlessness, dismay, anguish, and misery' (*Visioned Summits*). He also asserts that 'the thoughts of gold and glory are nothing but an eternal inferno' (*Visioned Summits*) and therefore, he requests God to give him 'an eye that can see others hearts in barter of gold' (*Visioned Summits*). In "Dome of Gold," the poet talks about the humans' lack of reason and their love for gold that acts as a mental poison. He affirms that humans become 'crazy and mad, passionate, eager and anxious, spirited, deadly and devilish' (*What the Himalaya... Said and Other Poems*) to become the custodians of gold and their attitude towards gold breeds: 'Adulteration and corruption, pollution and prostitution, day dreaming and deception' (*What the Himalaya... Said and Other Poems*). Moreover, they lost their meaning for existence and turned aimless. The poet demands the requirement of new consciousness to liberate humans from their 'captivating glorious dome' (*What the Himalaya... Said and Other Poems*).

In "My India," the poet desperately searches for the lost grandeur of India. He asks and wonders, what happened to 'the lilting lure of Vedas, Upanishads, the whispering radiance of yogis, Munis, Rishis...sustaining melodies of Ramayana, awe inspiring, harmonising drumbeats of Mahabharata...purity, innocence, love perpetuated by Maryadapurushottam Rama, pragmatism, dynamism, Niskama karma enunciated by Krishna, the Avatar,...the unity of God, of Kabirdas, oneness of man, universal brotherhood, and co-existence and harmony' (*Visions of Deliverance*). He identifies the replacement of the traditional virtues of the country and tries to find out the cause for the forlorn state. In the new culture of India, he discovers 'new cult of blurred youth, where tongues of hatred licking each other's brain' (*Visions of Deliverance*) and the people are fond of destruction through technology and express their perversion in various forms. He asserts that the people of India 'have lost their way' (*Visions of Deliverance*) and ends by questioning 'How would this blind prodigals trace their way?' (*Visions of Deliverance*) and 'How would this deaf delinquents hear their mother's call?' (*Visions of Deliverance*). The poet captures various forms of injustices and inhumanity happening in the world through his "Carrion Carnage." He pictures the plight of 'ill fated masses of Bosnia crushed by the diabolic ethnic forces,' 'the sighing Somalians,' (*Visioned Summits*) 'the fall of soviet and the rise of parochial spirit,' 'strange upsurge in Ayodhya in the sacred names of Ram and Rahim,' (*Visioned Summits*) and the 'cast and creed aberrations' (*Visioned Summits*) such as 'the Harijans, Girijans, and Daridra Narayans' (*Visioned Summits*). He wonders 'How long this bewildering humanity to be trapped in such a twilight of melancholy' (*Visioned Summits*) and inquires 'who will deliver these perplexed people' (*Visioned Summits*).

In "Visions of Deliverance," the poet points out the irregularity and obscenity present in the world and he also captures the plight of humans in it. He avers that humans are distracted by the evil things of the world and entangle their souls. 'Dark and despicable souls drowned in hatred and ignorance led by the fire flashing smithies into the abysmal sea of fire' (*Visions of Deliverance*) and are 'tortured to molten pieces' (*Visions of Deliverance*) after their death. They have to pass through much torture before reaching 'the pristine peaks of purity' (*Visions of Deliverance*). On the other hand, the souls that are 'true and righteous' (*Visions of Deliverance*) enjoy 'a spectacular panorama of life' (*Visions of Deliverance*) after their death. The poet feels that repentance is the only way 'to experience the eternity and the blissful-eternal bounty.' Finally, he affirms that Deliverance! could be achieved only through the realisation of 'The Sat-Chit-Ananda' (*Visions of Deliverance*). In "Peace in the Age of Space," he avows that it is not easy to achieve peace in this age. He identifies man's loss of faith in his spiritual bond as the reason for his loss of mental agility. Owing to man's imbalance of mind, 'confusion and chaos' (*What the Himalaya... Said and Other Poems*) become 'the blessing of our age' (*What the Himalaya... Said and Other Poems*) and 'clamour, hue and cry,' 'shriek, sound, and fury' (*What the Himalaya... Said and Other Poems*) turn as the achievement of the humans. The poet concludes saying peace will 'embrace' humans only 'when man recognises man, when an ideal recognises an ideal, when humanity regards humanity, when religion regards religion, and when realisation dawns in the individual' (*What the Himalaya... Said and Other Poems*).

In "Youth of Our Time," the poet says that the youth of the present day world are confused about the purpose of their lives and are caught in the whirlpool of life. They rush 'into the mire and sense around confusion and chaos amidst sound and fury' (*What the Himalaya... Said and Other Poems*) and 'are overwhelmed and intoxicated by the warm blood in their veins' (*What the Himalaya... Said and Other Poems*). Moreover, they are 'blind-folded and unaware in their pleasing pains of passion' (*What the Himalaya... Said and Other Poems*). The poet compares humans to dolls made of clay in "Dolls of Clay." He realises that man is an insignificant creature in this magnificent universe and his attempt to conquer the world and to master the universe is futile and impossible.

The poet informs about the meaningless activity of humans and the impending disaster of the world in "The Dreadful Doom to Come." The mind and the body of humans have become lifeless and they act as 'spiritless souls' (*The Dreadful Doom to Come*). Moreover, 'in his vain achievements of Science and Technology' (*The Dreadful Doom to Come*) and in his 'futile persuasions of progress and prosperity' (*The Dreadful Doom to Come*) man has 'harmed humanity to a very dreadful destiny' (*The Dreadful Doom to Come*). Further, man has ignored all that is 'eternal and divine' (*The Dreadful Doom to Come*) and 'shattered the mansion of virtue of the mystic path between Creation and the Creator' (*The Dreadful Doom to Come*). The poet reveals knowledge as deceptive and illusion as it is difficult to comprehend the functioning of the universe in "Ignorance" (*What the Himalaya... Said and Other Poems*). The poet also asserts that life's glory will never stay as known things have become strange. Though people learn about Philosophy, Religion, Materialism, Spiritualism, Politics, Economics, Society and Civilisation, it is difficult for them to understand everything thoroughly as 'the claim of knowledge in itself is ignorance' (*What the Himalaya... Said and Other Poems*).

The poet discloses the transforming power of hope in "Hope." He indicates that 'hope is a portal for the starving wanderer in rays' (*Visioned Summits*) and it is a goal for the 'pilgrimage of life' (*Visioned Summits*). As 'hope has a million embracing arms and a million prayer-answering eyes,' (*Visioned Summits*) humans should pursue their lives' 'voyage to the beckoning part of hope for rest and repose and for a delightful destination' (*Visioned Summits*). In "Life's Enigma," the poet radiates a ray of hope in the activity of the universe. He asserts that existence is a cosmic drama where life and death are 'interwined in struggle for a sustained sojourn in this world' (*Visioned Summits*) and 'solace, dreams and destinies, meaning and morality, virtue and wisdom' (*Visioned Summits*) are 'a hide and seek hoax' (*Visioned Summits*) and 'a perfect sham of surrealistic blabber' (*Visioned Summits*). Further, 'all human experience is a garbage accumulated' (*Visioned Summits*) and hence 'the day to day trivialities' (*Visioned Summits*) should not be treasured. On the other hand, humans should 'try to wake up at every new dawn like a fresh dew drenched petal' (*Visioned Summits*) and 'live a life for the day and leave the rest to oblivion longing for a new day and a new experience' (*Visioned Summits*).

By reflecting life as journey, Ameeruddin urges humans to cherish each moment and to accept things as they occur. He reveals different facets of relationship and finds out a way to establish peace and harmony in the world. Further, by his universal brotherhood, he transcends cultural and physical barriers and proclaims his concern for humanity. Through his portrayal of the calamities and chaos of the present-day world, he warns humans about the consequences of their irrational acts. Finally, by resting his faith in the transforming power of hope, he assures humans the way to attain liberation and to experience the bliss of the divine.

Works Cited

Ameeruddin, Syed. *The Dreadful Doom to Come*. Madras: Poet Press India, 1974. Print.

_____ *A Lover and A Wanderer*. Madras: Poet Press India, 1980. Print.

_____ *Visioned Summits*. Madras: International Poets Academy, 1995. Print.

_____ *Visions of Deliverance*. Madras: International Poets Academy, 2006. Print.

_____ *What the Himalaya . . . Said and Other Poems*. Madras: Kalaivendhan Publications, 1972. Print.

18

Syed Ameeruddin: A Wanderer with a Goal

—Mosam Sinha

Syed Ameeruddin is a unique signature in the field of Indian English poetry of the modern era. His poetry focuses upon lyricism, spiritual splendour, sublime images, sensuousness, feeling of consciousness, a blend of present and past, love for nature, romanticism in love, religious fervour, his strong faith in all religions and their teachings, concept of spiritual peace, patriotism, hollowness of modern life, ambiguity and mystery of life, insignificance of man, metamorphosis in woman, man-woman relationship, pathos in modern life, his philosophical attitude, optimism in life, depiction of beauty, love and its facets, sex and sense in love, morality in life, mysticism, his brood over social vices, etc. His poetry is symbolic and decked with the skilful use of metaphors, contradictions and epigrammatic force. His diction has a spark which illumines his thoughts and philosophy. He sometimes becomes descriptive, sometimes narrative, sometimes symbolic and sometimes epigrammatic.

Syed Ameeruddin's first collection of poems *What The Himalaya... Said* came out in 1972. The title poem gives a beautiful and vivid picture of the Himalayas. The spectrum of physical and spiritual in the poem is remarkably wonderful. After reading this poem the image of 'a saintly figure sitting by the edge of Himalaya giving sermons to the people of the world' comes to our mind. Like a saintly figure the poet says:

"Faith, Hope, Truth and Love,
The age old rites, the principles of life...
...It never too late, there is a way

Just to retrospect, repent-take a twist in your way.
Just remember! and follow the two principles
The self Discipline! and the self Realisation!"
'What The Himalaya... Said'

(*What The Himalaya... Said* 22-23)

Syed is perhaps the only poet of Indian English Literature who has defined and analysed the time so beautifully and majestically. The poem shows the poet's skill in teaching time management. People say that time is changing. But the poet says that time is not changing, our attitudes are changing. Time has eternal value and man must realise that.

"Its man and his attitudes that are changing
There is no Time, and there no change in Time
The mutable man
Must come out from the folly of time
And recognise....
The eternal value of Timeless-ness-from his-Time."
'Value of Timeless-ness'

(*What The Himalaya... Said* 27)

'Dome of Gold' is a symbolically philosophical poem on life and its facets:

Here life is....... In its lifelessness.......
Wisdom is .... In its ignorance.....
Awareness is.... In its unawareness...
Religion is... in its irreligiousness....
Beacause, the world is a dome of Gold,
Man and gold.....and Man's relations are of Gold.
'Dome of Gold'

(*What The Himalaya... Said* 31)

'Ignorance' comes out with the fact that knowledge is ignorance. The irony of the scheme is that one says one is knowledgeable even after not being so. The poet says:

....the man is unknown
unaware of everything and anything.
'Ignorance'

(*What The Himalaya... Said*.33)

Technology is at its peak and in this era of technology and science, peace has become a migratory bird gone to some forlorn place where scientific people and technocrat do not live. The poet surmises:

> Lack of peace is the gift of our age.
> Confusion and chaos is the blessing of our age.
> Clamour, hue and cry is our attainment.
> Shriek, sound and fury, is our achievement.
> 'Peace in the Age of Space'
>
> (*What The Himalaya... Said* 35)

Syed Ameeruddin becomes Wordsworthian in the poem 'Blessings'. The poem is a prayer addressed to the Himalayas, Ganges, Birds and Breeze. Nature is an eternal source of joy, a balm for ailing hearts. Under the intoxication of the beauty of nature the poet puts up:

> To share my bubbling mad joy
> To play and dance with my heart of gay
> To invoke with me, the blessings
> Of eternity-for a long happy wedded life.
> 'Blessings'
>
> (*What The Himalaya... Said* 38)

The poem 'Dolls of Clay' reminds us of Eliot's poem "The Hollow Man". The hollowness of man is depicted in the poem. The richness of the poem is in its prosaic style and realism. It is a symbolical poem on the insignificance of man and his vain achievements. The poet warns the people by saying:

> Here everything is transient, subject to decay.
> Even the Dome of gold will burst and break.
> This glitter and glory, of this vain life will vanish.
> Because we are 'Dolls of clay' and this is a city of clay.
> 'Dolls of Clay'
>
> (*What The Himalaya... Said* 40)

'Youth of Our Time' speaks of modern youth, full of dreams, ambitions and illusions. They have lost all sense of values. Addressing the youth of the day the poet gives them the lesson of *Bhagavad Gita* 'Bhakti, Gyana and Karma', a remedy to remove frustration.

Syed Ameeruddin's second collection of poems *The Dreadful Doom to Come and Other Poems* appeared in 1974. The title poem is on the hollowness of modern man. Corruption, pollution, filth, dirt, mess, mire, buzz, bewilderment and chaos have enveloped modern life. Man's supreme knowledge is his supreme ignorance. The dreadful doom is about to approach. It is high time for modern man to get up from his slumber to save himself from the doom. Divine messages, if followed, can save man from the dreadful doom. The poet says:

> Man of today
> Must get from his sensuous slumber
> And derive a lesson from his past...
> And immediately revive
> His entire activities of filth, flesh and fiction
> And must go back to these divine messengers.
>
> (*The Dreadful Doom to Come and Other Poems* 16)

'Where All This Leads To' is a saga of the pathetic life of modern woman. Like a great philosopher Manu, Syed Ameeruddin wants to make the point that God dwells where women are adored. He defines the woman using a number of adjectives calls her the basis of society.

> Woman is the basis
> And the very fibre of our society
> She is the centre...
> Of all Social and hereditary set up.
> 'Where All This Leads To'
>
> (*The Dreadful Doom to Come and Other Poems* 18)

Modern is full of difficulties. Darkness prevails everywhere. Modern man is in the midst of rough weather. Life has become a paradox today. The poet states:

> To be human
> Is inhuman Today.
> To be inhuman
> Is human Today.
> 'Despair of Our Age'
>
> (*The Dreadful Doom to Come and Other Poems* 24)

Life is fantastic, illusive, adventurous, sensuous and full of despair. The poet broods over life and its mysterious mystery. Like a philosopher the poet expresses:

What a mystic experience the life is
With its pulsating philosophies
With its redeeming religious messages
With its prophets and visionaries....
'What a mysterious Mystery the Life is'

(*The Dreadful Doom to Come and Other Poems*.28)

The poet becomes Keatsian and Wordsworthian in the poem 'A Craze for Supreme Beauty'. He is enchanted by the beauty of nature. For him, beauty is a joy forever. The poet asserts:

I love Beauty
And I long for Beauty
I am crazy about Beauty
I perceive Beauty
And I visualise Beauty
I live in Beauty
And Beauty lives in me.
'A Craze for Supreme Beauty'

(*The Dreadful Doom to Come and Other Poems*.33)

(The use of capital 'B' for Beauty shows that the poet spiritualises Beauty.)

The poet describes the three important phases of human life-Boyhood, Youth and Old Age as Shakespeare does in *'As You Like It'*.

Life a Journey
With its different stages
Alluring and fascinating
Shocking and Horrifying.
'Life is a Journey'

(*The Dreadful Doom to Come and Other Poems*.36)

Syed Ameeruddin's third collection of poems *A Lover and a Wanderer* appeared in 1980. The whole collection is rich in the use of romantic images. The touch of Romanticism is so powerful that it would not be wrong from any poet to put the poet in the category of Romantic poets like Wordsworth, Keats, Shelley, Byron and Pushkin. The collection is like a love epic having various turns, depicting love from different levels. Syed's use of imagery is delicate and fantastic.

> We sat together
> holding each pulsating rhythm
> in cascaded heart
> and eloquent in dumb deeds
> we felt the creep of velvety longings
> and eternity captured
> in mute mellow mystic night.
> 'Love Strings'
>
> (*A Lover and a Wanderer* 10)

Sex creeps into his love poems. The poet asks his beloved to come and celebrate the night of white shadows:

> Come, beloved
> Let us celebrate
> The flow of tides in scuttled womb of depths forlorn.
> 'Come, Beloved!'
>
> (*A Lover and a Wanderer* 10)

The poet's spiritual loneliness is observed in the poem 'Shattered Dreams'. The pain of separation is unbearable for him. He sees his beloved in different shapes. She is Radha or Parvati or Shakuntala or Urvasi or Rambha or Menaka. The poet becomes melancholic as he says:

> Now all my dreams
> Are scattered like shattered glass—
> My heart is frozen,
> But memories are still bitter
> With biting icy chill.
> 'Shattered Dreams'
>
> (*A Lover and a Wanderer* 10)

The poet uses the same tone and the spirit in the next poem 'Simmering Loneness'. The narrative tone of the poem makes him a great poetic story-teller. The contrast between present and past is highly romantic.

> Once.....
> We used to walk a quiet woodland path
> In perfumed air and dappled light,
> Locked arm in arm;
> With sensuous caresses warm.
> 'Simmering Loneness'
>
> (*A Lover and a Wanderer*.10)

'A Lover and a Wanderer' is about poet's life depicting his days of romanticism in love and the days of separation. The passion in love described in the poem is sublime. Sensousness is of high order. The biggest inspiration of a poet is his beloved. The poet exclaims:

> I am a wanderer. I have a goal. A purple purpose;
> Dear I need you! Dear I need you!
> Dark are the woods. Long is the Journey.
> But dear, you be my beacon light....
> 'A Lover and a Wanderer'
>
> (*A Lover and a Wanderer* 32)

The poet is pained to see the poverty everywhere. He makes the people aware of such a direful condition of society. The poet sympathises:

> These uncared
> And unwanted destitute
> Perishing everywhere
> Lead a hellish life.
> 'Clustered Clouds of Poverty'
>
> (*A Lover and a Wanderer* 34)

The poet beautifully paints the irksome life of modern man. Modern life has become corrupt and chaotic. The modern man feels:

> At every minute
> I am being crushed,
> Thrashed and tattered;

And this filthy flesh
Of mine being torn
To tilting tiny pieces.
'Irksome Everydayness'

(*A Lover and a Wanderer* 44)

Syed Ameeruddin's fourth collection of poems *Pettallic Love Times* came in 1988. Love in its varied forms is the theme of this collection. The poet is struck by the arrow of Cupid, the god of love. 'Petallic Love Times' is sweet in its lyrical tone and romanticism. Longing, anguish and separation in love make the poem highly touching.

You are still in my dream
The picture of my inward joy
I still fill my soul with your desire
I still live in your eyes and dream of your eyes.
'Pettalic Love Times'

(*Pettallic Love Times* 26)

The poet anxiously waits for his beloved. The company of his beloved is like rebuilding the paradise. There is lyrical splendour in his love. The poet asks his beloved to fill the cup of his heart with fragrance of her soul. Their love is eternal.

In my Joy allow me to love
And weave raiment of beautiful dreams,
And sing songs of petallic lovetimes,
Which will echo and resound lasting rhapsodies
In the glittering galaxies-from time to eternity.
'Love Song'

(*Pettallic Love Times* 31)

The poet calls his beloved his enchantress who has cast her magic upon him. He sees her in various forms. After reading the whole poem we feel that the poet has devoted his whole life to the love of his life. It is his love that pushes him to move further to set milestones in life. He feels that life without her is not a life.

My enchantress
You are my poetic Quest
You are my souls search
You are my hearts longing
You are my minds fancy
You are my dreams Diana
You are my emotions Radha
You are my passions Parvathi
You are my spirits Shakuntala......
'My Enchantress'

(*Pettallic Love Times* 32-33)

'A New Love' is poet's victory over all love poets of the world. The psychology of love which he has presented is so realistic and is nowhere found in the poetic works of any contemporary poet.

A new day breaks from our visual rhapsody
A gesture. A whisper. A word.
A new love springs. A new dawn dances.
'A New Love'

(*Pettalic Love Times* 35)

Love is highly sensuous and sexual here in the following lines:

When you caress my heaving breast
Gently turning the tips of my dusky nipples,
Cyclone centres
In a strange wasteland of my mind.
'I Am Alive Again'

(*Pettallic Love Times* 43)

The poem 'Unsung Song' reminds us of Keats' 'Heard melodies are sweet; /But those unheard are sweeter.' The whispers of his petallic love times of his romantic past create in the poet the feeling of excitement and love.

I feel nostalgic
With past blooms and bygone springs
That petallic Caress
That hushed whisper.
'Unsung Song'

(*Pettallic Love Times* 49)

Syed Ameeruddin's fifth collection of poems *Visioned Summits* came out in 1995. "There is no heavenly place on earth other than India" is echoed in Syed Ameeruddin's poem 'My India' from his rich collection of poems '*Visioned Summits*'. The poet expresses his feelings of sorrow at the loss of Indian culture and civilisation. His description on rich heritage of India reminds us of Nehru and his *Discovery of India* where he beautifully describes the rich heritage of our country and speaks on our culture. The poet's criticisim of degradation of values and belief in emptiness of modern life reminds us of T.S Eliot. The vision of the poet in the poem is that of Rabindranath Tagore in his Gitanjali where Tagore dreams of India as an ideal nation. Like Shri Aurobindo and Rabindranath Tagore, the poet wishes to change this earth into heaven. He thinks that by being united and having a firm faith in the unity of man and unity of God, our country can recover the loss and help us rebuild the nation it was in past. The poet echoes:

> What happened to the/Maxims of munificence
> care and concern
> Envisioned by Gurunanak
> The unity of man
> The unity of God, of Kabirdas
> Oneness of man,
> Universal brotherhood.........
> 'My India'
>
> (*Visioned Summits* 62)

The poet thinks of his past memories which fill him with joy and enthusiasm, and his comparison between his past life and present life is highly admirable. He wants to bring out the idea that memories of the past push us to fill enthusiasm in the present. The image of an alabaster soaring into nothingness compared to the poet's loneliness is beautifully designed and created:

> Today I am alone
> Like an alabaster soaring into nothingness
> Telescoping the purple moments we spent
> On the sand dunes of memory.
> 'Whispers of Beyond'
>
> (*Visioned Summits* 71)

His poem 'Ambiguity' is on ambiguity of life. Life is surrounded by dwindling destinies, delirious dreams and diabolic disillusions. 'What is Nirvana?' has been puzzle in our life. Different scholars give different point of view on the question of Nirvana. The poet says, Nirvana is:

> Reflecting on the smoky layers
> Of gloom and solace,
> and seeing-
> Meaning in Ambiguity.
> 'Ambiguity'
>
> (*Visioned Summits* 76-77)

The poet's social consciousness is seen in 'Wounded Dawn'. He laments at the suffering of the humanity. Man is in fire of pains and pangs of life and there is no way to come out. The poet cries out:

> Unhealed wounds sigh a pain
> Although the rain blanched night.
> Tears terminate to volcanic upsurge.
> Man in flames-in flames in man
> 'Wounded Dawn'
>
> (*Visioned Summits* 80)

'Pilgrimage' shows the poet's firm faith in all religions and their teachings. The ironical part is that even after going through scriptures of all religions and going on a pilgrimage, he could not understand the enigma of life. He gives the essence of all the religions and comes out with the fact that God is attained by those who realise God in themselves. Like a preacher, he preaches:

> Home of course is sweet and serene
> Foe those who discover symphonies of heart:
> Home is a place where your heart belongs.
> 'Pilgrimage'
>
> (*Visioned Summits* 86)

'Back Again' is the saga of poet's past memories. He feels happy and joyful when he remembers his petallic love times in the poem.

In 'The Pomp of Gold', the poet prays to God to grant him the feeling of love to be spread out to the whole of humanity and money to help others. Materialism has created a void in our lives. Spirituality is what we should look for to make our lives lovely, beautiful, virtual and delightful. Wealth is God if it serves like a warning and is used for helping others:

> Money is like water
> It flows towards the parching paths
> And it enlivens the others
> who turns upon his fellowmen.
> 'The Pomp of Gold'
>
> (*Visioned Summits* 98)

'Rainbow Acrobat' is on man-woman relationship. In 'Jigsaw Puzzle Life', the poet says that we should forget the forlorn hopes of jigsaw puzzle life and leave the question of creator and destroyer, reality and duality, virtue and sin, for the cynics, mystics and ascetics. The poet says:

> Why should we reflect
> All those mysteries
> of rigmarole Metaphysics
> Leave it to the cynics,
> Mystics and ascetics.
> 'Jigsaw Puzzle Life'
>
> (*Visioned Summits* 103-104)

Like true justice, the poet broods over the ill-fated masses of Bosnia, raped women and massacred infants, the sighing Somalians, the fall of Soviet, upsurge in Ayodhya, bellowing bomb blast of Mumbai and caste and creed aberrations in 'Carion Carnage'. He bemoans:

> Religion!
> The very word is nauseating
> with the stink/of human hatred and barbarism
> Then, where is God's benevolence?
> But the Question is, whose God??
> 'Carion Carnage'
>
> (*Visioned Summits* 111)

'Hope' is a masterpiece. The poet gives various definitions of hope. He calls it 'a portal', 'a goal', 'a lighthouse', 'a promise, 'a refuge', 'a remedy', 'a sparkling', and 'a mast'. Men must try to come out of sorrow and be hopeful. The poet says:

The searching soul
Must come out
of the path of
sounds and shadows
of darkness and density
To realise the splendor of HOPE.
'Hope'

(*Visioned Summits* 130)

'Beckoning Arm' is a call to the people to follow the path shown by God:

And before the growing Night
sheets up the earth
with bones of thunderbolts
and flesh of ashes
Fly over the wilderness
Guided
By the rhythmic waves
of His Beckoning Arm!
'Beckoning Arm'

(*Visioned Summits* 136)

In 'This is False: Our's Is Not This', the poet yearns for spiritual peace:

O, Let us fly
To tranquil peaks
And scale the heights
Of dim distance
And leap into leaps Nectarine
Where sapphire seers
Roam in Godly Glee!
'This is False: Our's Is Not This'

(*Visioned Summits* 143)

'Football Rings' reminds us of Tagore's mysticism. The poet hears the sound of the footsteps of God:

Beyond the flights
of Age's dreams,
Beyond the leap
of Eternities.
'Football Rings'

(*Visioned Summits* 147)

In 'Visioned Summits', the poet says that God is ultimate, truth and reality. He gives the concept of God in all religions: "Ekam Eva Advaitam Brahman!" The beauty and sublimity is excellent. In short, reading the poems of Prof. Ameeruddin's 'Visioned Summit' is like taking a dip into the pious water of Ganga and to purify one's soul.

Syed Ameeruddin's sixth collection of poems *Visions of Deliverance* came out in 2006. His poem 'A Prayer for My Grandson' is symbolic. His ardent love for his grandson is symbolic of his love for the whole of humanity. The metaphorical language used for the grandson is superb.

Who are you my little angel.......!
My genesis,
My progeny,
My harbinger.
You are my longing abysmal,
Beyond the constellation.
'A Prayer for My Grandson'

(*Visions of Deliverance* 40-41)

Syed Ameeruddin comes out as a great poet of beauty in his poems "A New Love", "My Beloved", "Love Song", "Love Times", "Your Eyes", "Broken Whispers" and "You are a Beautuful Poem". The poet speaks of spirituality in love in his poem "Love Song" when he says,

Allow me the strength to reach—
The spiritual heights
Form the scintillating sensuality—
Of your body.
'Love Song'

(*Visions of Deliverance* 87-88)

Physical love reaching the heights of sublimity finds abode in his poem 'Love Times'. The poet thinks of his times and becomes completely overwhelmed:

In your ecstasy, you possessed me—
Hard to yourself
To touch the dizzy zeniths—
Of exotic heights:
At that, I entered you as the evening sun
Enters into the dusky deep ocean.
'Love Times'

(*Visions of Deliverance*.106)

The biggest source of inspiration of the poet is his beloved. Eyes of his beloved are his poetic food:

In your eyes I watch fireflies light up
The future manuscript of my poems.

The beloved becomes his spiritual companion in 'You are a Beautiful Poem' when he says:

Let's love each other
To the depths and breadths and heights
Our souls can reach
To realise the ideal of
Sat-Chit-Ananda.
'You are a Beautiful Poem'

(*Visions of Deliverance* 118)

The poet cannot separate himself from his beloved. The intensity in his love is so high that he cannot see his beloved away from him. He laments:

Where are you, my beloved?
Withered leaves have scattered.
Barren boughs are weeping
Nature's bounty is ruined.

'Voyage' reminds us of 'Stopping By Woods By Snow Evening of Robert Frost where the poet says that he has to go miles before he meets his death. In the same spirit of optimism, Syed Ameeruddin says:

> I am wanderer, winding is my path.
> Journey is long. It's time to go.....
> 'Voyage'
>
> (*Visions of Deliverance*.62)

'My India' is a slap on the faces of those who do not regard the dynamic culture of the country. Like a true leader, the poet makes a call to Indians and says:

> How would these blind prodigals
> Trace their way?
> How would these deaf delinquents
> Hear their mother's call.

The poem is so touching that if one does not become a true patriot after reading it, one seems to have no feelings in one's heart. Syed Ameeruddin is like modern Tagore.

'Birthday Song-For My Son' is the most emotional song weaved with intensely chosen words and full of music which is unique. The poet says:

> The spiritual offspring—
> Our Flesh, Spirit and Blood—
> The Shining Star-of New Millennium
> The Jewel-The 'AMEEN'.....
> 'Birthday Song-For My Son'
>
> (*Visions of Deliverance* 93)

The poet gives a permanent new year resolution to us all to be taken at the advent of every new year:

> Let's celebrate this New Year
> With a resolve to harness
> The beast in Man, and to retain
> The smile on every Human Face.
> 'New Year'
>
> (*Visions of Deliverance*:99-100)

Like a true prophet, the poet says that life should be led with a vision. Love surpasses all:

> Man's life on earth a Visioned March
> From Darkness to Light:
> From Untruth To Righteousness:
> From Death to Immortality.
> When Love arrives, all needs and
> Flaws are gone.
> 'Turkey'
>
> (*Visions of Deliverance*.112)

'Mystery of Divine' is a warning to the people about the uncertainties of life:

> All this is warning to mankind
> To realise the reality
> Of uncertainty and the unknown—
> And the unraveling
> Mute mystery of the Divine
> 'Mystery of Divine'
>
> (*Visions of Deliverance* 120)

Time kills everything. Even love has to face the rough weather. The joy and the spiritual glory in love have to move into nothingness one day:

> The lyric splendor of our love's
> Spiritual glory and ephemeral joy
> Is twisted, trampled and crushed
> By the hissing hurricanes of horror
> And tumultuous eclipse of time
> Into the shrieking realm of vast nothingness.
> 'Realm of Nothingness'
>
> (*Visions of Deliverance* 142)

'Come Dancing Thine Way to Mine Arms' is like a romantic movie with pictures of youthful love in the lap of nature:

> In sensuous hastiness joyously flee
> And flickering shades of the evening Run!

Come dancing thine way to mine arms!
'Come Dancing Thine Way to Mine Arms'
(*Visions of Deliverance* 165)

The poem 'Drumbeats of Dampatya' is dedicated to the poet's wife. The poem has wonderful lyrical tone. It is the most beautiful song ever created by any poet for his beloved wife. The poet's wife seems to him no less than Mumtaz or Cleopatra. On the question of marriages being made in heaven, the poet says:

Who says, marriages
Are made in heaven?
Dear, let us create a Heaven
Out of mundane-marriage!
'Drumbeats of Dampatya'
(*Visions of Deliverance* 181-182)

Visions of Deliverance is like grand epic like *Paradise Lost*. Its sublimity is of high order. It is made ornate by the skilful use of similes, metaphors, epigrams, vivid images, mysticism and spirituality. Syed is like Bacon in the use of epigrams; like Keats in the use of imagery; like Milton in the use of mysticism, spirituality and sublimity.

19

Syed Ameeruddin's Poetry: Visions of a Pilgrimage to the Summits of Deliverance

—O.P. Mathur

The spiritual is ingrained in the Indian psyche right from the ancient days and is expressed in numerous ways—direct prayers to the Supreme Being and His manifestations in the various phenomena of nature, mythological and historical allegories and devotional poems or songs written from different perspectives. The spiritual, the mythological, the allegorical and the devotional have, by and large, withstood the philosophical and materialistic challenges from the West as far as the masses are concerned. Some of the works of the intellectuals, however, occasionally re-examine, or question them. Spiritual poetry in English, though somewhat at a discount, has a fairly large number of them, including even some illustrious ones like Rabindranath Tagore, Aurobindo Ghose, not to speak of relatively minor ones like V.K. Gokak, K.D. Sethna, Harindranath Chattopadhyaya, Niranjan Mohanty, R.K. Singh, Charu Sheel Singh, Mahanand Sharma and many others.

One of the acclaimed ones in this category is Syed Ameeruddin who has been recognised by no less a critic than K.R. Srinivasa Iyengar as having made a name for himself in Indian English writing by his 'thought-provoking poetry'[1] and as 'a rare phenomenon in the contemporary field of world poetry today'[2]. The combination of qualities which is indeed rare has been briefly focussed upon in this essay, with reference to his two published works *Visioned Summits*[3] and *Visions of Deliverance.*

Visioned Summits can be considered to be a loose series of monologues, the dramatic voice throughout being that of the poet himself, embodying a journey from depression and anger at the contemporary ambience of evil to the illumined peaks of 'benign Nirvana, Aham Brahman, Anal Haq ... The Sat-Chit-Ananda' (*Visioned Summits* 156-57). The bi-axial journey naturally consists of a whirling voyage from the agony of contemporary life to the ecstasy of having had a vision of complete harmony between the Self, the World and the Beyond. The first stage embodies his somewhat delirious reaction—the melancholy and the rage—at the 'opaque living' (*Visioned Summits* 39) of contemporary life in its various aspects—the new culture of violence, totalitarianism, greedy politics, the miserable condition of the masses, etc. depicting his emotions through the force of his language. He largely summarises the targets of his rage in an overview of the grievous environment that envelops modern life like a darkening cloud:

> What is this degeneration of values—
> Environmental holocaust
> Religious fundamentalism
> Ethnic and racial vandalism
> Political hegemony, national pride
> Economic disparity, social discrepancy
> Abnormality, obscenity
> Shallowness, shamelessness
> Sensuality, amorality
> Paranoid passions, devilish dareness—
> All this—echo a swan song—
> For the oncoming deluge of humanity
>
> (*Visioned Summits* 30-31)

The monologues that follow this opening poem 'voicing his rage at the opaque living' (*Visioned Summits* 397) of contemporary life consist of his varied musings exploring this 'decomposed jungle' (*Visioned Summits* 251) and his multidirectional reactions to it. He marches 'towards the eye of the storm' (*Visioned Summits* 50). Initially lamenting the lost grandeur of the country's past, he goes on to dissect his own loneliness, responsibility and prospects of redemption. This group of well over a dozen poems reveals the poet's stance from the existential to the humanistic, looking within the ambiguity of his own self to the carnage around him. This group of synergic poems is a valuable series of peeps into the poet's heart and his varied responses to life. Together they form an appropriately slow and undulating passage of the poet's journey from the depths of despair and rage to a "New Dawn" (*Visioned Summits* 113-14), the mystic's intuitive harking to the ringing of "His Footfall" (*Visioned Summits* 145-47) which is a prelude to the poet's final arrival at the summits of the Reality of the Cne, the Eternal, in whom all ambiguities and transient cycles spread over aeons dissolve (*Visioned Summits* 153-54).

Like the Bhakti poets, saints and sufis, he is suffused with the ancient wisdom of 'Aham Brahmasmi':

> The vibrant divine within me blazes.
> La Ilaha Illal Lahu
> Salam! Salam! Salam!
> Peace be with you!
> My crimson being further sparkles:
> Ekam Eva Adityam Brahman!
> Om! Shanti! Shanti!
>
> (*Visioned Summits* 156)

Like T.S. Eliot, Ameeruddin has seen that 'London Bridge is falling down falling down falling down', and with 'arid plains' behind him and passing these complex mental states, but without any 'Hieronymo', he again arrives at a similar conclusion, though perhaps with a spiritual splendour untouched by Eliot at least in this way—non-didatic, revelatory enlightenment, his stress on the true Eastern ethos with later poems being on the 'vision' and not on the *Wasteland* of this world. The depression, the lament, the rage of the earlier poems have, after tortuously passing through a maze of experience, feeling and reflection, liquified into this supreme wisdom syncretising the quintessential teachings of practically all the major faiths at his 'visioned summits'.

An important aspect of this powerful series of poems should not go unnoticed. Ameeruddin's style in it is largely synchronic with the progress of his 'long pilgrimage', his voice an appropriate vehicle for his vision. *Visioned Summits* can be considered to be a sequence of monologues, with the difference that throughout the convoluted journey the dramatic voice is that of the poet himself, without any Tiresias clearly taking it up here and there. Unlike *The Wasteland, Visioned Summits* can be called one loose allegorical discourse. Its comprehensive framework is enriched by the use of imagery, symbols, paradoxes and metaphors combining two or three of them in a phrase, a line or a sentence. The underlying onomatopoeic sounds are also modulated with the progress of the theme.

The opening monologue "Eloquent Serenade" is not a usual serenade of love, but an undulating song of a 'lover and a wanderer' (*Visioned Summits* 23) circumscribing a great deal of space and time and the predominance of evil with its impact on the poet's sensitive soul. He is puzzled and angered at the ambience of 'human bombs and AK 47s' (*Visioned Summits* 27), 'Darkness and deception', 'mirth and mutilation' (*Visioned Summits* 45) unmindful of

> The one and only Reality –
> Ishwar-Allah-Tere Nam
> (*Visioned Summits* 27)

Even before their visional summits can be reached one has to contend with the 'all-round degeneration of values' echoing 'a swan song/for the oncoming deluge of humanity' (*Visioned Summits* 30-31), the eternal enigma of 'cycling and recycling experiences' (*Visioned Summits* 48) of "birth, copulation, death" making him conclude:

> All is just a boomerang
> And a syllabled ding-dong song
> (*Visioned Summits* 48)

The poet's journey begins on a suppressed note with his decision to walk 'Into the alphabetic anarchy of starts' (*Visioned Summits* 24) while

All this—echo a swan song –
For the oncoming deluge of humanity.
(*Visioned Summits* 31)

All these extracts are marked by a concentrated feeling of repulsion and rage trying to burst out through personifications, synesthesias, series of metaphors, paradoxical phrases, deft use of onomatopoeic alliterations, which sometimes pass on from hard hammer-like consonant sounds followed by eerie serpentine hissings, to return soon to the hard sounds at the end. It is not easy to attempt a complete analysis of the artistic intermingling of emotion, imagery and sound in the poem.

To highlight a contrasted feeling of joy an entirely different sound pattern consisting of short playful vowel sounds and liquid consonants has been employed:

There should be laughter and smile everywhere
My hands should create the language of love
New alphabets of equality
New syllables of solace
So that, fire flies may weave the manuscript
Of man's rainbow dreams
(*Visioned Summits* 41).

In a few poems in the middle a tone is low and their movement slow which is quite in tune with their reflective content. The sound pattern and imagery of the last section are quite different, for they are marked by the poet's approaching 'The mysterious spiralling paths/of passion and peace' (*Visioned Summits* 149). In this section a web of ever-changing Proteus-like imagery, mesmeric metaphors, restful rhythms, alluringly altering alliterations hypnotise the reader as much as the 'spicy solace' and the tranquillising illumination of the orgasmic arrival does:

Dark night reaches the dawn
Midnight terror merges into mellowness
The trance comes to a poise
Fragrance of the ecstatic dream
Remain afresh lingering and
Lilting down the memory lane

Reminding the magnificent moon
Of 'Buddha Poornima'...
(*Visioned Summits* 157)

The summit of he poet's vision focussed in the illumination of the full moon highlights its universally tranquillising quality. This all-embracing, essentially Indian, message, arrived at through metaphysical mazes, is reminiscent not only of the inspiring discourse of the *Vedanta*, including the *Upanishads* and also of the Buddha, also of the quintessence of Christianity and Islam, as put forth not only by thinkers like Vivekananda, but also by the sermons of the *Bible* and the mystic poets like Kabir, the Sufis and Tagore, to mention only a few. Syed Ameeruddin also seems to have been inspired by T.S. Eliot, G.M. Hopkins and W.B. Yeats though in different ways. He is one of those poets who have grappled with the problem of penetrating the fog of worldly illusion and sighting the full moon of Divinity which radiates joy and peace over all alike.

Essentially, a poet of visionary fragments. Syed Ameeruddin's *Visioned Summits* was directed towards the attainment of propinquity with the Divine to deliver himself from the world perceived by the senses. Its difference from *Visions of Deliverance* is that of emphasis, but it is important as a focal point of these two complementary poetic collections.

Visions of Deliverance is an exciting collection of poems with both sensual and metaphysical overtones. It is also possible to read *Visions of Deliverance* as a wavy sequence of poems on love passing through various phases, not in any emotional order and also interspersed with poems on other subjects most of which have some relation to the theme of love in different fields, but ultimately touching the summits of Deliverance.

The underlying subjectivity of the sequence is rooted in filial love. In the opening poem "A Prayer for my Grandson" the eternal stream of love is a 'legacy' (*Visions of Deliverance* 27) of 'all the values or Moses, Jesus, Mohammed and Ram' (*Visions of Deliverance* 33), accompanied by a wish that his broad pluralistic vision of 'one Entity, one Creation, one Divinity' (*Visions of Deliverance* 44) may be inherited by his grandson, of course through the poet's son who is initially concealed in him only to be ultimately revealed (*Visions of Deliverance* 92).

These poems dealing with a 'spiritual family tree' (*Visions of Deliverance* 27) are naturally based on sexual love, the romantic side of which is celebrated in quite a few poems from the beginning of love in "A New Love", through 'Come Dancing Thine Way to Mine Arms', to its physical consummation in "Love Times" and its broadening out in "the zestful celebrations of Humanity" (*Visions of Deliverance* 182) in "Drumbeats of Dampatya".

However, what is remarkable is that almost all the love poems of Syed Ameeruddin, including the romantic ones gradually broaden out into spirituality. His romantic poems explore the presence of the radiance of divinity even in sexual love. Love gradually broadens out into spirituality by first including nature within its widening circumference. The last lines of one of his poems are a pointer in this direction:

> Our good-byes cast anchor in autographs of silence
> And in the seasonal jasmine blooming
> Where our partings remain embossed
> In the silvery dust of the flowery pollen.
>
> ("Broken Whispers," *Visions of Deliverance* 138)

In the poem "Love Song" he has begun to sense the spiritual in the beauty of his beloved:

> Let me dream in the simmering space
> Of your soul
> Allow me to reach
> The spiritual heights
> From the scintillating sensuality
> Of your body.
>
> (*Visions of Deliverance* 87-88)

He hopes that his songs

> Will echo and resound
> Lasting rhapsodies.
> In the glittering galaxies –
> From time to eternity.
>
> (*Visions of Deliverance* 88)

Thus he makes his love not only grow vertically into the spiritual but also horizontally into time and into the space of Nature as in the poem "My Beloved":

> Where are you, my beloved?
> Withered leaves have scattered.
> Barren boughs are weeping
> Nature's bounty is ruined.
> A spiritual drought is set on around
> A symphony of cemetry is echoed everywhere,
>
> (*Visions of Deliverance* 65)

The beloved becomes his 'spiritual companion' and in "You Are a Beautiful Poem" he finally seems to propose:

> Lets Love each other
> To the depths and breadths and heights
> Our souls can reach
> To realise the ideal of
> Sat-Chit-Ananda.
>
> (*Visions of Deliverance* 128)

Some of the poems in this collection indicate just worldly garb of divinity which include places, persons, important occasions etc. But through openings in that clothing, divinity does peep out every now and then. In "Voyage" during his wanderings he resolves to discover secrets of myself. The modernised Turkey symbolises 'the Essence of Spiritual Beauty.' A New Year should 'breathe in—Amity love for all,' and thus 'To let the dove flutter freely in the deep sky.' In the revised version of "My India" (the first one having been published in *Visioned Summits)* he leaves out the details about the different modes of worship in India's past and only highlights the present woes and misfortunes, wondering how we can regain our lost glory.

The last poem in this collection, *Visions of Deliverance*, reflects that which supplies the title of this book. It is presented as a "Vision", a dream, comprising of three parts, each unique in its own way. The first part projects the innumerable aspects of the repulsiveness of modern life through a powerful fusion of an amazing wealth of imagery with numerous linguistic devices to make the meaning burst upon the reader. Both the meaning and the language seem to have arrived at their very edge, as can be noticed in the following stanza:

> What is this rottening riot of glee
> And stinking stains of spree
> The splash of spirits on fumes ablaze
> The rhythmic plethora
> Of excited exits
> The fractured joys
> And furied raptures
> The puerile play
> Of flamy traumatic force
> The flash of purple woes
> In delirious souls,
>
> (*Visions of Deliverance* 187)

Freed by death from this nauseating phenomenon of worldly life, each soul is represented as charting its own path.

> Beyond—far beyond
> The timeless frontiers
> Roaring—Reverberating Neti...Neti...Neti...
>
> (*Visions of Deliverance* 192)

It ultimately reaches the tantalising light of 'the twin tunnels' in one of which its destiny, carved by itself, lies. One of them is Hell, with its frightful prospect of an ocean of fire in which the soul suffers for 'a space of timeless time' till, bathed in repentance, it is fit to receive divine grace. The other tunnel, meant for the virtuous, is illumined with divine radiance of the 'Eternal light' of "Eternal Bliss":

> The Moksha! The Maqfirat! The Nirvana!
> The blow of 'Soor'!
> the Drumbeat!
> The Shriek of Shankh!
> Deliverance! Deliverance! Deliverance!
>
> (*Visions of Deliverance* 202)

Thus after his *Visioned Summits,* Syed Ameeruddin in this book casts a backward glance at the worldly phenomena including love, which is often tremulous with intimations of the spiritual. In the last section of the book he has a "Vision" of the individual soul, reaping its punishment or reward in what is beyond this life, finally reaching its deliverance. What is indeed remarkable about his books is not only the powerful theme and expression but the essential unity of all important religions of the world as envisioned by our ancient scriptures and expounded by thinkers like Vivekananda. The words may differ but their essentials are almost the same, almost bringing them within the ambit of "My India". Another poet P.B. Shelley has expressed practically the same idea in his immortal lines in *Adonais.*

> The One remains, the many change and pass:
> Heaven's light for ever shines, Earth's shadows fly ...

Syed Ameeruddin seems to have envisioned the path of deliverance from 'earth's shadows' to 'Heaven', call it by whatever name you like.

Syed Ameeruddin's poetry does, of course, accept, like T.S. Eliot, the ambiguities of life and the multi-faceted evil that has gripped our world. But Ameeruddin sees it ultimately dissolve in the moonlight of divinity which, in spite of its various apparent differences and disputes, is essentially one. One of the ways to reach it, which Ameeruddin highlights, is love, beginning at the physical level, but transcending it by stages into the spiritual. This axial message is proclaimed by him in various ways with a verve, in a highly emphatic voice, almost verging on rhetoric with all the force of his rich and resounding vocabulary. T.S. Eliot also presents in a low but sharply suggestive way suitable for an intellectual the moods of depression and frustration in his many shorter poems like "The Love Song of J. Alfred Prufrock," "Aiuimila," "Whispers of Immortality" and "Sweeney among the Nightingales" as well as in his longer works like *The Murder in the Cathedral* and *The Wasteland,* which end with a sort of didactic curtain of the message of the Archbishop in one and of Prajapati's 'Da' in the other. Ameeruddin on the other hand, has glimpses of the oneness of the soul divine somewhat as in W.B. Yeats's "Sailing to Byzantium" in which even in a 'paltry thing' like "an aged man" we can notice how does:

> Soul clap its hands and sing, and louder sing
> For every tatter in its mortal dress....

The poetry of Syed Ameeruddin with its immortal message of uni' conveyed effectively and repeatedly has been acclaimed by critics, both Indian and foreign. Two reputed Indian critics have already been quoted in the beginning this essay. A few other critics have also been impressed by his poetry. A reviewer of *Visioned Summits* in *National Herald* (New Delhi) describes his poetry as 'a conglomeration of the metaphysical, the surreal and existential'[5], while a reviewer of *Deccan Herald* (Bangalore) recognises that 'Ameeruddin stands up boldly to release the dove of peace as he envisions the summits attained by world's religions'[6]. According to Justice S. Mohan (India), Ameeruddin's poetry is pregnant with far-reaching suggestiveness and that 'he combines a single moment with centuries.'[7] Dr. Joy B. Cripps of England is equally suggestive in saying that Ameeruddin's 'prophetic words are the living views of universe, holding keys to eerie secrecies.'[8] It would perhaps be proper to close with a remark by Dr. Naomi F. Faust of USA which covers many of the achievements of Syed Ameeruddin whom he calls 'an unique phenomenon for his poetic mission, spiritual vision, vibrating dynamism, symphonic symbolism, complex imagery and above all for his humanitarian and metaphysical concern's.[9] Perhaps it is high time that Indian critics and literary historians also pay due attention to the upcoming crop of modern Indian English poets among whom Ameeruddin should receive proper recognition for the characteristic uniqueness of his poetry.

References

1. K. R. Srinivasa lyengar's letter quoted in *Visioned Summits,* p. 778.
2. Krishna Srinivas, 'Syed Ameeruddin's Poetry,' *Visioned Summits* (Madras: International Poets Academy 2005) 21. All further reference to this book in this paper have been given in page numbers only, to b identified contextually.

3. Syed Ameeruddin, *Visioned Summits* (Madras: International Poets Academy 2005)
4. Syed Ameeruddin, *Visions of Deliverance* (Chennai: International Poets Academy, 2006). All references to this book in this paper have been give: in page numbers only, to be identified contextually.
5. Syed Ameeruddin, *Visioned Summits* (Madras: International Poets Academy 2005) 177.
6. Syed Ameeruddin, *Visioned Summits* (Madras: International Poets Academy 2005) 178.
7. Syed Ameeruddin, *Visions of Deliverance* (Chennai: International Poets Academy, 2006) 229.
8. Syed Ameeruddin, *Visions of Deliverance* (Chennai: International Poets Academy, 2006) 230.
9. Syed Ameeruddin, *Visions of Deliverance* (Chennai: International Poets Academy, 2006) 231.

20

An Elevating Spiritual Journey of Grace and Nobility through Syed Ameeruddin's *Visioned Summits* and *Visions of Deliverance*

—P.C.K. Prem

It is an experience to go through the poems of Syed Ameeruddin. He is a well-known name in Indian English Poetry and reading him, one feels unique thrills of an ennobling spirit pervading the entire mortal frame while a kind of distinctive catharsis takes place within without apparent feeling. He has an awe-inspiring religious bent of mind that infuses each word with a soul filling nectar. He is surprisingly rooted in Indian culture and traditions, ethical values and eternal belief in the existence of God in each particle of animate and inanimate. Somewhere, a thought continues to tease the inner consciousness with the feeling that perfection is possible only if sincere efforts are made to live a life of meaning and substance. It is a stupendous poetic effort with an immense philosophical and religious import directed at mankind involved in transient acts that make life meaningless. In another context, it is a humble attempt to reconcile the imperfections of the worldly life with the excellence of divinity, divinity that cannot be explained but can only be experienced provided man has faith. One has to reach the mental areas of the poet in order to comprehend the hidden meanings which are shrouded in mystery in the play of words he uses laden with intensity of images and stunning metaphors. The poet's play with the words is majestically unimaginable for he unceasingly bowls between earthly realities and ethereal possibilities bordering on truth of life on earth.

At times, a feeling is generated that poet is making concerted efforts to arouse the inner man of every one so that a better living is ensured on earth irrespective of the placing of man in the rough and jumble of life.

With extremely soft words he awakens man to the truth of living on earth and the divine pleasures awaiting man in the other world provided life on earth is pious and ethical. While treading this path, he is transparent in bringing out the frailties of human life. To the poet life is purposeful even in filth and sin, vice and violence, in case a genuine repentance enters the mind and heart of man.

The poet's lamentations reach a crescendo of woes and waitings when he looks around and finds that there is no safe place for 'Ishwar, Allah, Tera Naam' the one and only Reality; and crazy endeavour continues to determine an abode of that single Reality. He is conscious of the terrible specter of violence bowling the entire earth with dreaded weapons of annihilation. But man does not hesitate. Here man is confronting whirlwind of darkness, screams of solitude under the delirious sun, blaze of sensation with skies of sanity where 'myopic eyes with unbridles minds' dream of love and humanity. The poet tries to interpret he dilemma of modem anguish of man riddled with social and political bullets, finding no solace even in religious balm and thus he lives perennially in the shadow of cataclysmic despair with haunting images of ruins and inevitable calamity. There is inbuilt belief that salvation is possible if man dispels inner darkness while facing vicissitudes of life. The poet's staunch faith in God and in the ultimate deliverance of man, are his forte of strength. Life is a journey and man must go on to find the ultimate reality:

I am a wanderer,
I have a goal.
A purple purpose.
Long is the journey.
I must wander
Dark are the woods.
Its time for me to go
I have long buried the memories
of fractured sunsets
and long forgotten love times.

(*Visioned Summits*)

The poet is quite emphatic and dear about the destination. He wants to translate ideas and thoughts into reality. His compassion, sympathy and love for the poor and the underprivileged are evident. It is a perennial search for peace and harmony on earth and through the poor and the down trodden he wants to delve deep into the metaphysical question of life and existence.

II

The meaning of life and the purpose of man on earth continue to disturb the poet and a similar strain is apparent in "Voyage" where 'Haze and maze of—birth, copulation, death—All just a boomerang, All a syllabled ding-dong song...' Even love on earth, at times is just passion unlimited; and loneliness arising out of unfulfilled sensual love is immensely torturing.

Life for the poet is not only a mystery but a harrowing darkness and he exhibits tremendous guts to face it and straight way rushes towards the eye of the storm, and perhaps this way he exhorts man to fight out for existence. Life is a multi-fractured image where world appears crazy and divided into two halves of reality which is unstable; and the mad chase continues abruptly 'into the azure eyes of memory...yesterday, you touched me/with immutable pride/and longed for beautiful dreams.' And here again thought of beloved haunts the poet conceivably in the hope of resurrection. Here the symbol of the gypsy river is both mystical and earthy with sensuous undertones.

It is worldly anguish and anxiety of the poet when he speaks of 'violent waste' by men, on earth—a savage wasteland—indulges in'. Syed Ameeruddin probably hints at the terrible sense of loneliness in the crowd that a man feels on earth, and a the total vacuity within which continues to afflict. Though not clear yet it is the waste of natural and material resources on earth which are gradually resulting in suffocating living beings, including nature. A totally anarchic situation disturbs the poet and he feels he is in a dark deep vacuum; as the realisation of facts and truth speak of the ephemeral world's glory which is undoubtedly full of filth and sins beneath. But the eternal journey to find substance in life continues despite hurdles. It is immense faith in a roseate future for mankind which is the real strength and the poet even if alone, and a stranger is:

> A nowhere man
> With a lone son satchel.
> I shall march
> Alone in the shadow of ravines
> exploring the wasteland of hypocritical hybrids and tine shams
> Towards a strange and unknown destiny.
>
> (*Vicissitudes of Life*)

Worried about life, the poet is not unconscious of the deplorable plight through which the country passes through. He is a true patriot, and is quite remorseful of the contemporary sufferings of countrymen and the country *inter-alia*. At times he is straight and then silently oblique while hinting at the miseries and anguish of the people.

In spite of the failures and imminent obstructions, the search to seek answers to the enigmas of life continues unabated. In "Whispers of Beyond" a quaint attempt is made to foresee what lies hidden in the womb of horizons beyond the scope of eyes. It stirs and thrills the inner being. One is suddenly awakened to the make-believe reality of time. It is a state of mind where time stretches beyond the known parameters of past, present and future.

One comprehends the mystery but still remains in utter darkness and fumbles for words to describe a distinctive spiritual experience.

The poet observes:

> In the whirlpool of summer madness
> I dissolve into the yesterdays
> Where the past loafs *a* lilting march
> On the shimmering shores of time.

The poet is disturbed at the perennial ambiguities of life where nothing appears to open up clearly and there is a queer world where 'delirious dreams and diabolic disillusions' continue to stride like a Colossus and the world remains riddled with catastrophes waiting for deliverance and Nirvana. The poet is in love with unusual images and exclusively speaks of a man in flames, smoke and explosion where it is distress and agony but the optimist in the poet is unbending when he says that 'symphonies of heart' constitute the right destination where the heart must rest in peace. There are many impediments in life and man has to undergo sufferings so as to reach a stage of fulfillment. Even if defeats and failures challenge identity, the poet is unyielding in a determined march towards perfection where he ought to 'resurrect the symphony of love' of which he talked earlier.

The recurring theme with the poet is the enslavement of man by the forces of greed and avariciousness. Wealth is nothing but a carcass stretched over where vultures in men rejoice and thus a man is 'a prisoner of greed and mirth' and consequently life is a perpetuation of consternation, suffering and desolation.

The poet's prayer is:

> And bless me with the raiment of
> Nature's beauty and bounty
> Wealth is good
> if it serves like a warning.
>
> ("The Pomp of Gold")

If Syed is deeply involved in probing the mystery of man's birth and 'who am I,' 'why am I' and 'how am I' of life in its entirety while on earth and if these puzzles chase him throughout, it is a legitimate search in which the poet wants us to join. At the same time, he is conscious of the contemporary wide spread violence in many parts of the world. It a strange and deadly paradox of humanity that on the one hand it is the spirit of universality and catholicity engaged in extending the limits of humanism, on the other hand parochial, regional, religious and ethnic susceptibilities are corroding the very essence of man and humanity. "Carrion Carnage" is a poetic anguish at the widely spreading violence around and anarchy in the minds. Worries and anxieties of the poet about existence on earth are intense and harrowing.

He observes in "Life's Enigma":

> Existence is a cosmic drama
> Where life and death
> Are intertwined in struggle
> For a sustained sojourn in this world
> To suffer the trauma of ego-weakness.

While the poet confronts the reader with bewildering questions of existential meaning of life on earth, he is quite troubled within when country's present ailing scenario gives a clarion call for rejuvenation. In many poems, the poet's loneliness is agonising. In the deep recesses of heart, a lonely poet struggles to find meaning in existence but the social and political environment permits no respite to think, and he sits back to ponder over the fate of a miserable man. Guttural vacuity of man torments. Syed in the process imagines himself as a saviour of humanity and uses soft and yet rhythmically powerful words to convince man that peace and harmony are not far off provided he (learns to live as a man 'everywhere'. In the long uncertain journey he wishes to ameliorate the deplorable plight of man. As an inspired patriot and nationalist, he is worried about the destiny of India.

III

In *Visioned Summits* the poet is quite worried about the socially relevant moral issues with religious undertones. The humanitarian outlook is the fountainhead of his entire philosophy. One often observes in Syed's lyrics, an eternal bond of patriotism and cultural affinity among Indians despite appalling differences on the basis of caste, creed and colour. "My India" is a beautiful poem where the poet is unhappy with the present state of affair in India and wishes the ancient glory and splendour to be restored. India's prowess of spiritualism, mysticism, Vedic wisdom, art, culture and civilisation thrills and fascinates. India not only nursed various religions and religious men, saints and Sufis, it also permitted each to flourish and prosper without interference and thus it spread the message of universal brotherhood. India is the birthplace of towering saints and spiritual gurus who with the strength of yogic powers taught the perennial wisdom of life on earth and further communicated the lasting message of truth, love, compassion and sympathy. But this grand heritage is facing bad days now and the poet laments on the loss of values. The ancient grandeur has gone and now the poet wishes to regain that old beauty and might.

He is keen to revive the 'sustaining melodies of Ramayana/ Awe inspiring, harmonising/Drum beats of Mahabharata.' He wants 'unity and oneness of man' and the message of purity and innocence perpetuated by Rama to be translated into reality. If great teachings of religious gurus and saints, lasting wisdom of the *Vedas* and *Upanishads*, efforts of great men from Ramakrishna to Vivekananda to Gandhi have been partially or apathetically futile and ineffective and if on the other hand the sublime messages of non-violence, truth and service to humanity had not the desired result, it is because of:

> Some nasty finger has stuck
> Into your dreaming eyes.
> I know, I know
> You are sobbing and bleeding
> With bruises of infidelity
> And ungratefulness
> With manifold harms and hurts
> inflicted by your misled
> and miscreant children.
> Perhaps they have lost their way
> perhaps, they have gone astray-
> But the question is... How would this blind prodigals
> Trace their way?'
>
> ("My India")

This poem is simply magnificent for its historic perspective and truth whose narrative sweep takes the reader back to ancient times. The poet is not different in another collection *Visions of Deliverance*. The poet's anxieties about the enigma of life and living are quite discernible. He carries forward the strain of thought and emphatically makes out his mission clear. He visits and revisits unusual and striking areas of serious deliberation where he probes into the mysteries of life. Syed is worried about life on earth, he is really perturbed about life after death and then his worries are apparent when he makes strenuous efforts to understand the predicament of birth and rebirth. At times it appears he is concerned with the ancient values of India and suddenly he emerges as an advocate of modern Indian consciousness. Whereas *Visioned Summits* takes us to unknown beyond and gives an inkling of an exotic and stunning world created through impassioned expertise of imagination, in *Visions of Deliverance* the poet appears to confront us again in a more forceful manner with the questions of existence arising out of loneliness, lusty and greedy materialistic love and consequent vacuity in life.

For the poet, modernity creates inner turmoil and sufferings because a man is uncertain. "A Prayer—For my Grandson" is a beautiful invocation. The 'little angel' is an embodiment of divine light and an eternal truth is reflected through the little child. The child is a symbol of innocence and beauty and the poet hopes that appearance will infuse life and vitality to a 'murky mystic race.' Here questions arise as to the very basis of human race. To the poet, the child carries the heritage of not only a particular family but if the meaning is extended to the entire humanity, the little angel will ultimately salvage the world from its vicious and monstrous machinations.

In a kind of address to the self, the poet is conscious of modern sufferings and so it is also a serious and devastating commentary on the stupid and malicious ways of man. Moral values and ethical qualities as enshrined in the teachings of Moses, Jesus, Mohammed and Ram are in disarray and have almost ended up and now these are required to be rejuvenated and so the poet invokes the hidden saintly powers of the little child. He also speaks movingly of contemporary sins, vices, corruption and crimes and waits for a future man who would make this world worth living with virtues and truth prevailing around. It is a pious admission that the little angel is 'a genesis, a progeny, a harbinger of poet's 'longing abysmal' and hopefully the poet observes clearly that he must carry on:

> The mystic mantle of our heritage
> Into the inscapes and outscapes

Of times reality
Unforgetful of our glorious land
of Vedic love and Epical grandeur
And be rooted in our
Pluralistic culture that vibrates
Satyam! Sivam! Sundraram!
And the infinite cosmic confluence of
Anhal Hag'Aham Brahman! Nirvana!'

And then he eloquently waits for the dawn of humanism where man will 'share joy, sorrow and nature' to 'bring radiating brilliance—into the shrunken ghostly faces.' "New Love" is a search evidently to find meanings of love in 'social debris' but it is otherwise a journey to physical love, spiritual yearnings and the consequential haze. A genuine wish is expressed to get out of the corporeal gratification of life through a churning of the sensual and the spiritual that will lead to a life of divine ecstasy and rapture; and this constitutes the theme of "Moonlit Meanderings". This poem finds a more cogent explanation in "My Beloved" where passions unlimited and loneliness torture. In "Birthday Song" a realisation comes to the poet that meaning of existence is quite transparent when birth of a child indicates an unbroken continuity of human race and there all the spiritual and sensuous cravings find vivid evidence.

As usual, "New Year" speaks of a resolution to kill the beast in man so that a better world is born. "Love Times" reminds us of Omar Khayyam—a celebration of senses leading to something beyond physical. The recurring theme of love attracts indepth analysis as these are not only rejoicings of conjugal love with a passionately eager partner but the beloved is also a spiritual energy and inspiration. The following lines of "You are a Beautiful Poem" simply enchant and thrill:

I touched your breast with adoration
And caressed the contours of your waist
Then whispered in your ears
you are beautiful poem....
Let's love each other
to the depths and breadths and heights
Our souls can reach
to realise the ideals of Sat-Chit-Anand.

While "Your Eyes" is again a concerto of eternal love with unique sensuousness:

I drown and bask
In the white radiance
Of your eyes
Because
The sun never shines as bright as your eyes.

The poet cannot resist the temptations to envision feelings of love in different hues. In a slightly refreshing context, he observes:

You are away now, somewhere beyond
our memories play on the shores
Beckoning the summer evenings we spent together.
'Our goodbyes cast anchor in autographs of silence
And in the seasonal jasmine blooming
Where our partings remain embossed
In the silvery dust of the flowery pollen.

("Broken Whispers")

Visions of Deliverance is one of the most important poems that to some extent has epic dimensions. The theme is absolutely stunning and in an imperceptive way one goes through terrific experiences which are created by startling images and similes. Here one confronts doubts about the designs of nature. Poet is awe stricken with the 'magnificent extravagance of tumultuous devastations' The images of 'cluster of hurricane clouds' and 'shimmering shrieks of smithereens souls' are horrifying. The dreadful scenario indirectly tells man of the fury and terror of nature when angry and causes havoc around. It is almost a visit to hell one experiences. He talks of immense anguish and misery all pervasive and finds no respite or deliverance. Shocking and bizarre images at times confuse and it is difficult to reach authentic meaning. He is disturbed by the riot of glee where 'fractured joys' and furled raptures in 'puerile play' make life traumatic and painful.

The next few lines give sufferings of souls another dimension where poet is dreaded at the vast panorama of tornado blowing around and the escape is impossibility from the epicenter of infernos. The poet is visibly pained at the intensity of sufferings on earth.

The voyage is forlorn and excruciating when the poet observes that the voyage:

> From lone to lone
> From ethereal slumber
> to tyrannous trance
> Beyond the hissy hues
> of heathenly darks...

This journey is uncertain right from birth till one is driven to the grave but it is definitely spectacular.

The soul is thus entangled in nightmarish experiences with no hope of harmony and peace. Life on earth is entirely forlorn and miserable. Imprisoned in the pangs and sorrows of material pursuits it is almost a life of animals sans feelings, love, compassion and empathy.

The moment soul is liberated, it is a supreme experience saturated with divinity. This feeling defies description as the soul is set free and goes out of the worldly ensnares and narrow man-made precincts where prejudices and lethal voids govern. But when eternity opens doors it is a timeless feeling; and one feels liberated. One finds truth and seriousness of purpose in the poetry of Syed Ameeruddin; to use Arnold's words and this constitutes the poet's strength.

The poet observes:

> This phenomenon
> is hazy and smoky—
> Each soul must chart
> Its fleverecent flight alone
> And voyage it way
> To dwindling ups and downs

The mysterious vision continues with monolithic pressure and so also the spectacular odyssey of the soul to merge with the ultimate reality—the Brahman. And before this the 'dark and despicable souls' must undergo the travails of purification. It is a struggle eternal to achieve salvation. The purification is a painful exercise as the voluptuous soul has to face the 'whirlpools of torrential furies'. The poet interestingly uses symbol of fire in various hues which is both enervating and destructive. If is gives life and light, it also brings perdition and annihilation.

> The great churning begins and–
> Thus these souls in fumes
> Drifted into layers within layers
> of flames-multidimensional
> Till a space of timeless time
> Till the souls are cry stalled and crafted
> Moulded and shaped in molten lava
> to the pristine peaks of purity.

In a formidable and gruelling journey of soul, earthly realities and ethereal and metaphysical questions of life are quite evident. Burning of ego and sins by fire results in total purity and a new light is seen every where which opens up splendid panorama of divine living. It is a 'divine light and fire' with multi-fąceted hues which act as a great rejuvenating and resurrecting force; and thus the poet happily says:

> Thus, the souls of purple deeds
> Received and traversed
> through Labyrinthine vicissitudes of light
> Light upon light—Light within light
> Into the exalted layers
> Of munificence of light
> till the silvery souls
> Reached the gardens of 'Eternal Homes.'

It is in truth the journey to find the eternal light, the eterna bliss and the eternal Bounty where the realisation of Supreme fulfilment pacifies a hungry soul and thus deliverance becomes a near reality of life. Syed Ameeruddin is definite, clear and yet baffles with the use of words. He is sharp but at times overpoweringly repetitive. But the theme with the cosmic dimensions he handles perhaps needs this technique. It is a wonderful feeling when one flows quietly along with the rhythmic movement of his poetry.

He is remarkable in grafting and coining new words with musical undertones and wherever he indulges in poetic liberty, it stirs. His imaginative sweep defies restrain.

He takes cognisance of life's relation with nature in entirety and expresses it with a rare genuineness. Not for a while, does he ignore grace, instinctive Godly feeling and sublimity which an ideal life should have to ensure a harmonious existence. Poetry should ennoble a man with its all-pervasive power of beauty of grace, rhythm, and music and faith in life eternal. Syed is emphatic and confident in the strength of poetry as a force which in the ultimate analysis makes life better.

He fascinates and thrills with high sounding musical words and at the same time evokes feelings saturated deeply with an inexplicable divinity vanquishing all that exasperates man on earth and there lies its great healing power. Here one is reminded of poets of Pre-Raphaelites period who along, with a number of aesthetes, believed in the concept and theory of 'Art for Art's Sake' and vehemently espoused the cause of pure creative outpouring that serves the end of a particular art, thus ignoring the essential principle of creation that ought to make living on earth not only positive but purposeful. But the poet in Syed has specified a different objective where he wishes to idealise life and so he tries to infuse meaning and purpose to poetry. Through noble and lofty thoughts he wishes to make man's life better.

It becomes quite transparent that the poet is extremely comfortable when he, through the medium of poetry, wants to disseminate moral and ethical values and inadvertently here appear streaks of Miltonic touches—good and lofty. When one goes deep into the social concerns of the poet in the modern context, one may not find him very simple and flexible like Mathew Arnold but definitely he adheres to the spirit of sincerity and 'ever widening its knowledge' of the great critic Arnold.

Like Krishna Srinivas, Narsingh Srivastava and Aju Mukhophadhyay he is genuinely enthused by different religions and uses the cardinal teachings of various religions in his poetic art for the uplift of human intellect, heart and soul. Not so religious K.V. Raghupathi, also exhibits faith in the spiritual, moral and ethical values in poetry which can influence man's life, Syed Ameeruddin is deeply influenced by a kind of spiritual and religious fervour and it is expressed quite conveniently in poetry with a determined impact. Interestingly it appears, he is a believer in cultural and traditional values of life with ample scope and flexibility for corrections as the contemporary mind-set requires, and this alone is Syed's remarkable quality as a poet.

21

Poetic Style in Syed Ameeruddin's Poetry

—Rajeev Ranjan, R.K. Singh and M. Mojibur Rahman

Syed Ameeruddin has a considerable poetic output but he has not been academically explored by researchers and critics. Even various anthologies published in the last three decades have not given him the place he deserves. The study has been an attempt to reverse the trend by examining Ameeruddin's structural and textural characteristics.

Ameeruddin is a poet who reflects Indian sensibility in the choice of his themes, symbols and imagery, and use of the English language. He effectively Indianises the medium at lexical and syntactical levels according to his thematic requirements and needs of communication. He coins new words by blending or collocating them with words of other languages such as Hindi, Sanskrit, Urdu or Arabic. His innovations in the form of local borrowings, calques, translations and code mixing or mixing of elements of Hindi/Urdu/Tamil language makes him distinctly Indian. In fact the way he uses the English Language for communicative purpose is indicative of his attempt to acculturate English language.

His semantic or syntactical attitude is at best pragmatic in the sense that his rhetoric is guided by his native literary and cultural context which values stylistic embellishment. It is perhaps for this reason that Ameeruddin tends to borrow words and phrases of Sanskrit, Arabic and Hindi and indulges in phrase mongering with polite diction and moralistic tone. He is on the whole readable and communicable and his poems echo deeper meaning and broader vision even as his metaphoric expressions make him complex, thoughtful and serious. His sincerity of purpose, that is, a spiritual self discovery through the discovery of the country's spiritual past, however, is unquestionable.

Syed Ameeruddin is rich in his expression of Indian spiritual influences, Indian myths, legends and culture, and the socio political condition prevailing in the country. The poet himself believes in expression of Indian rich tradition and culture.

Syed Ameeruddin writes with a social and moral purpose with a view to changing the fabric of the society where man recognises man, religion recognises religion, and people abide by the concept of oneness of humankind. His poetry supports values of humanity, peace, love and harmony, just as the poet insists on respect and preservation of nature and ecological balance.

Ameeruddin's poetry revels with rebounded thought rather than spontaneous thoughts. He deliberately gives a twist—spiritual or metaphysical—to the various aspects of his vision. His adjectives tend to overload the texture of his poems. A poem like "Eloquent Serenada" echoes Walt Whitman with the Waste Landish awareness. He mixes up so many things in a single poem that it appears more a padding than a genuine poetic feeling. His poetic flights cross over a wide spectrum, cycling and recycling with linguistic liberty and verbal profundity.

The present study seeks to explore Ameeruddin's poetic style. Style is the linguistic expression or literary manner in which the poet couches his views, ideas, thoughts, messages and visions. It includes discourse features of the poem as gleaned from the form, symbol, imagery, versification, mood, attitude, tone, diction, language, etcetera. As Vinayak Krishna Gokak says, 'Style is really the exploitation, by the writer or poet, of a few of the possibilities selected out of many, under each of the following heads, to give a faithful and sensitive expression of his vision:language; rhythm; thought; imagery; mood; and attitude.'[1]

With his predilection for complexities of ideas and thought, and a tendency to turn inward, Syed Ameeruddin tends to be complex and evocative in his use of language. Sometimes he leaves his sentences incomplete, piling phrases upon phrases, or using sentence fragments in his attempt to construct impressive epithets or metaphors that mix with his narrative, descriptive or interrogative explorations. For example:

Life, a criss-cross crisis
Amidst dwindling destinies
Delirious dreams
And diabolic disillusions.

World, a frensied humdrum existence
of banality and triviality
of nauseating human experience
of cerebral jigsaw puzzles
of bated breath and
Spiritual destitution.

Reality, an elusive enigma
Between here and hereafter
A ravishing rainbow
Between life and death
A hazy horizon
Between material and metaphysical.

Deliverance, a dialectic
Of existence and evangelic
Poised on the horns of a dilemma,
The ambiguity and the ambivalence.

Then, what is Nirvana?
Reflecting on the smoky layers
Of gloom and solace,
and seeing—
meaning in ambiguity.[2]

Sometimes his sentences are very short and simple, but ideas gradually turn complex:

I am a wanderer. I am a nowhere man.
Gypsy river runs through my bones.
I walk with the thunder,
And share its magnificent pride.
I am a wanderer. I have a goal. A purple purpose.
Long is the Journey. I must wander.

Dark are the woods. Its time for me to go ...
I have long buried the memories
Of fractured sunsets
And long forgotten lovetimes.

My search stormed my quest quaked.
My secret grief of
Humanity and existence rigmaroled ...[3]

In his earlier poem he uses a lot of ellipses and exclamations which suggest some kind of a tension which he seeks to resolve pursuing his thought structure in a context. In fact, through a complex of thought pattern, imagery and linguistic devices, Ameeruddin seeks to add depth and force to his poetry. He may appear simple at some stage but soon he becomes complicated, intentionally or unintentionally, as he manoeuvres his way through his struggle of the mind, body, and soul. There may be some flashes of insight here and there but in most of the poems one notices a sort of surrealistic rambling, nostalgic sentiments and subjective musings as noticed in several poems, including his ambitious collection *Visioned Summits* (1995).

The poet's style may remind one of the style of Krishna Srinivas on the one hand and T.S. Eliot and Walt Whitman on the other. Most of his metaphors, imagery and phrasal constructions have distinct influence of Krishna Srinivas just as when he uses Sanskrit, Arabic or Hindi words, he seems to be recreating the Waste Landish style in certain poems. One notices a lot of culture bound expressions such as *Tandava, Nirvana, Moksha, Maqfirat, Dharma, Adharma, Iswar, Allah, Buddha Poornima, Bodhi tree, Mahaprasthan, Aham Brahman, daridranarayan, Anal Haq, Moksha*, etcetera. These are typical Indian culture words for which synonyms are not available in English.

Ameeruddin also presents several mythical characters. He uses either the name of deities or other religious or legendary characters: Ram, Krishna, Shiva, Parvathi, Radha, Shakuntala, Urvasi, Menaka, Rambha, Guru Nanak, Mohammed, Kabirdas, Khawja Ajmeri, Ram Krishna, Vivekanand. Gandhiji, etcetera. All these are direct examples of Indianness rather than Indianisation because these are the proper names in Indian context. The poet also uses proper name of places: Kurukushetra, Gurudwara, Masjids, Kailasanatha, Ayodhya, Bombay, Punjab, Kashmir, India, etcetera.

In his poetry we also find register bound lexical items based on Indian social culture such as *shankh, mehandi, patni, pati-dev, ardhangini, dampatya, izzat, khandan, dulhan, rathyatra, padyatra, salam, Ameen, Om shanti*, etcetera.

Ameeruddin also uses typical Indian adjectives for some well known iconic figures: 'Maryadapurushottam' used for Lord Ram, or 'Yugaprush' used for Gandhiji and epithets like Niskama Karma and serva jana.

He hybridises English as in 'Bhakti Singers, in the poem "My India" and makes plural of native nouns such as Yogis, munis, rishis, sufis, fakirs, masjids, avatars, etc.

The poet offers typical Indian collocations such as Ram and Rahim as in the poem "Carrion Carnage." He seems to translate typical Indian expressions as in 'interior of my soul', 'hidden dream', 'moon floors', 'bruised heart', 'hunting memory', 'hidden dream', 'purple moment', 'hissing hope', 'Dark savage sky', 'lilting lips', 'smithereen realities', 'Snaky arm', 'Fugitive moon', 'liquid moon', 'Moon-bathed', 'trembling moon', 'dreaming eyes', 'Opaque mind', 'hungry arm', 'Oncoming storm', 'empty river', etcetera.

Sometimes Ameeruddin coins words like 'halvesonned', 'whirly', 'wind', 'twillighty dawn', 'twilighty tapestry', etcetera to express his unique thoughts.

Ameeruddin uses verbal sounds to create deeper impact through alliteration, euphony, and onomatopoeic often on the verge of mysticism:

> Again... Mysterious—Unheard—Unimaginable ...
> Innumerable sounds of Distraction ... Broke out.
> From that ... a deadly thunder bolt flashed ...
> It roared ... roared ... roared ... thrice ...
> Each uproar ... conveying a Supreme sense ...
> Thrice it resounded ... with significant Meaning ...
> BH... K... TI... YO... GA !!
> ...GNA... NA...YO ...GA !!
> ...KA...R...MA... YO... GA!![4]

Syed Ameeruddin also makes use 'Hyperbole' to show his emotional musing:

My enchantress
You are my poetic quest
You are my souls search
You are my hearts longing
You are my minds fancy
You are my dreams diana
You are my emotions Radha
You are my passions Parvathi
You are my spirits Shakuntala ...[5]

Ameeruddin writes poetry in free verse like other contemporary poets but for musical effect he creates internal rhyme, alliteration and assonance:

"A teacher, poet ; enjoyed the
Pleasures and pangs of being
A lover, husband, father, friend and foe.."[6]

Here the poet creates alliteration through the repetition of |p|, |f| and |r| sound:

The night light burned, and we slept
Keeping the love we have we had stored inside.
We undressed in silent submission
Into the rippling force of the whirlwind.[7]

Here the poet creates internal music through the repetition of |i|, |t| and |s| sound.

Ameeruddin's style is also in tune with poetic themes which widely stress the Indian thought and philosophy as enshrined in the *Vedas, Upanishads, Gita, Quran*, Buddhism, Sufism and Jainism.

The poet also uses several Indian mythical characters as well as symbol and imagery which reflects his serious outlook. The varieties of symbols and imagery he piles in various poems show his thought provoking concept and emotional and sentimental mindset.

Ameeruddin offers different moods in his poetry. Sometimes he looks as a philosopher to follow divine principles of 'Bhakti Yoga,' 'Gnana Yoga' and 'Karma Yoga'; and sometimes he shows the mood of Nirvana. In love poems he depicts romantic and passionate mood and shows love and physical relationship to celebrate life as also to find the supreme bliss. In some other poems, he demonstrates a satiric and ironic mood to present his social consciousness. Thus, his different moods add variety to his poetry.

Syed Ameeruddin's poetic attitude is comprehensive. He echoes the path of universal brotherhood, universality of God and human values. Keki N. Daruwalla opines, 'Art has an aesthetic function. It gives the soul and your heart a different dimension. Religion and poetry came through the same upsurge of the soul.'[8] Syed Ameeruddin shows a similar attitude in his poetry giving to the soul and heart aesthetic pleasure. To quote R.K. Singh, Ameeruddin's intellectual and spiritual response to the "present social debris" invites exploration of the part for a 'New scintillating saga.'[9] The poet's intellectual and spiritual attitude makes him a poet of the high order who thinks about world peace and welfare of mankind. He sounds sincere.

Ameeruddin uses simple diction and vocabulary in his poetry. He avoids using complex words. Even in his concept of universal religion and brotherhood and philosophical ideas, Ameeruddin tries to be simple. As M. Mujeeb says, 'Mr Ameeruddin's diction is simple and lucid and his style sincere and effective.'[10] For example.

> Next morning we woke up
> To the twilighty radiance of morning sun
> Lilting, juvenile breeze of the dawn
> Tickled us into fresh vistas of smiling grass
> I held your dew-twinkling face
> On my serene palms—
> And saw you vibrant as new leaf
> Fresh from the cosmic touch,
> Newly plucked—and washed in rain.
> Then, I planted a fresh kiss on your rosy cheek.[11]

Syed Ameeruddin enjoys experimenting with words and ideas, be it love, nature, family or philosophy. He is also form-conscious. Without a good and well constructed form to think about good poetry is impossible. He mostly writes long and short descriptive poetry in the form of "Ode"[12] where he elevates and elaborates the theme of the poem in stanzaic structure. "Value of Timelessness", "Dome of Gold", "Peace in the Age of Space", "The Dreadfull Doom to Come", "Where All This leads to ..." "Despair of our Age, Life is a mysterious ... mystery," 'A Craze for Supreme Beauty,' "Life is a Journey,' "My India", "Eloquent Serenade", "Carrion Carnage", "Blessings" are some examples of his craftsmanship as an 'Ode' writer.

Thus, we find that Syed Ameeruddin's style is simple and effective. He has an understanding about form and structure but sometimes length of certain poems make them thematically weak and loose vis-a-vis the compactness of his phrasal construction elsewhere. But his style is notable as far as Indianisation of English is concerned. The way he uses the English language clearly makes him sound a non-native speaker who makes poetry serious, philosophic, metaphysical, mystic and thought-provoking.

References

1. V. K. Gokak, *An Integral View of Poetry: An Indian Perspective* (New Delhi: Abhinav Publication, 1975) 158.
2. Syed Ameeruddin, "Ambiguity," *Visioned Summits* (Madras: International Poets Academy, 1995) 75-77.
3. Syed Ameeruddin, "Eloquent Serenade," *Visioned Summits* (Madras: International Poets Academy, 1995) 35-36
4. Syed Ameeruddin, "What the Himalaya ... Said," *What the Himalaya Said... and Other Poems* (Madras: Kalaivendhan Publications, 1972) 23.
5. Syed Ameeruddin, "My Enchantress..." *Petallic Love Times* (Madras: Poets Press India, 1988) 32-33.
6. Syed Ameeruddin, "Lover & Wanderer," *A Lover and A Wanderer* (Madras: Poets Press India, 1980) 25-26.
7. Syed Ameeruddin, "Lover & Wanderer," *A Lover and A Wanderer* (Madras: Poets Press India, 1980) 20.
8. Quoted from *The Quest* (June, 2008) 81-83.
9. R. K. Singh, *Recent Indian English Poets: Expressions and Beliefs* (New Delhi: Bahri Publications, 1992) 18.

10. M. Mujeeb, *What the Himalaya ... Said and Other Poems. Recent Indian English Poets: Expressions and Beliefs* (New Delhi: Bahri Publications, 1992) 9.
11. Syed Ameeruddin, "Petallic love Times," *Petallic Love Times* (Madras: Poets Press India, 1988) 23.
12. Vinayak Krishna Gokak, "Introduction," *The Dreadful Doom to Come and Other Poems* (Madras: Poets Press India, 1974) 4.

22

Aju Mukhopadhyay: Voice of the Voiceless

—S. Kumaran

Aju Mukhopadhyay is a poet, essayist and fiction writer. His short stories in English have been published in various reputed magazines and also been broadcast through All India Radio. Further, he has written nine books in English and they include: novels, poems, biography, short stories, and environment literature. He has also received many awards and honours for his poetic excellence. This analysis tries to bring out Mukhopadhyay's reverence for nature, awareness of ecological principles, perception of human life, philosophy of Time, care for humanity, and concern for the world.

Mukhopadhyay reveals the sublime quality of nature and encompasses nature within human boundary through his poems. In "Nature," the poet feels that all the objects of nature such as 'remotest star,' 'nearest moon,' 'seas,' 'rivers,' 'primordial trees,' and 'very grass,' move 'forever from ports of the universe' (*In Celebration of Nature*). He compares humans to animals and affirms the similarity thus: 'animals are captives of physical-vital bodies humans are captives of their minds' (*In Celebration of Nature*). Further, he says that humans are very busy with their unfruitful attempt at 'taming nature' whereas nature manifests its presence even when 'man sleeps at night' (*In Celebration of Nature*). Nature's power is reflected in the five elements that include: 'Earth, Water, Fire, Air and Space' (*In Celebration of Nature*) but nature seems 'clam in the face' (*In Celebration of Nature*). The poet also believes that 'Nature acts and reacts according to its norms and claims humans to collaborate in all forms' (*In Celebration of Nature*) and the primitive men were aware of the invigorating presence of nature. Moreover, they understood nature as 'a bridge between human and divine force' (*In Celebration of Nature*) and maintained their correspondence with it. The poet elucidates the mysteries and secrets of the sky in "Sky." He thinks that 'the blue of the sky has many a grade' (*In Celebration of Nature*) which cannot be defined or segregated. Further, the poet points out the daily hardships of humans that distance them from observing nature and he kneels 'with gratitude' and offers his 'pranam with loving sense' (*In Celebration of Nature*). In another poem, "Colours of the Sky," the poet unveils sky as a wonderful and mysterious creation of a 'superhuman artistic consciousness' (*In Celebration of Nature*).

Mukhopadhyay's portrayal of the intrinsic value and inherent worth of nature is commendable. The poet asserts the purity and serenity of stars in "Bright Star Blooms." He says that the 'Bright star rooted in vast void sky during the cloudless night and still air' (*In Celebration of Nature*) and 'blooms in clean water without a frill' (*In Celebration of Nature*). The scene promotes love in the 'lovers' heart' and signifies purity' (*In Celebration of Nature*). In "The Lake," the poet accentuates the nobility of lake. He feels that a lake is 'a streaming tributary' (*In Celebration of Nature*) at times and 'sometimes sustained by sea' (*In Celebration of Nature*). Further, it is 'picturesque deep, ripply, vireous' (*In Celebration of Nature*) and 'quite voluptuous with hills and dales' (*In Celebration of Nature*) and it also holds 'many a face' like a 'damsel in life's race' (*In Celebration of Nature*).

The poet emphasises the awe-inspiring nature of waterfall in "Waterfall." Waterfall gushes 'forth from a pristine source' (*In Celebration of Nature*) and turns into a 'mighty force' and cascades like a 'sleek silver sheet violent and voluble, frothy at the feet' (*In Celebration of Nature*). Moreover, the poet points out 'it is neither moral nor immoral' (*In Celebration of Nature*) and does not hinder anyone approaching it. In addition, it is not 'tainted by philanthropy' and 'falls, foams and flows free' (*In Celebration of Nature*). The poet announces the invigorating nature of air in "Air." The poet finds air as a nourisher during 'sweats in stuffy weather' (*In Celebration of Nature*) and a comforter of all lives.

The poet's ability to identify the similarities between humans and non-human others promotes a healthy relationship between humans and non-human others. In "Life a River," Muhkopadhyay compares human life to a river and captures the unity between them. River is born in the 'snowy mountain' (*In Celebration of Nature*) and it crosses the hills 'like a mother passing through the fields' (*In Celebration of Nature*) and 'dancing like a bard along the city' (*In Celebration of Nature*) and finally, the 'experienced river reaches the sea' (*In Celebration of Nature*). Humans are born in the 'sunny meadow' and starts 'jumping like a doe.' They are laden with the burden of 'loss and gain' (*In Celebration of Nature*) and 'relish the fun before reaching the ocean' (*In Celebration of Nature*).

The poet reveals the various forms taken by a river during the course of its journey in "Riverine Character." A river is born 'out of the melting ice, snow and the raindrop' (*In Celebration of Nature*) and moves according to its wish. It becomes 'vast like a Brahmaputra' and sinks 'like a Saraswati' (*In Celebration of Nature*). Further, it dazzles like a 'dagger in the hills' (*In Celebration of Nature*) and floods like a 'devastator.' It also cares like a 'mother in the Villas' (*In Celebration of Nature*) and 'plunges at last with dignity' (*In Celebration of Nature*) towards the sea as it is its 'everlasting felicity' (*In Celebration of Nature*).

The poet again brings out the resemblance between humans and nature in "The Death of a Rose." As the 'rose-lovers' did not want to disturb the fragrances of the rose in the air, they 'stopped the robbery' (*In Celebration of Nature*). Though it was left undisturbed by humans, it 'kissed the ground' (*In Celebration of Nature*) on its own 'petal by petal' (*In Celebration of Nature*). Even after its fall, the fragrance could be noted in the wind that 'thronged around the body' (*In Celebration of Nature*) to wail from 'suppressed suffering' (*In Celebration of Nature*). The poet discloses that some humans also spread 'more fragrance after they cross the mortal space.'

The poets care for the non-humans proves to be good solution to 'ecocatastrophe.' He exposes the cruelty of hunting in "The Death of a Bird and Hunter." The bird had a joyful sailing a moment before but the 'weight of the bullet in the heart of the bird became a burden to the sky' (*In Celebration of Nature*). On the other hand, the jealous and 'murderous hunter is pierced in his treacherous heart by the 'greed and lust dwelled in his blood' (*In Celebration of Nature*). In "The Grass," the poet asserts the worthiness of grass. He believes that a blade of grass knows how to survive 'numerous of feet' (*In Celebration of Nature*) and looks 'hearty and healthy' (*In Celebration of Nature*) under all circumstances 'without a fuss' (*In Celebration of Nature*).

Mukhopadhyay expresses his concern for his fellow humans through his poems. The poet points out the havocs created by Tsunami in "Tsunami 2004." The poet declares that he had received the shock while sitting 'silently aspiring for beyond' (*In Celebration of Nature*). Tsunami, 'sea-borne juggernaut of nature' (*In Celebration of Nature*) ruined humans when they were unaware of its arrival and hit the 'shores of eastern countries' (*In Celebration of Nature*). It destroyed 'fish and fisherman,' 'pearl-oyster,' 'coral reefs' and created problems for 'prisoners' and 'Tigers' fights' (*In Celebration of Nature*). Moreover, it created 'pieces of human flesh scattered and devoured by vultures,' 'naked bodies,' (*In Celebration of Nature*) and orphans. Finally, he terms it 'an idiot hour of waning two thousand four destroyed what for aeons so far the centuries made' (*In Celebration of Nature*).

The poet's awareness of ecology is worthy and promising. He reveals his fond memories and the present condition of the Pondicherry beach in "Ode to the Sea and Beach of Pondicherry." He was very much attracted towards the sea shore when he was young and enjoyed swimming and bathing. He also remembered of his friends and companions with whom he walked on the calm beach. He mourns that the blissful state of the beach was disturbed by the course of nature including Tsunami and finally lost 'its sandy gold face' (*In Celebration of Nature*). Further, the poet points out the efforts taken by the humans 'to save the town,' and 'to receive the tourist;' (*In Celebration of Nature*). The authorities 'built a parallel road alongside the old promenade' (*In Celebration of Nature*) which is a 'makeshift toy-beach,' and a 'grandiloquent façade with broken, pulverised hills lifted and carried by modern Hanuman, the techno-giant' (*In Celebration of Nature*). The poet mocks at the efforts as they cannot restore the lost glory again. His 'hope remains that the Nature is protean and the Time to reckon is eternal.'

Mukhopadhyay's outlook towards human life is the need of the day. The poet encourages humans to shed their lifeless artificial life and to lead a natural life in "Living Naturally, Living Really." He questions the people, who seclude themselves 'within the air-conditioned four walls,' (*In Celebration of Nature*) whether they could feel the warmth and comfort of the soft wind that alleviates perspiration and 'gasp for breath' (*In Celebration of Nature*). Further, the poet thinks that they could possibly be 'choked with snuff and smoke' (*In Celebration of Nature*) as they are 'busy with thousand absurd things, paraphernalia' depriving 'many things real' (*In Celebration of Nature*). The poet asserts the transforming power of Nature in "Solace in Nature." The poet is disgusted with the filth of modern life and finds consolation in Nature. Mukhopadhyay points out the glory of morning in "Morning." He affirms that 'Nothing is as fresh as the morning and so hopeful of its journey' (*The Paper Boat*) because it is sweeter than honey and adds 'new phase' (*The Paper Boat*) to life. Further, nothing can be 'compared to its purity' (*The Paper Boat*) as it vibrates with 'serendipity' (*The Paper Boat*).

The poet announces his perception of life in "Lift Us Up." He says that humans are worried about insignificant things without knowing the dangers that are facing them. Moreover, humans have to undergo trauma and pain to identify the purpose of their lives. Further, the poet requests the Omnipotent spirit to help humans to 'reach the goal' (*The Witness Tree*). He also requests the 'dear Father' (*The Witness Tree*) and 'divine Mother' (*The Witness Tree*) to lift the humans 'from the world's quagmire' (*The Witness Tree*) to their 'secret bower' (*The Witness Tree*).

Mukhopadhyay announces his philosophy of Time in some of his poems. The poet identifies Time as a crucial factor in the lives of humans and elucidates it in "Time's Sovereignty." The poet avows that 'moments escape the eternity' (*The Paper Boat*) even before anyone could think of it. Further, the 'eternity remains a whole' (*The Paper Boat*) as it is the 'Time's sovereignty' (*The Paper Boat*). In "About the Time," the poet points out humans cannot revoke the foolish things they do in the passage of time as the apt word missed during a speech will not 'get a second chance' (*The Paper Boat*). The poet announces the uncontrollable nature of time in "With the Time." No one can halt time or 'no one can hear the silent footfalls of time' (*The Paper Boat*). The fleeting nature of time is expounded in "Time Flows." The poet avows that time 'always escapes through the clinched fist very stealthily' (*The Paper Boat*) and none could 'stop time's flow even breathlessly' (*The Paper Boat*).

Mukhopadhyay explores different phases of Night in "In the Last Phase of the Night." The poet says that all are 'wide-awake' (*The Paper Boat*) in the first phase of the night and 'hedonists are awake' (*The Paper Boat*) in the second phase. The third phase is filled with thieves and 'Yogis get up fresh in the fourth phase of it' (*The Paper Boat*). The poet considers the fourth phase as the hour of intense happiness as 'in the space azury' (*The Paper Boat*) many 'happy dreams,' 'new hopes' (*The Paper Boat*) and love do grow.

Mukhopadhyay's vision of day-to-day life is practical and inspiring. The poet recollects his childhood days and its blissful state in "The Days have Passed By." He used to sit amidst trees along with his friends and enjoy 'brick-red gold spreading sun dipping down into the fathomless ocean' (*The Paper Boat*). Those days 'have passed by' (*The Paper Boat*) and the places that comforted them have lost their status due to the advent of technology. He finds 'the wood is dwindled' (*The Paper Boat*) and 'villages are metamorphosed to hybrid creatures' (*The Paper Boat*). Further, the poet says that he and his friends are living now in 'separate corners of the globe' (*The Paper Boat*) and they cannot 'recreate the things' (*The Paper Boat*) or the time they 'lived then' as 'modern hydras are growing up out of the pristine nature' (*The Paper Boat*). As an antidote, Mukhopadhyay appreciates reverie in "A Dream Like State." The poet identifies dream like state as an antidote to miseries of humans and asserts that one who enjoys such a state 'cannot be dishonoured in his dream like state' (*The Paper Boat*).

Mukhopadhyay rests his faith in the power of human body and spirit. In "Worship the Body," the poet points out the importance of human body. He finds body as the 'receptacle' (*The Paper Boat*) and a 'kingdom for mental and vital progress' (*The Paper Boat*). Moreover, he identifies it as a storehouse of 'life's secret' (*The Paper Boat*) and affirms 'serving is always its primary duty' (*The Paper Boat*). Further, he urges humans to 'pay respect, worship' (*The Paper Boat*) the body as 'its image is a remembrance to all posterity' (*The Paper Boat*).

In "A Poet Violated," Mukhopadhyay reveals how great geniuses, thinkers, and philosophers were put to hardships by the fanatics and how they were 'persecuted and killed at last' (*The Witness Tree*). Further, he shows the poet as a 'wonderful creator' (*The Witness Tree*) who does not belong to any country rather an 'asset to all humanity' (*The Witness Tree*). In "Soliloquy," the poet highlights the stoic courage of the human soul. The soul is haunted by 'pristine pleasure' often by its 'hide and seek' (*The Paper Boat*) nature but 'Life's urge is not to surrender but to fight till the time's there' (*The Paper Boat*).

In "The Inner World," Mukhopadhyay explicates the correspondence between human mind and the universe. The poet feels the dwelling of 'the wide of the sea at night' (*The Witness Tree*) in him and experiences the 'calm of the forest' (*The Witness Tree*) in his heart. Further, he pronounces that 'the chaos of the city fumes inside him' (*The Witness Tree*) and 'the bright of the star calls' (*The Witness Tree*) him 'forever' to it. In "Talks about Immortality," the poet brings out the impermanence of things and 'the divine maya' (*The Witness Tree*) of this universe and reveals immortality as a 'distant dream of humanity' (*The Witness Tree*). Moreover, he exposes the difficulties and hurdles that block immortality and asserts that immortality can be achieved 'with the support of an expedient body' (*The Witness Tree*). Though 'the body alone is certainly a non-entity,' (*The Witness Tree*) it is proposed as a means to attain immortality by 'the Mother' (*The Witness Tree*). Finally, the poet avows that 'immortality will remain a far cry until Sri Aurobindo's and Mother's ideas fructify' (*The Witness Tree*).

Mukhopadhyay's exploration of the different facets of human relationship is remarkable. The poet points out the aspects of human relationship in "The Relations." The poet unearths relationship in different forms such as friends, relatives, and spouse and also discloses the failure of people in maintaining relationship as they trample one another's feelings and even fail to understand 'many soft hearts, tender feelings' (*The Witness Tree*) throughout their lives. At times people are reminded of the lost relationship and feel content with the revival of the 'memories' (*The Witness Tree*). Further, the poet says that 'the dear ones appear like the fading stars in the twilight sky' (*The Witness Tree*) when one is in 'solitude or a rarefied mood' (*The Witness Tree*) and sometimes, 'our cherished guests of life fade away under the rolling pressure of time' (*The Witness Tree*).

In "Strange Relationship," the poet points out the loss of relationship between parents and children. Parents 'see their own image in their children' (*The Witness Tree*) and bring them up with so many dreams. On the other hand, the children are carried away by the corrupting influence of 'hybrid cultures' (*The Witness Tree*) and fail to maintain their sacred bond with their parents. The poet asserts that 'all these are laughing moments for the one who ever remains a witness, living among us everywhere, indistinguishable from our friends and foes from our relations and ourselves' (*The Witness Tree*).

The poet bemoans the present situation of India in "What an Age We are Passing Through!" He feels that the word democracy has become meaningless and the politicians manipulate the resources of the country to their own advantage. Further, 'they give anything to anyone, of any denomination' (*The Paper Boat*) and are ready to 'destroy the land we stand on to secure their position of power, right to misrule' (*The Paper Boat*). There is no security for the people of the country as they 'commit suicide' (*The Paper Boat*) and are afraid to lead their lives. Further, the moral values and traditional wisdom of the country had been discarded for the convenience of people and they do involve in all sorts of inhuman activities. Moreover, humans have disconnected themselves from Nature forgetting the laws of ecology and are faced with ecological imbalance.

The poet reveals the complication of the present day world in "Misadventure." He says that 'Everything moves fast in this cybernetic world' (*The Witness Tree*) and 'each one is very close to the other, mechanically' (*The Witness Tree*). He finds the impact of computers on the lives of humans and also exposes the fear about 'bugs, viruses or pilfers' (*The Witness Tree*). He also exposes how 'calculators have robbed men of their mental agility' (*The Witness Tree*) and how 'men have worried to destroy their atomic weapons' (*The Witness Tree*). The poet cautions that 'if computers can replace the buddhi, there are other aspects of the mind like chitta, manas and yet higher siddhi' (*The Witness Tree*). Further, he declares that 'human life has myriad hues, many an aspect beyond the structure of the machines to report' (*The Witness Tree*). He also questions about the death of innocent people and the dryness of children's skeletons in Ethiopia and urges humans to solve these issues before relishing their misadventure. Finally, the poet asserts that the knowledge about where 'to give' and 'where to refuse' 'emanates from real wisdom' (*The Witness Tree*) and 'to know where to stop, how much to utilise is the real science' (*The Witness Tree*). The poet concludes saying 'it is dangerous to produce things which are beyond man's capacities to retain or use.'

Through his portrayal of the intrinsic value and inherent worth of nature, Mukhopadhyay declares the independence of nature and by elucidating the resemblance between humans and non-human others, he affirms the interrelation between humans and nature. Moreover, Mukhopadhyay reveals his awareness of ecology and urges humans to cherish ecological principles. By proclaiming the importance of Time,

Mukhopadhyay cautions humans to seize it and by pointing out the sanctity of human body and spirit, the poet asserts the dignity of human life. Further, the poet analyses different facets of human relationship and upholds the necessity of safeguarding it. Finally, Mukhopadhyay scrutinises the plight of modern world and warns humans about their loss of human values and moral principles.

Works Cited

Mukhopadhyay, Aju. *In Celebration of Nature*. Aligarh: SL Publications, 2007. Print.

_____ *The Paper Boat*. Bareilly: Prakash Book Depot, 2007. Print.

_____ *The Witness Tree*. Calcutta: Writers Workshop Publication, 2000. Print.

23

Purifying the Contemporary Inherent Irritants: A Critical Appreciation of Aju Mukhopadhyay's *Poems on Sri Aurobindo and the Mother* and *The Paper Boat*

—P.C.K. Prem

Aju Mukhopadhyay is a poet, feature and fiction writer and has appeared in various anthologies and periodicals. He has authored nine books in English which include: *Sri Aurobindo's Ideal of Freedom and Human Unity* (Essays), *Mother of all Beings* (Biography), *Lord Ganesha* (Monograph), *The Witness Tree* (Poems), *Short Verse Vast Universe*, *In Celebration of Nature* (Poems), *A White Bird and its Black Shadow* (Short Stories), *In Trains* (Novel), *Water and Pondicherry Environment* and twelve books in Bangla. He is a keen student of nature and environment and has bagged many literary and social-service oriented awards from different renowned organisations.

To read the poetry of Aju Mukhopadyaya is an experience at once fulfilling and ennobling. If one is looking out for some effective influence of poetry on the life of man, it is here. Aju is a poet of positive and optimistic view of life, and in him one finds that life is always a storehouse of harmony and benign richness. It is only a devout heart and intellect that is required to fathom the delicacy of life of humanism. In a tiny but beautiful collection of poems on *Sri Aurobindo and the Mother* the poet pays rich tributes to Sri Aurobindo who was not only a great scholar but was also imbued with the spirit of nationalism.

The poet is genuinely attracted to the wonderful spiritual and intellectual genius of the great sage Aurobindo who inspires him to pen down lyrics in his sacred memory and sagacity. To the poet, the great soul was 'destined to emit a brilliant light' so that he could enlighten the path of people still groping in the dark—the dark period of slavery in the history of India. He observes:

> The light shall shine for ever
> Like a polestar
> to guide the eager traveler
> Towards a morning yet to be born
>
> ("The Fireborn," *Sri Aurobindo and The Mother* 8)

Aurobindo was a grand soul whose presence infused immense aura of harmonious fragrance around and he was also a great source of strength and courage to the disheartening people in the midst of extreme enslavement and cruelty. But his birth on earth was 'like a tree he was peaceful, unhurried and calm with perseverance/among the thousand resounding words his existence was silence' and could take the people away from the 'mundane' to the 'cascading light' of hope and beauty, prosperity and health.

It is interesting to know that very early in the childhood Aurobindo got education at Manchester where he lived with the family of a clergy. In Cambridge, he proved a wonderful scholar. It was in England that he was filled with patriotic fervour. He could have easily got a lucrative job in the British administration but he was made for a much nobler cause. Soon he returned to India much against the wishes of his father and devoted himself to the service of the nation. After a very short stint in Baroda, he came to Calcutta and joined as the principal of a college. He was meant to serve the nation so again he resigned and began to take active part in Nationalistic Movement. Finding many renowned persons including Gandhi in the struggle, he also jumped with an intense fervour in the fight against the British. He always insisted on total independence for Indian. Later on, he was arrested on a serious allegation of treason and suffered lonely confinement for a year.

This period in the prison proved a turning point in his life for here he had fundamental spiritual experiences which revealed the truth of spiritual power. Thus various spiritual experiences brought him near the truth of ever eternal religion of humanity—Sanatana dharma—together with the eternal spiritual wisdom of ancient India. He was steeped in the ancient wisdom of the *Vedas* and *Upanishads* and this brought about a great transformation in his attitude towards life, society, the country and the world at large. He was essentially an apostle of humanism. This background is necessary to understand the mind and heart of the great soul and this is what Aju Mukhopadhyay emphasizes. The poet is a great admirer of Aurobindo and the Mother, and this inspired him to share his experiences with the readers. Thus, the collection is quite unique and relevant to man in the contemporary scenario.

When he talks of "Two Birthdays," he has in mind the birth of the saint (Aurobindo was born on 15 August, 1872) and the birth of free India (on 15 August, 1947). The poet says:

> Apostle of spiritual nationalism,
> he raised the nation to the height
> with spiritual force and light
>
> ("Two Birthdays" 10)

But unfortunately, the poet is pensive as the great ideals for which Aurobindo stood were soon ignored, as the leaders begin to follow apathetically and selfishly a different path. The poet regrets:

> And ideals other than spiritual were focused
> As the leaders at the end had their personal demands
> To fulfill, a sick India was last born;
> Maimed, bleeding profusely and torn.
>
> ("Two Birthdays")

And therein, he makes an appeal that 'let us not cripple her further, nor divide the mighty Himalaya' and to 'rejoin her limbs, making the union happy and free' strenuous efforts have to be made. He is compared to an ever flowing river that ultimately merges with the mighty sea and 'the sea into the river brought; a dual citizen of earth and heaven'. It may be symbolic of his return to Pondicherry but in the final analysis it is about:

> ...living on earth in divinised nature
> your greatest boon to humanity this,
> the greatest of revolutions
> without any killings.
>
> ("Om Sri Aurobindo" 11)

An indirect reference to non-violent freedom movement where Gandhi was a great force makes it more authentic and further he says –

> the inner being pushed him from one to the other theme
> He was poet revolutionary yogi journalist writer and thinker
>
> ("A Complete Human Being" 13)

The poet in truth underlines the stupendous qualities of head and heart of Sri Aurobindo who was a man of astounding multi-dimensional virtues. Aurobindo was a true yogi and taught that the spirit of yoga is essential to bring harmony to mankind. It is yoga of the physical and spiritual which makes a complete human being leading consequently to a happy and peaceful society. Here, he speaks not only for man but for the total humanity. He says:

> The existence of institutions is sufficient
> to abrogate the need of insisting on the spirit
> that made the institutions
> But spirituality is .. Nothing
> if it is not lived inwardly and if the outward life
> does not flow out of this inward living.
>
> ("All Life is Yoga" 18)

The poet is impressed and fascinated by the spiritual strength of mother to whom Aurobindo had ultimately handed over the responsibilities of running the Ashram. The timing is perfect as the continuity is an eternal feature of life. The poet says:

Out of the womb of time she was born
A divine consciousness in mortal form
She was our earthly Mother who knew herself
From the age of five, faintly as the divine incarnate.
… …
To be close to her is a profound happiness,
We live basking in her Sunshine.
Protected and rejoiced by her divine smile.

("One in Our faith" 26)

That is how he describes the overwhelming spiritual aura of Mother. Little poems like "A Seed of light", "Maa", "Femme Divine" and "She lives in His Heart" guide to a different kind of experience which opens resplendent and dazzling doors to divinity soothing an agitated emotional state of mind and heart:

her image blooming in his heart space
she lives there, dwells in his breath and pulse
the song of his life is tuned
by her purest divine presence.

("She Lives in His Heart" 35)

All the poems in fact pay homage to the two great souls: Aurobindo and the Mother which invariably bring into focus vaguely the revolutionary zeal and the freedom movement thereby rejuvenating the sagging spirit of Indians with the power of ancient values with an objective to usher in an era of love and harmony for the suffering humanity. It is an awakening of the dormant spirit. It is a conscious and serious effort to give a clarion call to all Indians to rise above petty squabbles and make this world a better place to live after a period of darkness that foreign rule was. It is pure Indian consciousness with a spiritual experience that is needed to make life better.

The poet delicately sustains the flow of sublime thoughts and feelings through out while penning lyrics in praise of the great souls. Not for a moment he appears burdensome and in a subtle poetic style, makes us conscious of the truth of birth, life and death and its apparent transitory nature while emphasizing the immortality of soul and the presence of divinity in each of us. To this extent poems on Sri Aurobindo and the Mother are relevant to grief-stricken men. It is elevation of man, soul and deeds that structure a meaningful edifice of life. From here, he moves on to another powerful journey of lofty and noble thoughts and relates them to contemporary time, man and life and a definite continuity is maintained in the lyrics of *The Paper Boat.*

The Paper Boat is again a journey into little experiences of life which often remain unnoticed but if one is observant, there is sufficient nature's bounty spread about that can heal wounded hearts and thirsty intellects. It is an eternal coming back of a prop to its master so as to inspire him to embark afresh upon an adventure to make life more purposeful. The poet makes it evident in the following lines:

> The paper boat
> I set adrift
> In my childhood
> On the flooded road
> Of a metropolis
> Has just arrived
> This rainy evening
> At my doorstep
> Under full sail
> Inviting me
> To set out on it
> For a nouvelle
> Adventure.
>
> ("The Paper Boat" 37)

In "Morning" the poet speaks about the freshness and eternal message of nature when he tells in simple words that 'Nothing is ever so simple as morning, Resonant, loving, forever beginning'. Next poems are a tribute to the all pervading presence of time. Its sovereignty can't be questioned. It is this moment man when must act with a cool and harmonious heart and intellect and if he makes a mistake, he will not get a chance. Time's movement is eternal and none can stop it.

> no one can halt it
> no second no minute

hour day month or year
no one can hear
the silent footfalls of time.
("With the Time" 4)

In another little verse, "Time Flows" the poet feels that even if a man tries hard to hold time, it is impossible to do so.

you can't hold it
stop time's flow
even breathlessly
realising the futility
be with it/in all humility.
("Time Flows" 5)

Man must accept that before time he is just helpless. What a man experiences during the night is something quite inexplicable. It is a journey into many unmeasured areas of thoughts, dreams and realities but still nothing is certain for one fails to comprehend whatever is hidden in the womb of 'grayish orange dawn.' Nature never permits man to understand its movements. The poet is nostalgic about the destruction of Deccan Sultanate brought about by ups and downs as the time rolled on. Transience of life is permanent, is the message the poem "Silent Witnesses of the Bygone Ages" appears to convey.

Little enticements play havoc with life. "Soliloquy" urges man to continue the fight against temptations of worldly pleasures and says—'Life's urge is not to surrender/But to fight/ Till the time's there.' and immediately it is observed that 'Concentration fixed on the absolute nothingness/helps the one to possess the being/to fulfill the emptiness/Toward an unknown bliss leading.' ("On the Way" 15) and this is the message eternal to salvage a broken life. "The Days Have passed By", "A Dream Like State", "A Vision Sublime" and "I and Me" are poems that fill a lacerated heart with a sublime feeling. Surprisingly, the poet turns to the present and underlines the sufferings in "From Darkness toward Light" that man confronts:

> Falsehood has spread everywhere
> greed is covered by carcass
> darkness in the nether world
> dark hole in the sky.
> . . . .
> man has threatened nature and earth
> warming nuking aiding with AIDS
> Nature is a helpless spectator.
> Religious fundamentalists
> swarm like snakes on earth
> Whole body covered with burqa like things
> they look at your heart
> With vile eyes.
>
> ("From Darkness toward Light" 20)

The above lines make clear the world in which we live. The poet talks of corruption, pollution, religious bigotry, falsehood, hatred and every thing evil which make life so dreadful. Again the next verse 'What an Age we are Passing through', p.22, vividly exposes us to a shocking scenario when he bewails over the dismal performance of democracy and 'after all, a rule by the people, for the people' has only made people vulnerable and:

> everything they lose to the politicians
> who possess kaleidoscopic characters
> verily, the chhaya of the ancient maya...
> and suddenly the picture is changed.

The poet's anger and protest appear to stop nowhere when he talks of hunger, greed, love for industry, death of farmers, caste, politics of votes, conditions of women, media, global warming, violence, communism, dirty politicians, ecology, technology, science, terrorism and so on. It is the system that is under the scanner and 'we the people of India' create a deplorable and highly miserable state of affairs not only for the people but for the country as a whole.

The poet undoubtedly is very penetrating and also anguished at the miseries and erosion of value system and the system as such in the country but the words he chooses to convey the feelings of a wounded heart do not look repulsive or disgusting. It is the language and the idiom, he puts into practice to communicate the sublimity of a dignified thought that enchants, captivates and impresses a reader evocatively. This way it is poet's strength to make an appeal without being didactic.

> What an age we are passing through
> Ecology destroyed, disharmony brought to Nature
> Man-Animal relation worsened
> by killing daily thousands of dumb creatures.
>
> ("What an Age We are Passing through!" 23)

This thought continues to flow in the poems like "The System" and "To the Gallows" but then at once he strikes a note of optimism in "Age of No-War Dawn of Peace" and "Hope" He says, 'Relation with the divine is intimate, individual/beyond the sphere of religion, truly spiritual;' and then he affirms:

> artificial dams over the rivers of logic
> are gradually breaking down
> men have realised the fault of creating
> ecological imbalance
> adjustment at every step is perceptible
> even amid terrorism and destruction.
>
> ("Hope" 29-30)

There is no change whatsoever in the mood of the poet. Poet, "In Memoriam", "A Real Day", "A Real Choice", "Frankness" and "Worship the Body" are truly poems of beauty and grace of thoughts. All these little pieces are born out of a serene mind who is eagerly observing everything around with a pious and melodious frame of mind. Nothing is left unrevealed in the scheme of life and nature and nothing is opened up which does not exist. If it exists, it is irritating and not quite suited to the finer sensibilities and so it is left out. The poet maintains a remarkable attitude of grace and dignity while giving vent to his humane feelings.

A lover of good poetry while reading the poems of Aju Mukhopadhyay finds the going as smooth and musical as a hill stream in a deep gully with resounding echoes of bliss and divinity. And here ends a symbolic journey of the poet who believes in absolute harmony in life. If poetry is an art of instilling grace, beauty and nobility in man's life, then the poet is quite successful. Mukhopadhyay uses simple words with unassuming condour and meaning, which flow in a musical rhythm. He inspires, stirs quietly, gives a message and beautifies all of us but he is not compulsive or irritating.

Long back, the Pre-Raphaelites and a few aesthetes forcefully advocated the theory of 'Art for Art's Sake' but it did not find favour later on. Poetry must serve society and man and to this extent, poetry to Aju Mukhopadhyay is an aid to elevate and ameliorate the moribund prevalent in the society. Here, the poet appears to be 'sincere, simple, flexible ardent ever widening its knowledge' like Mathew Arnold, the great critic. It is quite obvious that the poet is comfortable with the moral and social values of poetry like the ancient poet-philosopher and like many other Indian English poets namely Krishna Srinivas, Narsingh Srivastava and Syed Ameeruddin he draws inspiration from religion to a great extent and uses poetic art for the uplift of human mind and soul. Though not totally religious, K.V. Raghupathi does believe in the ethical poetic influence and to that extent Mukhopadhyay has unique similarity with Raghupathi. It can easily be inferred that the poet is a staunch believer in traditional value system but to an extent he is open to thoughts which have cathartic influence on the minds and hearts of men. For him, poetry is a vehicle to carry such thoughts and there he is quite successful.

Works Cited

Mukhopadhyay, Aju. *The Paper Boat.* Bareilly: Prakash Book Depot, 2007. Print.

_____ *Poems on Sri Aurobindo and the Mother.* Bareilly: Prakash Book Depot, 2009. Print.

24

An Ecoaesthetic Rendering of Aju Mukhopadhyay's Poems

—M.S. Raj Sree

Aju Mukhopadhyay celebrates the beauty of nature in his poems. Though he is romantic in spirit, he is aware of the deformities nature suffered in the hands of mankind. He sings not only of the beauty of nature but also its power and at the same time its helplessness against technological invasion of man. *The Witness Tree*, with its vibrant images, depicts the beauty and cruelty of nature. In the collection *The Paper Boat*, he uses nature to convey his philosophical thoughts on time, history in ruins etc. *In Celebration of Nature,* he reaches the zenith in exalting the beauty of nature. His poems fascinate us with nature's appealing beauty. He gives importance to the indigenous veneration of nature over Western anti-ecological notions towards nature. His poems celebrate eco-centrism. His poems critique the anthropocentrism of the West. He is aware of the redemptive powers of nature that can heal the fragmented self.

Poems celebrating nature can be read resorting to the critical tool of ecoaesthetics. Ecoaesthetics is a theory of evaluation and appreciation of nature and its beauty. It is a non dualistic approach to analyse the relationship between nature and man in an ecocentric framework. Mukhopadhyay's poems are essentially biocentric and hence an ecoaesthetic rendering of his poems is inevitable. In *Reading the Earth,* Michael P. Branch explains ecocriticism as 'not just a means of analysing nature in literature; it implies a move toward a more biocentric world view, an extension of ethics, a broadening of human conception of global community to include nonhuman life forms and the physical environment'. Ecocriticism (in USA) or Green studies (in UK) refer to the critical approaches, which began in the USA in the late 1980s and in the UK in the early 1990s. Ecocriticism emerged as a recognisable discipline within literature as study of nature writing and reading literature by contextualising ecological issues. Texts are read in terms of their environmentally harmful or helpful effects. 'Ecocriticism seeks to redirect humanistic ideology, not spurning the natural sciences but using their ideas to sustain viable readings' (Howarth 164). An ecocritical reading of Mukhopadhyay's poems bring forth the essence of his poems.

Ecological perspective played an important role in carving the worldview of Indians. It is evident in their routine of worshipping the sun in the break of dawn. European conventions read nature as a God given space which is separate from man. Man perceived land or nature as an object to impose his will upon it and man is divinely sanctioned as evident in Genesis 1: 28: 'Then God blessed them, and God said to them, "Be fruitful, fill the Earth and subdue it: have dominion over the fish of the sea, over the birds of the air, and over every living thing that moves on the Earth.' But Aju Mukhopadhyay contradicts this notion of anthropocentrism which is predominant in the western metaphysics. Anthropocentrism places humanity at the centre of everything and other forms of life as resources to be consumed by human beings.

Aju Mukhopadhyay views nature as a spiritual anchorage and therapeutic to the psyche bruised by modernity and its mechanical giants. For Mukhopadhyay, the river, the sun and the sky serve as solace to human mind. "Solace in Nature" is a fine example. His poems bring forth the idea that man should not rule nature but instead protect nature and there by insuring his life. In "Life a River", the river is equated with mother who gives life to a new being and to a poet who nourishes the human craving for beauty. Man is viewed in relatatedness with nature which 'is a discursive herbarium and a bestiary, part of an archaic, unchanging world of immanence'

(Conley 152). It is not that river exits for man's needs but man exists because there is a life giving river. This is the core of ecocentrism. The poem begins with the river 'jumping like a doe', untouched by human civilisation. But later human encroachment made it 'bent with the burden of loss and gain' (*In Celebration of Nature* 8). In "Nature", he perceives nature as a bridge between human and divine force. In "Autumn Sky", sky is lovely and 'trees are dreamy, drenched with rain'. But the poet implies that 'it was the hour before the men awake' when nature was unaltered by human activity. When humans interfere, it won't be the same.

Aju Mukhopadhyay's description of nature is in accordance with three major concepts pivotal in ecological discussion. Kate Soper distinguished the metaphysical, the realist and the lay ideas of nature. According to the metaphysical idea, nature is the concept through which humanity thinks its difference and specificity. In "Ode to the Sea and Beach of Pondicherry", man differentiates himself from the sea and tries to build walls to separate sea from him. The splendour and the beauty of the beach were destroyed in man's attempt to protect themselves.

> To save the town, beautify it out of fear and greed
> To receive the tourist they became the real spendthrift.
> They built...A makeshift toy-beach, grandiloquent façade
> With broken; pulverised hills...
>
> (*In Celebration of Nature* 16-17).

In "The Death of a Bird and Hunter" also man takes a role detached from nature by killing birds thinking that he is purifying nature. But little did he know that he is destroying life which is part of nature, part of man himself. The hunter finds pleasure in killing the bird, without realising the fact that the bird also has its ecological niche on this planet Earth. Ecological niche refers to 'an overall design in nature that furnishes a place for every species...' (Kerridge 535). However, human activities can tamper that niche and it can just disappear. Man fails to appreciate beauty of nature which is central to ecoaesthetics as 'greed and lust dwelled in his blood' (*In Celebration of Nature* 20). Instead of perceiving beauty in the bird, the hunter satisfies his greed. By killing the bird, he enforces his dominion over natural resources. He sees the bird as an object devoid of reason and emotion. On the contrary, the poet tries to give the message that we should value and preserve nature.

The realist concept refers to the process and casual powers of nature which humans can neither destroy nor escape from, as expressed in the power of the raging sea in the Ode. In "The Death of a Rose," he pictures a rose which is protected from money minded traders. But it faded away. Man cannot change the laws of nature however hard he tries.

The lay concept of nature is most often used in Mukhopadhyay's poems. This is the nature of immediate experience as well as of aesthetic appreciation, the one which is often destroyed and polluted, the one which is to be conserved and preserved. Mukhopadhyay depicts nature in opposition to culture, as an immediate experience, a source for aesthetic pleasure, the nature we have. "Autumn Sky" is yet another example of an appreciation of nature.

The ecological wisdom in the "Ode" gives insight into the poet's worldview on nature. In the first two stanzas, the poet exalts the magnanimity and the past glory of the sea and the beach of Pondicherry. The beauty and calmness of the sea is emphasized. 'Dolphin's snouting and seraphin's song wafting in the air./On your beach calm and quiet we walked, O sea!' (*In Celebration of Nature* 16-17). It is a nostalgic account of poet's childhood life in relatedness with nature. The sea is venerated as 'a wonderful solace'. But the rest of the poem takes us into the consequences of human encroachment and violation of natural forces. He describes the raging sea after Tsunami hit the land. The human intervention is reciprocated by nature in various forms like Tsunami. The beauty and the quietness are lost. It's now 'an unfathomable sea, treacherous in calm' (*In Celebration of Nature* 16-17).

The poet pictures the technological inventions which destroy and deform nature in a satiric manner. The bulldozer which is often used to destroy natural landscapes is referred to as 'modern Hanuman, the techno-giant'. In the latter part of the poem, sea is considered dangerous. 'O Pondy Sea, you too have become the killer of men/who might have been deceived by the siren' (*In Celebration of Nature* 16-17). The poet depicts man in battle against nature. Without realising the reason behind Tsunami, man fights nature to protect himself, forgetting the fact that if he protects nature, his life is secure. This clearly portrays the anthropocentric nature of the people and the biocentric nature of the poet.

The poet says that Pondicherry is attractive for the sea and not for man-made statues and pillars. Man-made structures are not that appealing like that of nature's wonders. He views the man made world as ugly and harmful to human life as well as to flora and fauna. This clearly brings out the biocentric view of the poet in turn underlying the anthropocentric nature of man.

> Pondy is attractive mainly for you, the sea!
> And for you the Beach!—washed by the waves constantly
> Few are the things and sites attractive which are man-made
> Alas! The slim and golden beach is at last dead.
>
> (*In Celebration of Nature* 16-17)

In the "Ode", he laments "the death of the golden beach". Though the scenario is very bleak and pathetic, the poet puts his hope in the healing power of nature. 'The only hope remains that nature is protean/and time to reckon is eternal' (*In Celebration of Nature* 16-17). The protean nature of nature may bring out wonders even in the worst of situations. This is ecological wisdom one gets on reading this poem. He expresses deep anguish about the general callousness towards ecological issues. The ever-increasing mindless dependency on technology has corrupted the human mind and has also brought havoc to the planet. Mukhopadhyay very deftly deals with the most rampant issue in ecological discourse. His nature poems foreground the ramifications of human intervention towards nature.

Mukhopadhyay offers 'deep ecology' as a solution for protecting nature from destruction. Advocating a biocentric view, deep ecologists reject technological and managerial solutions which constitute human dominance. Similarly, Mukhopadhyay exhorts us to recognise the non human world as having value irrespective of its usefulness to mankind who has no right to destroy it except to meet vital needs. 'Deep ecology proposes drastic changes in our habits of consumption, not only to avert catastrophe but as spiritual and moral awakening' (Kerridge 536). Thus we can not only preserve nature but also protect ourselves from impending calamities.

The dogma that culture will always master nature is deconstructed in his poems. Though the tradition of man/nature dualism can be found in his poems like "Ode" and "The Death of a Bird and Hunter", he conveys the principle of stewardship. Though the poet rejects the anthropocentrism of the West, he advocates the biblical principle of stewardship. It suggests that man is a steward of all natural resources and he is accountable. In this way we can preserve nature. He tries to see nature and man as one organic body. In *In Celebration of Nature,* nature predominates, not man. His poems are environmentally oriented. The non human environment is not merely a framework or device but a pointer, pointing to the fact that human history is implicated in natural history. He depicts the effects of culture upon man, with a view of celebrating nature and demeaning its spoilers. His poems relate human self to the natural other in a relationship of heterarchy rather than hierarchy.

In "The Death of a Bird and Hunter", a bird is the centre of focus, in "Autumn Sky", the sky; in "The Death of a Rose" the rose; in "Ode" the golden beach. He does not see human interest as the only legitimate interest; instead, he views human interests as harmful to the ecological balance and beauty of nature. Human interests deprive the sky of its flocking birds and the beach of its calmness. In "The Death of a Bird and Hunter" the poet says that 'the weight of the bullet/ in the heart of the bird/became a burden to the sky' (*In Celebration of Nature* 20). The hunter's attack caused havoc not only to the flock of birds but also the sky. Again, the interrelatedness of nature is foregrounded. Human intervention causes discordance and cacophony in the harmonious framework of nature. 'Under the hush of the early devout hours/An immaculate calm and a mystic silence prevailed' (*The Witness Tree* 9) which is disturbed by human activities. Mukhopadhyay sees plucking flowers and other similar acts as acts of robbery: robbing nature of its resources. Man robs nature of its fragrance and beauty.

> When the rose was there
> Fragrance wafted in the air
> Bees were busy at sucking
> Traders were going for plucking
> Stuck by wanton beauty
> Rose-lovers stopped the robbery.
>
> (*In Celebration of Nature* 24)

Like Romantics, Mukhopadhyay also recognises the congruency between creativity in art and in nature. In "The King and the Artiste", the artist paints the picture of a crown. The process of artistic creation is compared to 'the great creation on the western sky' (*In Celebration of Nature* 6). Like the artist who moves to paint something else, nature is always in the process of making something.

> But the colours faded soon rendering the crown dry
> Unmoved the artist move to the other corner of the sky
> To create town and hill and river
> With golden bricks and rocks of silver.
>
> (*In Celebration of Nature* 6)

The artist and the poet like a tree extracts nourishment from the depths of the Earth. The organic metaphors used by Mukhopadhyay are essential to the concept of Deep Form which offers us the knowledge that an authentically deep ecology is required to place mankind in a sustainable relationship with nature. Mukhopadhyay's poetry is an expression of Deep Form. Deep Form refers to the correspondence between formative process of mind and formative process in nature. It unravels the intricate design or web of vital relationships embedded in all things. It offers the poet 'a new repertory of gestures instead of grasping, seizing, mastering, struggling, it attempts a tender touching, non interfering gaze, a receptive bonding with Earth and the other' (Roszak 226). In "February Twenty First" dawn is portrayed as a complicated yet beautiful process of nature which is to be relished for its aesthetic appeal.

> Then came the moment when all get drenched
> By the heart-blossoming and joy-flowering showers
> Of Divine's transcendent powers
> The throat and the lips and the tongue
> Remained unstirred; not even a whisper was heard
> Yet an unnamed name, a wordless cry
> Keep repeating and throbbing in the occult depths of the heart
> It was to commemorate a divine birth
> A fathomless emotion was blissfully conscious
> That it was February Twenty First.
>
> (The *Witness Tree* 9)

His poems give the message of symbiosis. Man should see the reality. The reality is symbiosis—that is, to coexist, cooperate and flourish in the biosphere. Ecocriticism is the analysis of literature as though nature mattered. Mukhopadhyay's writes poetry 'as though nature mattered.' In the post modern world corrupted by excessive humanism, his poetry remains as a testimony to deep ecology.

Works Cited

Branch, Michael P., Scott Slovic and Daniel Patterson, ed. *Reading the Earth:*

_____*New Directions in the Study of Literature and Environment.* Moscow: University Of Idaho Press, 1998. Print.

Conley, Verena Andermatt. "Helene Cixous: The Language of Flowers." *The Green Studies Reader: From Romanticism to Ecocentrism*. Ed. Laurence Coupe. London: Routledge, 2000. 148-53. Print.

Howarth, William. "Ecocriticism in Context," *The Green Studies Reader: From Romanticism to Ecocentrism*. Ed. Laurence Coupe. London: Routledge, 2000. 163-66. Print.

Kerridge, Richard. "Environmentalism and Ecocriticism." *Literary Theory and Criticism*. Ed. Patricia Waugh. Oxford: OUP, 2006. 530-43. Print.

Mukhopadhyay, Aju. The *Witness Tree*. Kolkata: Writers Workshop, 2000. Print.

_____ *In Celebration of Nature*. Aligarh: Skylark Publications, 2007. Print.

Roszak, Betty and Theodore Roszak. "Deep Form in Art and Nature." *The Green Studies Reader: From Romanticism to Ecocentrism*. Ed. Laurence Coupe. London: Routledge, 2000. 223-26. Print.

The Holy Bible, New King James Version.